Action Research for Language Teachers

CAMBRIDGE TEACHER TRAINING AND DEVELOPMENT
Series Editors: Marion Williams and Tony Wright

This series is designed for all those involved in language teacher training and development: teachers in training, trainers, directors of studies, advisers, teachers of in-service courses and seminars. Its aim is to provide a comprehensive, organised and authoritative resource for language teacher training development.

Teach English – A training course for teachers
by Adrian Doff

Training Foreign Language Teachers – A reflective approach
by Michael J. Wallace

Literature and Language Teaching – A guide for teachers and trainers*
by Gillian Lazar

Classroom Observation Tasks – A resource book for language teachers and trainers*
by Ruth Wajnryb

Tasks for Language Teachers – A resource book for training and development*
by Martin Parrott

English for the Teacher – A language development course*
by Mary Spratt

Teaching Children English – A training course for teachers of English to children*
by David Vale with Anne Feunteun

A Course in Language Teaching – Practice and theory
by Penny Ur

Looking at Language Classrooms – A teacher development video package

About Language – Tasks for teachers of English
by Scott Thornbury

Action Research for Language Teachers
by Michael J. Wallace

Mentor Courses – A resource book for trainer-trainers
by Angi Malderez and Caroline Bodóczky

Alive to Language – Perspectives on language awareness for English language teachers
by Valerie Arndt, Paul Harvey and John Nuttall

Teachers in Action – Tasks for in-service language teacher education and development
by Peter James

Advising and Supporting Teachers
by Mick Randall and Barbara Thornton

* Original Series Editors: Ruth Gairns and Marion Williams

Action Research for Language Teachers

Michael J. Wallace

CAMBRIDGE
UNIVERSITY PRESS

CAMBRIDGE UNIVERSITY PRESS

Cambridge, New York, Melbourne, Madrid, Cape Town,
Singapore, São Paulo, Delhi, Tokyo, Mexico City

Cambridge University Press
The Edinburgh Building, Cambridge CB2 8RU, UK

www.cambridge.org
Information on this title: www.cambridge.org/9780521555357

© Cambridge University Press 1998

First published 1998
15th printing 2011

Printed in the United Kingdom at the University Press, Cambridge

A catalogue record for this publication is available from the British Library

Library of Congress Cataloguing in Publication data
Wallace. Michael J.
    Action research for language teachers / Michael J. Wallace.
        p. cm. – (Cambridge teacher training and development)
    Includes bibliographical references and index.
    ISBN 978-0-521-55495-4 Hardback
    ISBN 978-0-521-55535-7 Paperback
    1. English language – Study and teaching – Foreign speakers –
    Research. 2. Language and languages – Study and teaching – Research.
    I. Title.   II. Series.
    PE1128.A2W228   1997
    428′ 007′2 – DC21
                                                            97-33569
                                                            CIP

ISBN 978-0-521-55495-4 Hardback
ISBN 978-0-521-55535-7 Paperback

For Eileen

Contents

Acknowledgements

The author and publishers are grateful to the authors, publishers and others who have given permission for the use of copyright material identified in the text. While every endeavour has been made, it has not been possible to identify the sources of all the material used and in such cases the publishers would welcome information from copyright owners.

City Polytechnic of Hong Kong for the extract on p. 63 from 'Journaling together: collaborative diary-keeping and teacher development' by M. N. Brock, B. Yu and M. Wong (1992), in J. Flowerdew, M. Brock and S. Hsia (Eds) *Perspectives on Second Language Teacher Education*; Oxford University Press for the following: the article on pp. 68–75 'An experiment in role-reversal: teachers as language learners' by T. Lowe, *ELT Journal* 41 (2), © 1987; the article on pp. 92–103 'Six writers in search of texts: A protocol-based study of L1 and L2 writing' by V. Arndt, *ELT Journal* 41 (4), © 1987; the extracts on pp. 139–141 and pp. 143–145 from 'Language development provision in teacher training curricula' by G. Murdoch, *ELT Journal* 48 (3), © 1994; the article on pp. 153–159 'Learner strategies and learner interviews' by E. Pearson, *ELT Journal* 42 (3), © 1988; the article on pp. 172–180 'Developing a course strategy for learner autonomy' by S. Cotterall, *ELT Journal* 49 (3), © 1995; the article on pp. 195–206 'Survey review: two series of Business English materials' by B. Reed and S. Nolan, *ELT Journal* 48 (1), © 1994, all by permission of Oxford University Press; Cambridge University Press for the extract on pp. 121–123 from *Teaching Talk: Strategies for Production and Assessment* by G. Brown, A. Anderson, R. Shillcock and G. Yule (1984) and the extract on pp. 220–221 from *Language Teaching: The international abstracting journal for language teachers and applied linguists*, 28 (4), 1995; British Education Index for extract (a) and ERIC Document Reproduction Service for extract (b) on p. 219; Multilingual Matters Ltd. for the extracts on pp. 224–225 from *Introspection in Second Language Research* edited by C. Faerch and G. Kasper (1987); the article on pp. 243–250 'Research Update on Teaching L2 Listening' by R. L. Oxford, *System* 21 (2), 1993, is reprinted by permission of

Elsevier Science Ltd, Oxford; Phoenix ELT for the article on pp. 251–252 'Forging links: an idea for reviewing superlatives . . . and a bit more!' by D. Buckeridge, *Modern English Teacher* 3 (3), 1994.

We have been unable to trace the copyright owners of the figure on p. 60 and would be grateful for any information which will enable us to do so.

Thanks

I would like to begin by thanking all the EFL/ESL teachers (both practising teachers and would-be teachers) who have worked through the materials in this book, and, through their feedback, helped to shape it into its present form. I only hope that the content of this book has been at least as helpful to them, as reading their action research projects has been rewarding for me.

I am grateful in the first place to my colleagues in Moray House for providing such a stimulating and facilitative professional and academic environment in which to work. In this respect I'd particularly like to mention: Gordon Kirk, Pamela Munn, Jim Morrison, Gordon Liddell and Iain MacWilliam.

As always, I'm very grateful to the library staff of Moray House for all their unstinting help. Special thanks to: Denny Colledge, Steve Scott, David Fairgrieve, Sally Wilson and Hazel Robertson.

I'd like to record here my appreciation of the sterling efforts of the series editors, Marion Williams and Tony Wright. Their comments and suggestions, from the detailed to the organisational, were always thoughtful, considerate and helpful. Thanks also to my editors at Cambridge University Press, Alison Sharpe and Jane Clifford, for their unfailing courtesy and helpfulness. Thanks to Liz Driscoll, copy editor, for saving me from many egregious errors.

In its long gestation and succeeding versions, this manuscript has tested the secretarial skills of several people, all of whom have managed to cope both cheerfully and efficiently. I'd particularly like to thank Edith Young for all her help; and also Carole Jackson and Janine Fox. Thanks also to Barbara Thomas for her assistance.

Thanks, as ever, to my wife Eileen for her unfailing support.

Introduction

This book is written out of the conviction that one of the most effective ways of solving professional problems, and of continuing to improve and develop as teacher, teacher-trainer, or manager in ELT (English Language Teaching) is through reflection on our professional practice.

Reflection on practice can be managed in many different ways. The approach that will be explored in this book is the one that is sometimes called *action research*, by which I mean the systematic collection and analysis of data relating to the improvement of some aspect of professional practice.

This approach is not for everyone. For one thing, it makes demands on our time, and also requires the ability to look at evidence of our own practice in a more detached and objective way than we normally do. Nevertheless, if we can find the time and energy to do it, and we find it congenial, there is ample evidence that this approach can provide all sorts of interesting and helpful professional insights.

It is becoming quite common for ELT professionals to improve their qualifications through further studies, which very often require the completion of some kind of extended study, professional project, etc. Most people would prefer these studies, projects, or whatever, to relate as closely as possible to their normal professional action. For them, this book should be particularly useful. It should also be useful for pre-service trainee teachers facing similar requirements, providing they have had a reasonable amount of teaching experience, perhaps gained through a period of extended teaching practice.

If you are a practising teacher with a keen interest in professional development you might like to consider the action research approach presented here. If you do, hopefully, you will find certain of the techniques described to be of some practical use.

Special features of this book

As well as providing an approach to action research which is intended to be reasonably 'user-friendly' for interested practising ELT teachers, the book has certain other features which you may find helpful.

Examplar articles and extracts

These examplars are intended to achieve a number of aims. They show how the research techniques being described can work out when implemented in a specific context. They demonstrate how research findings can be reported. They give examples of the kinds of interesting results which an action research approach can yield. And I hope, also, that you will find them worth reading in their own right.

'Personal review' sections

The 'Personal review' sections are intended to give you a chance to think about the ideas being discussed and to relate them to your own situation. In many cases this will be done by involving you in various aspects of the process of action research – in other words a kind of 'learning by doing'.

Commentaries

Most 'Personal review' sections are followed by 'commentaries' which usually discuss possible responses to the questions raised in the 'Personal review' sections, and expand or elaborate on the issues involved.

Summaries

Each chapter concludes with a summary which briefly reviews the main topics dealt with in the chapter.

Glossary of research terms

In the text, a number of technical terms related to research are used. These will all be explained as they occur, but they will also be listed in a glossary at the end of the book for easy reference.

Suggestions for further reading

The present book is very much an introduction to a limited range of research methods. If you wish to explore further, this section will provide some suggested titles, with brief comments.

1 Why action research?

1.1 Aim of this book

As professional people, most teachers would accept that our expertise should progressively develop as we continue in our chosen occupation. My aim in this book is to demonstrate a particular strategy for accelerating and enhancing that kind of development, with special reference to language teaching.

This strategy is basically a way of reflecting on your teaching (or teacher-training, or management of an English department, or whatever it is you do in ELT). It is done by systematically collecting data on your everyday practice and analysing it in order to come to some decisions about what your future practice should be. This process is essentially what I mean by the term *action research*. In this first chapter, I am going to try to locate action research within the context of professional development.

1.2 Professional development

The value that is placed on 'experience' in most job-descriptions shows that the expectation of improvement after a period of practice is true, not just of professions, but indeed of a wide range of other employment. However, in some jobs, the expectation may be that the process of professional development levels off after an adequate level of competence is reached. This may be after a shorter or longer time, depending on the complexity of the tasks involved in doing the job, the aptitude of the person engaged in those tasks, and other factors. People working in a profession like teaching, on the other hand, may have more demanding expectations of themselves and their colleagues, because they regard the process of professional development as continuous and on-going.

One of the qualities that we should therefore expect in the strategies that we consider for professional development is that these strategies should help us to turn the problems we face in our professional careers into positive rather than negative experiences. In other words, how is it possible for us to turn our felt need for self-improvement into a challenging rather than a threatening process?

In fact, most of us tend to use a wide variety of strategies for our professional development, some formal, some informal. One informal but very effective strategy is discussions with our colleagues on classroom experiences or problems relating to specific students. This kind of 'talking shop' can have a whole range of useful functions: accessing useful background information, articulating possible solutions to everyday classroom problems, improving self-esteem, relieving tension, and so on. A very different kind of activity (much less common!) is reading professional journals for ideas and suggestions. Perhaps at this point you might wish to reflect on the 'strategies for professional development' that you currently use, or have used in the past.

PERSONAL REVIEW 1.1: Strategies for Professional Development

What are the strategies, formal or informal, that you either as a matter of policy or perhaps almost unconsciously use for your professional development? (I am thinking of things like attending conferences, reading professional journals, etc.) How useful/helpful do you find these 'strategies'? (Use a scale of 1–5, where 1 = not really useful/helpful and 5 = extremely useful/helpful.) How congenial do you find these strategies? In other words, do they come easily to you, or does it take a real effort of will to embark on some of these strategies? (Use the same 1–5 scale, where 1 = least/worst and 5 = most/best.)

	Strategy	Useful?	Congenial?
1.			
2.			
3.			
4.			
5.			
6.			

1.3 Commentary

How many different strategies did you come up with? Were the six spaces sufficient, or did you want to list more? There are many possibilities, of course. You may have listed the *membership of a professional association* as one of your strategies. This has many of the advantages of *informal discussions with colleagues*, and in addition a wider scope for social interaction. Membership of an association may or may not go along with *attendance at conferences*. If you listed this, you may have found it difficult to grade, since conferences can vary so much in their impact upon one. *Departmental meetings* and *membership of working parties* can also be very positive or very frustrating experiences, partly depending on one's relationships with the colleagues involved! *Evening/week-end/twilight* (i.e. after school) *classes* can also vary widely on their effectiveness and congeniality. Taking up *new challenges*, for example by career moves from one post to another, is another way in which many people expand their professional expertise. There is also, of course, *private reflection*: sometimes we do our best professional thinking while silently driving to or from our place of work, or while reading a book on some aspect of language teaching.

There is clearly a wide range of possibilities, and as I have already noted, the aim of the present book is to extend that range of possibilities still further.

1.4 Areas for development

Some teachers tend to be very self-critical – sometimes too much so. But this is better than being totally complacent, since self-development will never take place without the perceived need for it. Self-awareness of potential areas of improvement is therefore helpful provided it goes along with a reasonably good self-image. The leap into the unknown is unlikely to take place unless it can be done from a secure and stable platform of self-esteem. In this spirit, let us attempt two further 'Personal review' sections.

Just because something is a 'strength' does not mean, of course, that it need not be developed further – particularly if it is an important or 'key' strength in your professional repertoire. This point should be remembered when we turn to our next topic.

PERSONAL REVIEW 1.2: Strengths

Pick six areas of your professional competence which you feel are strengths of yours. The figure 'six' is quite arbitrary, of course, but go on – stretch! (If you have more than six – write them all down. Don't be modest!)

If you are working in a group and you feel this task is a little too 'personal' then set yourselves this task: What are the teaching strengths that you would say are most common among the teachers that you know?

Can you rank them in importance? (Or, alternatively, put an asterisk beside the key strengths.)

	Professional strengths	Rank/importance
1.		
2.		
3.		
4.		
5.		
6.		

1.5 Increased effectiveness

The next 'Personal review' section should be easier because it is concerned with areas of our expertise that we feel could be improved. In my experience, teachers and colleagues in the education field generally, are much more conscious of such areas than they are aware of their strengths. I would like you to imagine that you wish to become a more effective teacher, inspector, adviser, administrator, project organiser, head of department, teacher-trainer – or whatever. The 'Personal review' section will also ask you to think of the possible application of action research to these areas of concern.

PERSONAL REVIEW 1.3: Areas for Improvement

Use the chart below to make a list of, again say, six areas in which you think you could be more effective in your work. The areas can be very general (e.g. keeping discipline) or very specific (e.g. finding interesting topics for composition tasks).

As before, if you are working in a group, this task may be a little too private. In that case ask yourselves this question: In your experience, what are the areas in which most teachers could be more effective than they are now?

When you have done that, go back over the areas you have listed, and ask yourself if there is any serious possibility that 'research' (whatever you understand by that term) is likely to be of significant help to you in addressing some of those concerns. If you think it is, put a tick (✔) in the final column of the chart.

	I (most teachers) could be more effective if:	Would research help? (✔)
1.		
2.		
3.		
4.		
5.		
6.		

1.6 Commentary

Since I don't know what you put, let me give an example of a statement that many teachers have made in doing such an exercise: 'I could be more effective if I had more time to prepare my teaching.' This is probably a sentiment that many of us would share!

Putting to one side, for the time being, the issue of 'research', let us just look at this statement in terms of some questions it might raise:

- How much time do I currently spend on school work out of class?
- Is that a rough estimate? If so, how could I make it more accurate?
- How much of that time is spent on preparation (as distinct, from, say, correction)?
- Have I any idea of how these figures compare with my colleagues?
- Are there any ways in which class time could have been used for preparation without reducing the effectiveness of my teaching?
- Have I discussed this with my colleagues at all – have they any ideas?
- How about my use of time generally? Would I say it was efficient?
- What do I know about time management? Have I read any books on time management. If so, what do I think of them?

Please note two things about these questions which make them useful questions to ask. Firstly, they relate to your *personal practice* – so the answers ought to be relevant. Secondly, they are *answerable*, even if occasionally the answer is a matter of judgement rather than fact.

These questions might be of much greater interest to you if they applied to one of your own areas of concern. The next 'Personal review' section gives you an opportunity to do this. Just in case you haven't been able to think of a 'suitable' topic, the 'Personal review' section includes suggested areas of concern which you can use if you prefer.

PERSONAL REVIEW 1.4: Generating Questions

Take one of the areas that you have specified in PERSONAL REVIEW 1.3 and see whether you can generate some questions on the topic. Alternatively, you can try one of these areas, which have been suggested by other teachers:

I could be a more effective teacher if:

1. I could keep better discipline
2. I knew a wider range of teaching techniques
3. I didn't have to follow such a tightly-specified syllabus
4. I had more teaching resources
5. I wasn't so disorganised

Note: if you have trouble generating questions, try relating the topic to the question-words *Who/Whom?, What?, Why?, Where?, When?, How?* Remember to ask questions that are *personal* and *answerable*.

1.7 Commentary

You were asked to make up questions to this 'Personal review' section which were 'personal' (i.e. specific to your own professional practice). However, just as a check that you are on the right track, I would like to show how questions could be generated from one of the given topics. Let us take the first one (*I could be a more effective teacher if I could keep better discipline*). This topic could generate questions like these:

- *When* have I experienced indiscipline this session?
- *What* form did the indiscipline take?
- *How* did I react?
- *Did* I react appropriately, or not?
- *How* should I have reacted?
- *Who* was responsible?
- *Why* did the indiscipline take place? *What* were the immediate causes? *What* were the underlying causes?
- *What* is the appropriate strategy for me to take? In the short term? In the long term?
- *What* sources of help or guidance are available to me?

These are only some of the possible questions: others may have occurred to you. Asking the questions does not of course solve the problem. But even the act of writing the questions and perhaps writing out the answers may help to 'objectify' the situation and enable you to think your way through to a proactive plan of action (instead of merely *reacting* to problems as they arise). At the very least your questions should give you a range of options.

1.8 Inquiry

Let us briefly review where we have got to so far. It has been suggested that a continuous process of professional development is a rational and intrinsic part of the good professional's life. The motivation for this development is often an interest in, or perhaps even an anxiety about, some aspect of our professional performance. We have seen that there is a wide range of possible activities that we can get involved in to develop our professional expertise.

One possibility which we have just been exploring is to isolate an area and ask ourselves some questions about it. This is not very far from what Cohen and Manion (1994) have called inquiry. *Inquiry* in its most basic sense simply means the act or process of seeking the answer to a question. So academic inquiry means seeking to answer academic questions. Some examples within ELT might be:

- What makes a good ESP syllabus?
- How do you design good materials to develop listening skills?
- How should I teach the present perfect tense?
- What are the relative advantages of teacher-centredness and student-centredness?
- Is teaching English as a foreign language a form of linguistic imperialism?
- What are the processes by which someone learns a foreign language?
- How effective is task-based learning?
- What happens when people try to learn a language without the help of a teacher?

Notice that I have deliberately made these questions of very different types in order to show the range of questions that 'inquiry' can convey. Some of them (e.g. What makes a good ESP syllabus?) could be answered without collecting any *data* (facts) at all, but could be argued from certain principles (e.g. principles concerning the nature and function of ESP).

Other questions (like the last one: What happens when people try to learn a language without the help of a teacher?) are purely descriptive and any worthwhile discussion would have to be supported at some point by data recording the successes or failures of people trying to learn languages on their own.

Depending on the job we do within ELT, the answers to such questions might be quite important or completely irrelevant. But for someone, somewhere, any one of them may be a question worth answering, or at least attempting to answer, with reference to his or her particular practice.

Knowing what questions to ask, and how to ask them, is by no means as straightforward as it might appear, and this is an issue that we will have to return to later. In the meantime, let us have another look at questions that were raised about the 'not enough time for preparation' problem.

1.9 Research

Looking at these questions, you will notice that many of them relate to established *facts* (e.g. How much time do I spend on school work out of class? How much of that time is spent on preparation? How do these times compare with my colleagues?). Some have to do with collecting *views* and *opinions* of colleagues – what are their suggestions about preparation time?

Both these sets of facts and these opinions can form the raw data, which, after a period of reflection or analysis, we can use as a basis for our decisions on what, if anything, we are going to do about the problem we have identified.

This process of *data collection*, the setting up of a *database*, and the subsequent *analysis* of the data we have collected forms the core of what we call *research*. There are many other aspects of research, and other procedures may also be involved, but this process forms its essence. We see that, according to this definition, research is a special kind of inquiry, since not all inquiry is based on data collection and analysis. Some inquiry, for example, takes the form of pure reasoning from first principles and is especially common in disciplines like mathematics or philosophy. This form of inquiry, or something approximating to it, is also quite common in ELT. Many of the influential writings on methodology of teaching languages have been based, not on data about classrooms or language learners, but on deductions from principles of what constitutes good language teaching, or what is the appropriate philosophy for a teaching programme. So, we find that some national language teaching syllabuses specify that the syllabus should incorporate moral teaching in a systematic way. Other foreign language programmes contain elements designed to create mutual understanding between cultures, because this is felt to be a desirable pedagogic aim. And so on.

We have already used in the previous paragraph the expression 'deductions from principles': this kind of inquiry or investigation can be characterised as *deductive*. This is often contrasted with the *inductive* kind of inquiry which is derived from data collection and analysis (i.e. 'research' in our terms). It will hopefully be clear from what has just been said that *research* is here being viewed as being included in the term *inquiry*, just as, for example, *rose* is included in the term *flower*. I am labouring this point about the distinction I am making between *research* and *inquiry*, since *research* can be used with a wide variety of meanings, some of them very close to what I have here called *inquiry*.

1.10 Research, inquiry and professional development

By this time, you may feel that we have wandered quite a way from our starting point of professional development. Let me, therefore, try, to pull these issues together at this point.

I have elsewhere (Wallace, 1991) proposed a model for teacher education at the core of which is a process of *reflection on professional action*. I suggested that it was this process (called the 'reflective cycle') which provided the momentum for increased professional competence.

In the present context, the process involved could be summarised by the representation in Figure 1.1.

The whole of the present book is essentially an exploration of certain ways in which the 'reflective cycle' can be managed. Putting it another way, it is concerned with providing 'tools for reflection'.

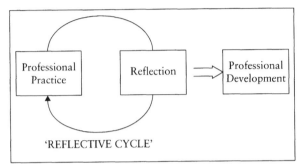

Figure 1.1 The reflective cycle and professional development

1.11 Research, inquiry and the reflective cycle

If you now look at Figure 1.2, you will see that I am suggesting that there is more than one way into the reflective cycle. This has to be the case, since the *process of professional development varies from one person to another.* We all have our own different kinds of professional experience, knowledge, background and expertise. Strengths and needs may vary from one individual to another. What may be of great importance to me may be totally irrelevant to you.

You will therefore note in Figure 1.2 that after 'Strategies for PD' there is a fork in the diagram. On the right-hand side are listed a few of the strategies which many of us have used (e.g. attending conferences, informal discussion with colleagues, etc.). Such activities very often give us information or ideas which cause us to reflect on our practice, and perhaps change it. Hence the arrow leading into the REFLECTIVE CYCLE box (which refers back to Figure 1.1).

1.12 Informal reflection

It has to be recognised, however, that not all these strategies are equally effective. Certain types of informal reflection can be more therapeutic than productive. Contemplating problems does not necessarily lead to

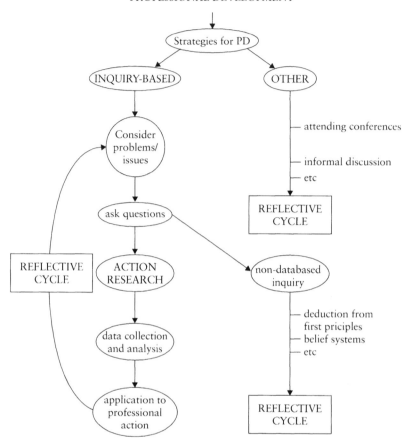

PROFESSIONAL DEVELOPMENT

Figure 1.2: Professional development strategies (excluding 'conventional research')

solving them. Indeed, sometimes such a process is not even therapeutic: mentally rehearsing certain experiences can lead to an intensification of unpleasant emotions without suggesting any way forward.

1.13 Structured reflection

There is therefore a case for also having available as a source for our reflection certain systematic approaches and techniques which will help us to make sense of our experiences, and perhaps through such *structured reflection* come to a solution. It would be extremely naive, of course, to imply that all our professional problems are capable of 'solution'. Some can only be investigated; some we might have to walk away from; others we might have to live with. However, it is the received wisdom of those working in caring professions that most problems benefit from being aired and discussed in some controlled or structured way; and this should also be true of professional problems. It is suggested here that action research is a form of structured reflection. Since action research is the main concern of this book, it has been separated and positioned on the left hand side of Figure 1.2. To simplify the diagram I have excluded 'conventional' research from the diagram (see discussion below in Section 1.18).

1.14   Action research is problem-focused

Some of our professional development is open-ended and relatively unfocused. We sometimes skim through professional journals just to see if there is anything interesting. We occasionally even enrol on training programmes without a very clear idea of what the criteria will be in terms of our professional development.

Action research is different from this in that it nearly always arises from some specific problem or issue arising out of our professional practice. (We looked at some possible problems of this kind in PERSONAL REVIEW 1.3.) It is therefore very problem-focused in its approach and very practical in its intended outcomes.

1.15   Action research and inquiry

As we saw in PERSONAL REVIEW 1.4 and the discussion leading up to it, problems/issues give rise to *questions*. Generating questions gives us the lead into various possible areas of investigation. As we have already noted, action research is therefore a sub-area of *inquiry*, which simply means the process of answering questions by using various kinds of evidence in some kind of reasoned way.

If you look again at Figure 1.2 you will see that two kinds of inquiry are featured:

1. non-databased inquiry
2. research

1.16   Research and non-databased inquiry

We saw earlier in this chapter that questions can be answered by a process of data collection and analysis (*action research*), or by other means (e.g. by arguing from general principles or by coming to certain conclusions according to certain things we believe – 'belief systems'). Some questions can be answered by either of these processes, or by combining them, but other questions can be answered only by using one method or the other.

Any conclusions or ideas we derive from databased inquiry can also feed back into the reflective cycle. To take a very simple example, when faced with a particular problem, I may go to a more experienced teacher and ask his or her advice. I may reflect on the advice, and then decide to follow it implicitly, modify it, or do something else.

However since we are mainly interested in action research, we will not pursue this any further, and go back to the left-hand side of the diagram. But before that, let us just explore a bit further this business of how we can go about answering professional questions, by doing PERSONAL REVIEW 1.5.

PERSONAL REVIEW 1.5: Answering Professional Questions

Look back at the ELT questions that were listed in Section 1.8. Pick any one of these questions. How would you go about answering the question you have chosen?

More specifically:
1. What sort of evidence would you look for?
2. What procedures would you use to collect the evidence?
3. Would the evidence involve the collection of data or not?

To give an example: the answer to 'How should I teach the present perfect tense?' could be found to be appealing to an authority (e.g. checking up in a teacher's book on methodology, asking a more experienced teacher), or by observing various teaching methods (a form of data collection), or by trying out various approaches and seeing how they work. Or you may be guided by certain principles/belief systems (e.g. 'I don't believe in the formal teaching of grammar, so this question really doesn't make much sense to me').

1.17   Action research and the reflective cycle

Action research involves the collection and analysis of data related to some aspect of our professional practice. This is done so that we can reflect on what we have discovered and apply it to our professional action. This is where it differs from other more traditional kinds of research, which are much more concerned with what is universally true, or at least generalisable to other contexts.

This is a loop process, in the sense that the process can be repeated (reframing the problem, collecting fresh data, rethinking our analysis, etc.) until we have found a solution that satisfies us.

1.18   The status of action research

To some readers, it may seem that we have come a long way round to a statement of the obvious. I suspect that for many people, however, the role of action research as an activity for practising teachers is by no means obvious. It is likely that the attitude of the majority of teachers varies between indifference and downright hostility. So it has to be made clear precisely what is being argued for here.

It has been assumed here that it is natural, and appropriate, for teachers (like other professionals) to develop their expertise by reflecting on their practice. It is not being argued, however, that every teacher can be, or should be, a 'researcher' in any traditional sense of that word. This seems to the present writer to be an unreasonable requirement. As Wright (1992: 203) has noted: ' . . . teachers may sense that they are being asked to take on yet more duties in addition to those which already burden them . . .' As we have previously established, there are many avenues of professional development which different professionals will find more or less useful and/or congenial. It seems unduly constrictive to isolate one of them as a route that must be taken.

Action research has been proposed as an 'empowering' procedure. But, as Widdowson (1993: 267) has pointed out, if it becomes another top-down requirement, it turns into the reverse: not only is it an additional burden upon teachers, but it also creates a new kind of dependency on (non-teaching) 'experts'. Various conditions have been laid down from time to time as to what constitutes proper action research. Some writers recommend that action research should be collaborative or team-based. Others suggest publication or at least sharing of the process and results of the investigation in some way. It has also been suggested that the same stringent requirements of *validity*, *reliability* and *verification* for conventional research should also apply to action research. (These terms will be discussed in Chapter 3, which deals with issues relating to the collection of data.)

If reflection is to be of any real value it must be valid (i.e. the data analysis must be relevant and appropriate). However, since the position being taken in the present book is that action research is primarily an approach relating to individual or small group professional develop-

17

ment, the generalisability of the findings to other contexts will not in most cases be of primary importance. The important thing is that the processes involved are helpful to the practising teacher's reflection, irrespective of whether they can be verified by someone else.

Action research, in this definition therefore, overlaps the areas of professional development and conventional research, and for some practising teachers may well form a bridge between the two. The aim, however, is not to turn the teacher into a researcher, but to help him or her to continue to develop as a teacher, using action research as a tool in this process.

If you have identified some problems and you are not clear about the kind of data available or the method of collection, don't worry: this book is intended to help you with these problems!

1.19 Summary

It is assumed that most language teachers wish to develop themselves professionally on a continuing basis. They have access to a wide variety of methods of doing this. One method is by reflecting on interesting and/or problematic areas in a structured way. In this book, we shall be looking at various ways of structuring this process of reflection through the systematic collection and analysis of data. This is what I have called 'action research'. Action research is different from other more conventional or traditional types of research in that it is very focused on individual or small-group professional practice and is not so concerned with making general statements. It is therefore more 'user-friendly' in that (for example) it may make little or no use of statistical techniques. The main function of action research is to facilitate the 'reflective cycle', and in this way provide an effective method for improving professional action.

PERSONAL REVIEW 1.6: Professional Problems and Available Data

At the end of this chapter, it might be appropriate to see if you can think of any problem areas in your professional life that might be tackled through collecting or analysing data in a systematic way.

'Problem areas' could cover a wide range of possibilities, for example:

1. problems of classroom management

2. problems of appropriate materials

3. problems related to particular teaching areas (e.g. reading, oral skills)

4. problems relating to student behaviour, achievement or motivation

5. problems relating to personal management issues (e.g. time management, relationships with colleagues/higher management)

These are only examples, and the topics given are probably too broad. Try to be specific.

As before, if you are doing this as a member of a group, and do not want this exercise to be too personal, ask yourselves this question: What are the problems which an average teacher in our context might encounter or be concerned with? What kind of data might be available to him or her?

	Problem	Kind of data that might be available and how it might be collected
1.		
2.		
3.		

2   Selecting and developing a topic

2.1   Introduction

In this chapter, we will be discussing how you might go about selecting
and developing a topic on which you want to do some action research.
You should therefore not look upon everything in this chapter as a
prescription of what *must* be done. Rather it is an indication of what
might be done depending on the scope of project you are undertaking.
Clearly, if you are going to spend only about ten hours in total on your
piece of action research, then five hours spent on planning would be out
of proportion. But if you estimate that you will probably spend one
hundred hours in total, then five hours spent on selecting and developing the topic might be fairly minimal.

PERSONAL REVIEW 2.1: Time Allocation

1. What is the total amount of time, in hours, that you think
    you can afford to spend on your action research project?

2. Let us assume that selecting and developing the topic will
    take up to 10% of that time. How much time does that give
    you?

2.2   Overview

The decisions you make about selecting and developing a topic can be
absolutely crucial, in two ways. Firstly, if you are a teacher who is
thinking about how action research can help you reflect on your
teaching, it is essential to embark on an appropriate topic in an
appropriate way, because your experience with it will obviously colour
your attitude to the whole business of doing action research. Secondly,
if you intend to devote a substantial amount of time to an action

research topic, for whatever reason, success or failure may be predetermined by how you select and develop the topic. (Some would-be action researchers start off by asking themselves questions which are essentially unanswerable!)

Selecting and developing the topic will be dealt with under the following headings:

1. **Purpose**   Why are you engaging in this action research?
2. **Topic**   What area are you going to investigate?
3. **Focus**   What is the precise question you are going to ask yourself within that area?
4. **Product**   What is the likely outcome of the research, as you intend it?
5. **Mode**   How are you going to conduct the research?
6. **Timing**   How long have you got to do the research? Is there a deadline for its completion?
7. **Resources**   What are the resources, both human and material, that you can call upon to help you complete the research?
8. **Refocusing/fine-tuning**   As you proceed with your research, do you suppose you will have to rethink your original question?

2.3   Purpose

Try to be very clear about why you are doing this research. As we have said, your investigation is much less likely to be involving or productive if you are doing it because you have to, for example, as part of a course. If you are in this situation, think very hard about how far you can relate the task to your real personal/professional interests. *This is a very important consideration and you should devote some time to it*. If the topic you have chosen does not relate in some direct way to your professional needs, then it is by definition not action research.

2.4   Topic

If you have worked your way through the 'Personal review' sections of Chapter 1, particularly PERSONAL REVIEW 1.6, you may very well already have some ideas about the topic area in which you wish to do your action research. You may decide that you want to tackle several related topics, devoting only a short time to each, just to see what you come up with. Or you may decide that you cannot afford to do that but must choose one area: but which one? The answer to this may depend on the answers to the other questions that have been listed in Section

2.2, and will be dealt with in more detail in the rest of this chapter: practical considerations, including feasibility, are crucially important.

However, before we can go on to discuss your choice of topic, there is another issue which we must look at, which is how far it is within your power to change the way that you teach.

2.5   Boundaries of decision-making

Sometimes teachers reject action research as a possible mode of professional development because they say, in essence, 'There is nothing we can change. Everything is decided by the Ministry or the Inspectorate.' If this is truly the case, then of course these teachers are right. Action research presupposes that there are certain areas of professional action where teachers can choose to do one thing rather than another, and to evaluate the results. The response of these teachers does not, it should be clear, undermine the rationale of this book. It has already been established in Chapter 1 that action research is only one among many forms of professional development, and the position taken here is that it is not an activity every teacher will want to undertake.

Having said that, it is hard to believe that teachers in certain contexts have no personal decision-making powers. If this were the case, one would expect the quality of teaching in such contexts to be almost identical in every class (which is perhaps what some bureaucrats aspire to!). Experience shows that in such contexts, as in other more unconstrained contexts, there is in fact a wide range of teaching quality. It is possible that these differences are attributable to personality traits or the degree to which the teacher flouts the 'rules'. But it seems equally possible that the differences (or some of them) are due to decisions taken by individual teachers in terms of, for example, classroom management, interaction with the class, motivation, pacing of lessons, task-prioritisation, feedback, disciplinary routines, and so on. Now try PERSONAL REVIEW 2.2.

When you have filled in the table for PERSONAL REVIEW 2.2, look again at the areas NOT within your decision-making domain.

Note that there may be different aspects of such areas: for example, you might not be able to *change* the syllabus but you may be able to *modify* it or *interpret* it in different ways. Similarly, selecting your colleagues might not be within your decision-making domain, but choosing *how to relate* to them might well be.

Within the topic areas that are open to you for change of professional action, the most important factor in selecting a topic for your own action research is your sense of *personal involvement* with the topic. How important is it to you? If it is important enough, then you will be

PERSONAL REVIEW 2.2: Decision-Making Areas

Before we go on any further, therefore, it may be useful and, for some, perhaps even liberating, to think about some of the areas in which we do or don't have decision-making powers. For some teachers, for example, 'the syllabus' may be something given or imposed, whereas for others the syllabus might be entirely within their own decision-making domain. Another example would relate to how rigidly the coursebook has to be followed. Two further examples are given below. Use the rest of the chart for your own answers.

Some professional areas within my decision-making domain	Some professional areas NOT within my decision-making domain
which tasks I give for homework	what topics are to be covered in the syllabus

much more likely to overcome the various practical difficulties you may encounter.

Important is an ambiguous word, in a way. For example, you may say: 'This is important to me because I need to do some action research for a Master's Degree.' This kind of extrinsic (externally driven) motivation may be sufficient encouragement for you to persevere, but it would be preferable if you had intrinsic (personal) motivation as well. All this means is that you should, if possible, choose a topic which matters to you in terms of your own professional development. Although it is sometimes inevitable, it is usually unwise to follow someone else's agenda.

The final 'Personal review' section in Chapter 1 asked you to list 'any problem areas in your professional life that might be tackled through collecting or analysing data in a systematic way'. The next 'Personal review' section asks you to consider a slightly different but related question.

2.6 Focus

Your prioritisation of importance/interest should have given you the grounds for an overall prioritisation of the areas for investigation. If you are lucky, one topic will have ranked 1 for both importance and interest. If you have to choose between importance and interest – you should probably go for interest! We now have to turn the *topic* into a *research focus*. In other words, what particular *aspect* of the topic/area do we wish to investigate? If we are doing action research for a dissertation, this focus will have to be expressed in the form of a *working title*. (We will use the term 'working title' because, as you will have previously noted, you will probably have to modify the title as you get further into your research.)

2.7 Example: group work

Let us say, for example, that you are interested in researching *group work*. We now have to start answering many other questions, such as:

What aspect of group work is it that is bothering you, or intriguing you?
– Is it the business of setting up groups?
– Is it the composition of groups?
– Is it the personality clashes within groups?
– Is it the use of the mother tongue in groups?

PERSONAL REVIEW 2.3: Prioritising Areas of
Investigation

Look back at the answers that you wrote to the 'Personal
review' sections in Chapter 1, particularly PERSONAL
REVIEW 1.3 and PERSONAL REVIEW 1.6. Having done
that:

1. make a list of up to six 'areas for investigation';

2. say why you have chosen these areas;

3. prioritise them in rank order (1–6) according to how
    important and interesting you feel them to be.

When you are listing the areas for investigation, do so in the
form of a statement/phrase (e.g. implementation of group work;
use of visual aids, etc.). An example is given below. You can
use the rest of the chart for your own answers.

Areas of investigation	Reasons for choice	Priority	
		Importance	Interest
interaction in group work	some students are very passive in group work—are they learning anything?	3	1

- Is it the dynamic of groups – how the individuals within a group work together?
- Is it the issue of group leadership?
- Is it the effectiveness of group work?
- Is it the selection of the best materials for group work?
- Is it the effect of different tasks on group work?

This list of questions could be much longer. Perhaps you are interested in not one simple aspect but a combination of aspects. Perhaps you are interested in group work related to something else – the school ethos, or the curriculum, or whatever. Now do PERSONAL REVIEW 2.3.

This, therefore, is one important element in achieving focus: that is, specifying the topic as precisely as you can. Another element relates to the *population* that you are researching. 'Population' simply means the group that you are interested in investigating. Sometimes it is not possible to investigate the whole population directly, so you have to take a *sample*. Are you interested only in learners at a certain level – beginners, say, or intermediate? Are you perhaps thinking of a particular class, or of a particular group, or of a particular individual within a group?

You may read somewhere of the advantages of group work, but wonder if it works well in your school, in this class, with this particular group, for this particular individual. How closely focused you want to be is entirely up to you. Here is an example of how we might specify our focus:

1. An investigation of group work
2. An investigation of *the use of the mother tongue* in group work
3. An investigation of the use of the mother tongue in *task-based* group work
4. An investigation of the use of the mother tongue in task-based group work *in a French school*
5. An investigation of the use of the mother tongue in task-based group work among *intermediate-level learners* in a French school
6. *'Monique': a case study* of the use of the mother tongue in task-based group work among intermediate-level learners in a French School (and so on)

The first three examples are probably not sufficiently focused. In the last example, 'Monique' is presumably the name given to an individual learner to protect her true identity, as frequently happens in *case studies*.

The examples we have been looking at are the kind of informative titles required for dissertations. For an article or a talk, you might need something more informal.

2.8 Narrowing the focus

There is therefore much to be gained from trying to make the focus of your topic as specific as you can. Look at these examples, still in the area of group work:

General topic	More focused topic
group interaction	I'd like to look in detail at how two of my groups interact during an information-gap activity. I am especially interested in the amount of participation: does everyone participate? If not, why not? Are there differences in the patterns of interaction, and, if so, can I think of reasons for these differences?
group interaction	I'd like to take one sample group and monitor the level of language that is used. What kinds of mistakes are being made? What action, if any, should I take about these mistakes?

It will be seen that the same general topic can end up with quite a different narrow focus.

PERSONAL REVIEW 2.4: Narrowing the Focus

Look back again at PERSONAL REVIEW 2.3. Pick one of the areas/topics that you are interested in and see if you can be more specific about exactly which aspect of the area/topics it is that you wish to investigate, along the lines of the example that has just been given. If you have access to a group, share your ideas with others in your group. Each person should take it in turn to explain what he or she intends to do.

2.9 Product

What is the intended outcome of your research? Here are some possible answers.

1. I have no idea. I intend just to do it and then see what I come up with.

27

2. I hope to be able to apply the results of the investigation to my own teaching.
3. Like (2), but if I come up with anything interesting, I'll share it with colleagues in my department.
4. If the results look interesting, I intend to give a talk to our local branch of the English Language Teachers' Association.
5. If the results look interesting, I might publish it:
   - in-house
   - in an Association newsletter
   - a journal
   - a refereed journal (i.e. a journal where the articles have to be approved by experts before they are published)
6. This is going to be the subject of:
   - a module assignment
   - a Master's dissertation
   - a PhD thesis.

Clearly, your answer to this question will affect how you go about doing your research. If your answer is (6), a number of decisions (e.g. about length, format, etc.) will already have been made for you. If your answer is (1), (2) or (3), it might still be worthwhile to keep all your data and findings in some accessible form: they might turn out to be useful to you at some later stage of your career.

2.10 Research modes

How are you going to conduct the research? One of the purposes of this book is to widen your range of choices. There may come a time when you have to commit yourself to a particular research methodology (or a selection of methodologies), but in the meantime, keep an open mind. Stay on the lookout for new ways of collecting and analysing data, in the same way that, as a teacher, you are always on the lookout for new teaching ideas. Most people beginning research have very fixed ideas about what constitutes research (e.g. experiments, questionnaires), but one of the advantages of action research is that the choice is very wide. Now try PERSONAL REVIEW 2.5.

2.11 Timing

We started off this chapter by looking at the issue of time allocation. The availability of time in which to do the research is a major issue, and it will influence the scope of what you can do. A further issue is whether or not you will be working to a deadline.

PERSONAL REVIEW 2.5: Brainstorming Different
Research Techniques

See how many different techniques for conducting research
you can think of. Make a list. Now glance through this book
and see if there are any techniques you can add to the list
(even if you are not sure exactly what they mean). Keep the list
somewhere and add to it whenever you come across a
technique that is new to you. You can start the list with the
techniques we have just mentioned:

1. experiments
2. questionnaires

There are two possible approaches to this issue of time:

1. If the action research is purely for your own professional development, then you will not have the disadvantage (or perhaps it is an
   advantage?) of working to a deadline. It also means that you can
   scale down the scope of the research until it fits into the time you
   have available, even if that is only a matter of some hours.
2. If the action research is for a formal qualification, then the chances
   are that you are working to a deadline, and the write-up will have
   to meet certain criteria such as length, etc. In this case, you will
   somehow have to 'scale up' the time available until it matches the
   requirements of the project.

For both approaches, a little extra time spent in planning may save a lot
of time in implementation. There is not enough space to fully discuss
time-management (see 'Suggestions for further reading'), but three
points can be made briefly:

1. If you need to save time, and you have a choice of research topics,
   then choose one which requires activities that you would do
   anyway (e.g. it should take up less extra time to experiment with
   different kinds of feedback on written work, since this is an activity
   you would be required to do anyway).
2. Is it possible to involve students in some of the data collection in an
   ethical (moral) and *productive* way? One has to think carefully
   before involving students, since issues of professional ethics may be
   involved (see next chapter). It may be however, that, for example,
   getting students to monitor their own group behaviour might be
   beneficial for them, as well as providing useful data for an action
   research programme.

29

3. We all have a human tendency just to get on with the next thing that is to hand, and there are arguments for sustaining motivation by doing what is congenial to you. Nevertheless, if you are working to a deadline, it really is worthwhile to make a timetable of what you intend to do. Always put cut-off dates for the different stages of the research, as you should be aware of slippage as quickly as possible. If there is slippage, consider ways in which you can save time without undermining your project (e.g. by being more selective in data collection).

PERSONAL REVIEW 2.6: Allocating Time

If you have a project in mind, ask yourself:

1. How many hours is it going to take?
2. How are you going to make this time available? You might find it useful to take a sheet of paper and divide it into two columns: **Sacrifices** and **Gains**, for example:

Sacrifices	Gains
reading newspaper on train	30 minutes reading per day = 2.5 hours per week

3. Is there any way you can economise on time (e.g. through the co-operation of colleagues, students, management)?

Make a provisional timetable for the project. (Two of the possible formats are provided, which you can modify to suit your needs. Examples have been given in the first format; comments can either be things to remember, or a note how the task was completed.)

If you are working in a group, without having any particular project in mind, see if you can brainstorm as many ways as you can in which action researchers could save time while doing their research. You could also, as a group, brainstorm a list of ways in which you could work together to use your time more effectively.

TASK-TIME FORMAT

Project: _____

Completion deadline: _____

Task	Cut-off date	Comment
interview three students (15 mins each)	30 June	only two interviews completed

MULTIPLE-TIMELINE FORMAT

PROJECT: _____

COMPLETION DEADLINE: _____

WEEK NO:	1.	2.	3.	4.	5.	6.	7.	8.
Planning								
Reading								
Data collection								
Analysis								
Writing-up								

Note: in this format, you can put more detailed information. For example, for **Planning**, Week (1), you might put: 'Brainstorming initial ideas'.

2.12 Resources

Apart from your own energy, interest and time, you may also need other resources to help you to do the research you want to do. It is probably a good idea to think about resource requirements earlier rather than later.

You can think of these other resources under two headings:

1. material
2. people

By 'material resources', I mean things like a video-recorder, video tape or audio tape, playback facilities, etc. You will probably also need help from certain people (e.g. camera operators, secretarial help).

Even if you don't think you actually need extra resources, it is perhaps worthwhile reviewing what is available to you: this may give you some ideas for other activities.

PERSONAL REVIEW 2.7: Listing Resources

1. Make a list of the tasks you intend to perform as part of your research project and match them with resources required. Put an asterisk (*) beside any resource requirements that look problematic.

2. Make a list of any other resources readily available to you. Are there any possibilities here that could enrich your research?

3. Look back at the resources you have asterisked. Is there any other way in which you can acquire:

   – the same data?
   – equivalent data?

2.13 Refocusing/fine-tuning

As we have already said, there is, or should be, a dynamic relationship between the problem you set yourself at the beginning of your research, and your conceptualisation of that problem as the research proceeds. From time to time you should go back to your initial statements. Did you ask yourself the right questions? Should the problem be reframed? On a major project such changes should not be undertaken lightly, but the questions have to be asked. It has to be said that, realistically speaking, it is almost inevitable that your initial conceptualisation of what you are researching will be changed at least to some extent.

2.14 Summary

In this chapter, we have been looking at some of the necessary planning issues involved in selecting and developing a research topic. We began by considering the topic and looking at how it could be more focused in terms of the research questions. We then considered a number of practical issues, particularly the use of time and other resources. Finally we noted that in most research projects the initial topic will almost inevitably have to be refocused and fine-tuned.

3 Collecting the data

3.1 Overview

In the last chapter, I suggested that one of the key issues in developing an action research topic had to do with choosing the *mode* of research. In other words, when we choose an action research topic, we have to ask ourselves: Which particular research methods are going to be applied to this topic? It is one of the main functions of this book to widen and deepen the range of your choice of action research methods. However, before going into a more detailed discussion of the various methods of action research, I will present in this chapter a brief survey of the range of possibilities that will be discussed.

The second aim of this chapter is to look at some ways of broadly categorising the various research approaches. Thinking about these categories may help you to decide which action research methods are the most appropriate for you.

The chapter will conclude with a discussion of some key issues related to ethics and protocol in implementing action research. It is appropriate to discuss these issues before you start collecting data as breaches of ethics or protocol can undermine action research and make it counter-productive.

3.2 Ways of categorising research

In this section we are going to look at some ways of categorising action research. These different categories are summarised in Figure 3.1, where they are related to some of the action research methods that I am going to describe in this book. You will notice that, by and large, the categories are not exclusively applied to the methods – words like *usually* and *either* are frequently used. This is because most action research techniques can be implemented in various ways.

However, before we get on to the categories listed in Figure 3.1, there are two terms often applied to any kind of research which I would like to discuss briefly at this point: the terms are *reliability* and *validity*.

3.3 Reliability

You are probably already familiar with the concept of reliability from your professional studies in language testing. In testing, the issue of fairness to all candidates is very important, so we have to ask ourselves questions like: Is the marking scheme for this test such that any competent marker (Marker A) would give Candidate X's paper the same grade as any other competent marker (Marker B)?

The same kind of questions can be applied to research results: If the research procedures used by Researcher A are exactly followed by Researcher B, will the *findings* (results) be the same each time? Another way of putting this question is this: is the research exactly *replicable* (repeatable)?

It has to be said that sometimes action research data are not very reliable in this technical sense. Sometimes, achieving a high degree of reliability means controlling nearly all the aspects of the situation that can change or vary (i.e. the *variables*). In many action research situations this is impossible or undesirable. If you are doing action research for yourself, you may be happy to trust your own judgement as to how 'reliable' your findings are. If you wish to convince others, for example, through publication, you may make your findings more credible by being very explicit about the nature of your original data (e.g. by putting complete transcripts of interviews in an appendix, etc.).

You may also remember from your knowledge of testing procedures that one way of making subjective assessments (e.g. grading essays) more reliable is to have more than one marker. In the same way, another way of increasing the reliability of research findings is to have more than one source of data. For example, if you interview a teacher about a lesson he or she has taught, it might be useful to have carried out *observation* of the lesson yourself, to have a video and/or to interview some of the learners who have taken part in the lesson. (This procedure of getting more than one perspective on the topic being researched is sometimes called *triangulation*.)

3.4 Validity

This is another concept that you will probably be familiar with from what you know about testing. Validity means testing what you are supposed to test, and not something else. For example, let us imagine that I want to test someone's reading comprehension ability, and I decide to do this by asking him or her to write a summary of a certain text. Is this a valid test? Am I actually testing reading comprehension, or something else – writing skills, perhaps?

Categories / Techniques	Quantitative/ qualitative	Introspective/ empirical	Individual/ collaboration	Intrusive/ complementary	Illuminative + heuristic/ conclusive
verbal reports (think-aloud)	usually qualitative	introspective	individual	usually complementary	usually illuminative/heuristic
observation	either	either	usually collaborative	usually intrusive	usually illuminative/heuristic
interviews	usually qualitative	introspective	either	either	usually illuminative/heuristic
questionnaires	either	introspective	either	either	usually illuminative/heuristic
case studies	usually qualitative	either	usually individual	either	usually illuminative/heuristic
evaluation	usually quantitative	usually empirical	either	either	either
trialling	usually quantitative	usually empirical	either	either	either

Figure 3.1 Some common research techniques related to categories

Similarly, let us suppose that I want to know if my students like my method of teaching them. I decide to do this in an *interview* with each student individually. Will the results be valid? Or will my students conceal their real feelings, either out of self-interest or because they don't want to offend me? Perhaps I will get more valid results if I give the students an anonymous *questionnaire* to fill in.

Whether you are researching purely for your own personal development, or because you want to share your findings with others, validity is clearly an extremely important issue: there is no point in reflecting on data that are misleading or irrelevant.

3.5 Quantitative and qualitative approaches

Probably the most common way of classifying research studies is by categorising them as using either quantitative or qualitative approaches. *Quantitative* is broadly used to describe what can be counted or measured and can therefore be considered 'objective'. *Qualitative* is used to describe data which are not amenable to being counted or measured in an objective way, and are therefore 'subjective'. Thus, in researching a language lesson, it is quite easy for us to measure (with a stop-watch, for example) the amount of 'teacher talk' as against 'pupil talk', or the amount of use of the target language as opposed to the mother tongue. Such data are amenable to a quantitative approach.

Alternatively, you could interview the teacher (and/or the students) involved in the lesson and ask what comments they had on the lesson. Ask the teacher, did everything go according to plan? Was he or she pleased or disappointed with the lesson as a whole? Would he or she teach it the same way next time? Ask one of the students, how interesting was the lesson for him or her? Was it easy to understand? The responses to individual interviews cannot easily be measured quantitatively, but the data (i.e. the replies) might actually be more interesting to practising teachers than statistics about the quantity of teacher talk.

The truth is, of course, that there need be no real opposition or contradiction between the two approaches. Quantitative data can throw light on qualitative insights and vice-versa. The dangers arise when larger claims than can be sustained by the data are made for either kind of investigation. For example, with reference to the quantitative approach, there is a temptation to isolate a category of behaviour (e.g. pupil talk rather than teacher talk) as intrinsically a positive aspect, to quantify its presence or absence, and then use these 'objective' data to evaluate a teacher's performance. The fallacy of such evaluation is obvious (What if the pupil talk is a 'sharing of ignorance'? What if the teacher talk is charismatic and motivating?). With reference to the qualitative approach, the dangers of bias are obvious, and all such evidence has to be weighed carefully, otherwise there is the danger of simply confirming existing prejudices rather than achieving new insights.

Where does this leave the action researcher? An early step in many investigations will be that of collecting facts or *hard data* (i.e. objective, quantitative data that can be measured in some way). (See PERSONAL REVIEW 3.1.) The researcher has to interpret the significance of these facts for his or her own professional development as a matter of analysis, interpretation and evaluation. So at some stage a qualitative element is almost inevitable

3.6 Introspective and empirical data

Research techniques can also be categorised according to whether the data is generated by, as it were, 'looking inward' (*introspective data*), or by 'looking outward '(*empirical data*).

Classic empirical research is done by 'looking outward'; in other words, by closely observing certain aspects of the world around us. It is concerned with examining objective, material things. These observations can usually be checked by other people.

It is also possible to 'look inward' through examining our own thoughts and feelings and giving an account of them: this yields what is sometimes called introspective or *mentalistic data*. Such ways of collecting data fell into disrepute because there is usually no way of checking on their reliability, or even their validity. If I say I am thinking something, I could be lying (for some reason) or I could be confused or mistaken. On the other hand, there may be no other way of even getting a hint of how people think. Also, what people think or feel may be just as important as any other kind of data: this explains, for example, the amount of attention that is paid to public opinion polls.

3.7 Individual and collaborative approaches

Individual approaches to action research are those which do not directly involve anyone else except the professional concerned; obvious examples are writing personal *field-notes* and keeping a *diary*. The advantages of such approaches are that they tend to be more flexible, less professionally risky and more easily implemented than others.

PERSONAL REVIEW 3.1: Using Hard Data

1. Think of your existing classroom practice. What sort of 'hard data' do you find useful in exercising professional judgement? (For example: How far in assessing written work are you guided by hard data, such as the number of times certain types of errors occur? Are the errors categorised and weighted for seriousness?)

2. Are there any areas of your professional action (teaching, management, etc.) where you would like to get some more hard data but because of lack of time or any other reason, such data are not available to you? How would you go about getting this information if you had the time/ resources? (You might find it helpful to check back to PERSONAL REVIEW 1.6 when doing this.)

An example is given below. You can set out your information like this:

Professional area	Source of data
student motivation	questionnaires to students

3. Are there any areas of your professional life where you are conscious of having to rely heavily on your intuition, judgement and/or previous experience? Can you think of any ways in which such judgements, etc. could be made more reliable?

Collaborative approaches involve others, usually other colleagues in the same institution. An example of collaboration would be sitting in on a colleague's lesson to observe it, or tape-recording discussions about various aspects of teaching.

With the right kind of co-operation, collaboration can do much to sustain motivation, save time by the allocation of different tasks as appropriate, and generate richer input from the combined talents and insights of those involved. Possible difficulties are: the emergence of different, incompatible positions between action researchers, varying amounts of commitment, different work-schedules so that committed time cannot be synchronised, and different levels of status within the team (e.g. between full-time researchers and classroom teachers).

PERSONAL REVIEW 3.2: Collaborative Research

1. What are your own views about the advantages and disadvantages of individual and collaborative research respectively? Complete a chart like this:

	Advantages	Disadvantages
Individual		
Collaboration		

2. What sort of institution are you working in? Are there structures or support mechanisms either inside or outside your institution which might support collaborative research? Are there any such structures/mechanisms which it would be feasible to introduce? (Some possible examples are: dedicated times for staff development, official recognition of action research as an appropriate activity, etc.)

3.8 **Complementary and intrusive approaches**

Perhaps the most interesting categorisation of action research method-ology for busy professionals is between those approaches which are complementary to their normal routines and those which are intrusive or disruptive. Clearly, the most convenient approaches for professionals to put into effect are extensions or elaborations of what they would normally be doing anyway. The table below shows how complementary, or minimally intrusive, activities could be developed from normal teaching activities:

NORMAL TEACHING ACTIVITY	MORE HIGHLY-STRUCTURED REFLECTION (ACTION RESEARCH)
1. trying out new materials	comparative data between old and new materials, (e.g. former textbook and present textbook)
2. error correction	logging and categorising errors
3. monitoring quality of target language use in group work	audio recording of a group to monitor target language use
4. promoting group interaction	use of an interaction chart to log group interaction
5. encouraging student response	delaying teacher response time and monitoring effect of this
6. motivating learners (1)	case studies of motivated and unmoti-vated students, perhaps by using inter-views
7. motivating learners (2)	questionnaires on preferences, likes/dis-likes

(Adapted from Wallace, 1993)

Figure 3.2 Normal teaching and structured reflection

Intrusive techniques, on the other hand, either disrupt one's own normal professional action (therefore intruding on the normal learning processes of one's students, for example), or disrupt the professional (or private!) lives of others. Questionnaires, interviews, experiments and observation are potentially intrusive techniques. Very often the degree of intrusion can, however, be mitigated by sensitive handling: interviews, for example, can be kept short in duration, and questionnaires can be part of a normal evaluation process.

PERSONAL REVIEW 3.3: Devising Complementary Data Collection Techniques

Look again at Figure 3.2. Can you add to that list? Are there any other normal professional activities that you or your colleagues are engaged in which are amenable to extension or elaboration in the way that is described? Use the same format to list 'normal teaching activities' and 'complementary activities'. You may be able to use (or adapt) some of the suggestions you put forward to PERSONAL REVIEW 3.1.

3.9 Illuminative/heuristic and conclusive approaches

Another aspect of the qualitative/quantitative distinction that we discussed earlier relates to this issue: do we want to conclusively prove that something is the case, or do we simply want to throw some new light on a topic or problem (*illuminative research*) or discover something about that topic/problem that we were not aware of before (*heuristic research*)?

Most scientific research relates to the first ('conclusive') approach. Most traditional research scientists would see it as their task to prove that some facts or laws relating to natural science are true. This kind of research is very important to language teachers. It is highly relevant for us to know how people learn languages, whether their mother-tongue or a foreign language. It is extremely useful for us to know about how the languages we teach are structured. If we use group work a lot, then it would be helpful to know what has been discovered about the various ways in which groups interact. We could obviously go on in this vein for a long time.

It is widely agreed, of course, that all scientific theories are provisional: such theories are only valid until some better explanation comes along. But this does not mean that these theories are not useful: Newtonian physics was an amazingly fruitful scientific theory, even though the theory of relativity later revealed that it was flawed in certain key areas. In the area of language study, Noam Chomsky's theories (e.g. on the nature of language competence) are the subject of much controversy. But there is no doubt that, whether true or not, they have vastly increased our awareness of the complexities of language.

During their professional training, language teachers should therefore be given the opportunity to learn about the scientific findings that are relevant to what they do, and also given the opportunity to update this knowledge regularly. It must be said, however, very few practising teachers will be in a position to add to the store of scientific knowledge of their profession through their own research, unless they have funding, institutional support or an unusual amount of free time.

Illuminative or heuristic research is much more feasible for practising professionals: gaining insights into one's own teaching or discovering something about oneself as a professional that one didn't know before is the very essence of action research. It is again clear that these approaches are not in opposition to one another, but rather complementary.

Illuminative/heuristic research can be used to discover whether the findings of conclusive research actually apply to one's own particular context. The issue here is that, in fact, only a minority of research findings in the social sciences aspire to the 'law-like' status of many of those in the natural sciences such as physics. Quantitative findings in the social sciences are often averages or central tendencies covering a range of behaviours. *The question for the professional is: does this finding relate to my particular case?* This is an especially valid question in an international discipline like ELT. To take an obvious example: it might be possible to prove statistically that a certain group-work task has had specified positive results. But will it have the same results in another country with different cultural norms? Or even in the same country, in another context with different institutional norms? In this sense, many, perhaps most, findings in an area of social sciences like education are indicative rather than truly conclusive, as far as professionals in the field are concerned.

Working the other way, illuminative/heuristic research can often provide ideas or hypotheses which can be more widely generalised using appropriate empirical procedures.

PERSONAL REVIEW 3.4: Applying Research Findings to Personal Experience

In an article in *The Modern Language Journal* (1991), Batia Laufer addresses the issue of the vocabulary development of advanced language learners. Will the vocabulary level of such learners continue to develop simply by exposure to the target language, or is it advisable to incorporate specific vocabulary development exercises into their programme? The subjects of the study were 47 first year University students in a Department of English Language and Literature. The students' development in language was measured by their progress in the 'lexical richness' of the language used in their free compositions. The finding of the research was that, without specific vocabulary development, the students tended to reach a certain 'threshold' level, and to remain at that level. The conclusion was that exposure to the target language was not enough: in order to develop a richer active vocabulary, vocabulary has to be 'consistently and systematically practised and tested'.

I would like you now to think about how the findings of this piece of research correspond to your own experience: do these findings correspond with your own experience of language learning either as a teacher or as a learner? Do you think this is true for your own students? What are the implications of Laufer's findings for classroom practice? What kinds of activities would be involved?

3.10 Research techniques: a brief survey

From Chapter 4 onwards, we shall be concerned with looking at various techniques of research, discussing them and reflecting on them in some detail. Some examples of reports of investigations using the different techniques will also be given.

It seems useful at this point, however, to briefly describe the main techniques. As previously noted, this is being done for two reasons:

1. First, it might save your time if you have already embarked upon or are just about to embark upon an action research project by directing you to the techniques that might be of immediate relevance to you;
2. Secondly, it will relate the different techniques to the various ways of thinking about research that we have just been looking at.

3.11 Field-notes, logs, journals, diaries, personal accounts and verbal reports (think-aloud)

This group of techniques ranges from the making of field-notes while one is teaching to keeping *diaries, journals* and *personal accounts*. It also includes 'think-aloud' techniques which involve verbalising one's thought processes while engaged, for example, in professional action or in a learning situation. These procedures are by their nature *private* rather than *collaborative*, although they can be made collaborative. The contents of diaries, for example, can be shared in various ways. The procedures also tend to be *qualitative* or *illuminative/heuristic* because they reveal people's attitudes and private thoughts.

3.12 Observation techniques

These techniques involve some form of observation of professional action or of learning processes. This may involve the use of video or audio techniques, or of checklists/observation schedules. Observation of professional action is most easily done on a *collaborative* basis, although *individual* observation of learning processes is quite feasible. In the same way, while observation of professional action is usually quite *intrusive*, in the sense that it requires the presence of someone else in your classroom, observation of learning need not be, since you can do it on your own as you teach. Observation studies can be either *quantitative* or *qualitative*, depending on the data-collection procedures used. Similarly, the findings may be either *illuminative/heuristic* or *conclusive*.

3.13 Evaluation and trialling

Evaluation and *trialling* is something that comes naturally to teachers. We very frequently evaluate our students' work, our syllabuses, the textbooks we use, our own methods, a particular technique, our managers, the way the school is administered, and even our colleagues!

This 'evaluation' is very often done in an informal, unstructured way. Similarly with trialling: having evaluated something and found it deficient, we try something else to see if it works better: a different textbook, a new technique, a variation in the syllabus, or whatever. Action research may therefore be simply a matter of handling in a more structured way an evaluative process that we would be engaged in anyway.

3.14 Interviews and questionnaires

These two techniques are usually bracketed together since they both involve eliciting something from informants: usually factual information about themselves and their teaching situation, or attitudes/ opinions on some issue. Some interviews are simply questionnaires in oral form. For the action researcher, the interview, especially in its less structured form, would seem to have more potential: at its most unstructured, the interview is very like a professional conversation ('talking shop'), and therefore quite complementary to normal professional behaviour. Generally, however, interviews and questionnaires require a lot of thought and organisation, and involve intruding on other people's time. Interviews tend to be more *qualitative*, and *heuristic*, whereas questionnaires tend to be *quantitative* and more easily generate conclusive findings. Both techniques involve the collaboration of subjects to be interviewed or surveyed by questionnaire, but the interviewing/surveying can be done by one researcher or by many.

3.15 Case studies

By 'case study' we mean the systematic investigation of an individual 'case', whether that refers to one teacher, one learner, one group, one class, or whatever. The nature of case studies means that they can be *complementary* rather than intrusive (especially, for example, if you are investigating a pupil or a group in your own class), but this depends obviously on the nature of the 'case'. Because one is investigating, in effect, a sample of one, the results tend to be *qualitative* and *illuminative* rather than conclusive. It is, of course, possible to investigate a number of related case studies, but the results are still not usually claimed to be conclusive, in any statistical sense. Again, the potentially smaller scale of a case study means that it might be more possible for action research on it to be done on an *individual* rather than collaborative basis.

3.16 Experiments

The term 'experiment' in everyday usage can cover a huge range of activities from what Huberman (1992) calls 'tinkering', on the one hand, to full-scale classical empirical *experiments*, on the other. The 'tinkering' end of the spectrum (i.e. trying things out to see if they work) may be characterised as *individual, heuristic, complementary* and possibly *qualitative*. Classical experiments, however, probably involving *experimental* and *control groups*, careful sampling, etc. are clearly *quantitative, intrusive* and are usually intended to be *conclusive*; they may be conducted on either an *individual* or a *collaborative* basis.

PERSONAL REVIEW 3.5: Assessment of Techniques

Below is a list of the techniques that have been briefly described in this chapter. On a scale of 1–5, indicate how attractive or otherwise the techniques seem to you as possible modes of action research. Why do you find the techniques attractive/unattractive?

Research technique	Attractive ←——→ Unattractive				
diaries	5	4	3	2	1
'talk-aloud'	5	4	3	2	1
observation: taped (audio or video)	5	4	3	2	1
observation: checklists	5	4	3	2	1
evaluation/trialling	5	4	3	2	1
interviews	5	4	3	2	1
questionnaires	5	4	3	2	1
case studies	5	4	3	2	1
'tinkering'	5	4	3	2	1
experiments	5	4	3	2	1

3.17 'Cutting corners'

Time is the enemy of nearly all action researchers, but most of all perhaps for those who have to combine a full-time job with involvement in research activity. In choosing your mode of research it is therefore probably worth spending a little of the same precious commodity (time!) on thinking about ways in which you can pursue your research more efficiently without, hopefully, any loss of effectiveness.

One obvious procedure in action research is collaboration, which as we have already noted, can share around the burdens of data collection and also help sustain motivation.

Another method is to look for ways in which data collection can be made more complementary and less intrusive. Is it possible, for example, to involve learners in data-collection activities which will help them with their learning, while at the same time providing you with the data you need? For example, a group observation procedure sometimes used is the 'fishbowl' technique whereby a group of students sit around observing an inner group and noting group behaviour.

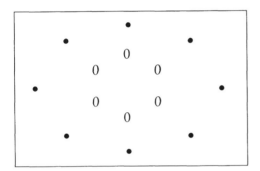
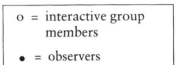

Figure 3.3 Fishbowl technique

The data generated by the observer group could obviously be used by a teacher investigating group behaviour. They could simply hand him or her the checklists, etc. that they had been using. Alternatively, an observer-reporter in each of your class-groups can observe and report back on the group's interaction. Now try PERSONAL REVIEW 3.6.

One must be careful, of course, that such learner co-operation does not turn into exploitation on the part of the teacher, and it is to this issue that we turn next.

3.18 Ethics and Protocol

The examples that have just been given remind us of the ethical dimension (*researcher ethics*) involved in all research, including action research. The issue that we have already raised is *abuse of authority*. It is not ethical to use up our students' time and effort on activities which do not contribute in any way to success in their studies. The same considerations apply at a higher level to managers with respect to those

PERSONAL REVIEW 3.6: Involving Learners in Data Collection

In this 'Personal review' section, you have to see if you can think of ways in which learners can collect 'data' in a way which might also benefit themselves as learners ('payoff'). I have given a few examples.

Topic Area	Learner Involvement (Payoff)
learning process	learners keep *logs* of their study time and how they use it (may enable them to use their time more effectively)
attitudes to learning	learners interview one another about their attitudes to learning English and write up the results (may help to develop motivation)

over whom they have authority. It is not fair to force others to work on research which does not benefit them.

Another key ethical issue is that of *confidentiality*. This issue arises when we wish to publish or share the results of our research with others. Colleagues or students may have co-operated with us without knowing at the time (or perhaps at a later time) that it was our intention to publish the findings. If we invite the co-operation of others, it is only right that they should know what we intend to do with the data we collect. Even if we have the subjects' permission to use the data, they may not wish to be personally identified in any resulting talk or article. A learner may be self-conscious enough about making errors, without his or her lack of proficiency being immortalised in, say, a published article! One should be even more careful with video material since that is much more potentially hurtful (and much more difficult, perhaps impossible, to make appropriately 'anonymous').

Another obvious ethical point is the avoidance of *plagiarism*. All quotations from, and, summaries of others' work must be carefully documented so that one's readers or listeners know what the original source is, and exactly how to refer back to it. As well as being fair to the author one is quoting or summarising, this is also a courtesy to one's audience. When speakers give talks about their research, all too often references are given in a way which makes it virtually impossible for the listener to get back to the original sources.

Sometimes, the issue is not so much ethics as *protocol*, or even just plain good manners and consideration of others with whom you work. Whether you are working in your own institution or in another institution, it is important to think of all those who might be affected by your research, or who might feel that by doing the research you are somehow operating within their area of responsibility. This means going through the correct channels, obtaining clearance from heads of department, headteachers, perhaps even local education officials. Clearly, this is a matter of common sense and judgement: who is likely to feel offended if they discover that I have started doing this research without clearing it with them first?

Some further important areas of action research protocol and good manners are:

– to make arrangements (e.g. for an interview) *in good time*, and not at the last minute;
– to give adequate *advance information* of what is involved;
– to *keep conscientiously to the arrangements* that have been made (e.g. if the interview was scheduled to last ten minutes, it should not go beyond that);
– in some cases, it may be advisable to allow interviewees, for example,

PERSONAL REVIEW 3.7: Ethical and Protocol Issues

If you are already involved, or about to be involved, in some action research, take a sheet of paper and divide it into two columns. On one side put the heading *Ethics/protocol issues* and on the other *Necessary action*. List any issues that you are aware of, and what you propose to do about them.

Keep this list for reference, and check it from time to time to make sure that the necessary action has been taken. You may have to add issues that were overlooked or not foreseen at the time of making up the list. Check the list through again before publishing any findings.

Some examples are given below. Use the rest of the chart for your own answers.

Topic: Management of an English Department	
Ethics/protocol issues	Necessary action
Heads of Department (HoDs) must be aware that I am going to interview staff members.	1. Give full details to HoDs. 2. Request permission to interview.
Replies have to be kept confidential.	1. No department to be identified. 2. Identity of all respondents to be concealed. 3. All respondents to get opportunity to read final draft of report.

to *check* that your interpretation of what they said corresponds with their own understanding;
- to *formally thank* everyone who has helped you;
- and, where appropriate, to *send copies of your findings* to anyone who has been of substantial help to you.

The smaller the scale of your action research, the less you are involved in these issues. It is one of the advantages of purely individual, complementary action research that such involvement may be minimal; but no matter how small-scale the action research, it is always worth giving at least a few minutes' thought to possible problems of ethics and protocol. See PERSONAL REVIEW 3.7.

3.19 Summary

In this chapter, four topic areas were discussed:

1. validity and reliability
2. ways of categorising research modes
3. a brief survey of the main research modes
4. the ethics and protocol of implementing research

Research techniques were categorised in terms of: quantitative and qualitative; introspective and empirical; individual and collaborative; complementary and intrusive; illuminative/heuristic and conclusive.

The following research techniques were briefly discussed: introspective techniques; observation techniques; evaluation and trialling; interviews and questionnaires; case studies; experiments.

The main issues covered under ethics and protocol were: abuse of authority; confidentiality; plagiarism; and various basic issues of protocol involving, essentially, good manners, efficiency and consideration for the feelings of others involved in the action research process.

In the chapters which follow we will be looking at the various techniques which have been briefly discussed here.

4 Field-notes, logs, journals, diaries and personal accounts

4.1 Overview

In the first chapter, we noted that one of the common means of professional development is by private reflection-on-action (i.e. the process of privately thinking back on our teaching). This may only happen occasionally. Such reflection may take place when we are driving home from our place of work, and the process may arbitrarily finish when we reach home. Similarly, in driving to our place of work, it may be our custom to mentally preview what has to be done that day.

In what ways can these everyday happenings be made more systematic? How can these very subjective data be made more 'solid', so that they can be studied and analysed? In this chapter we are going to look at some ways in which private reflection can be made available for systematic analysis.

A way into this chapter would be for you to think of your current practice in private reflection, using PERSONAL REVIEW 4.1 which follows. (If you are one of a group, you can fill this in individually, and then compare notes.)

4.2 Teachers, learners and teachers-as-learners

Before we go on to examine reflective techniques in detail, we must ask ourselves who is reflecting. There are at least three possibilities:

1. **Teachers**   Most of the professional *literature* in this area deals with the reflection processes of teachers on their teaching. This also extends, however, to trainee-teachers: in some courses (see, for example, Bailey, 1993), the keeping of a journal may be one of the elements in the training course (an optional element in the course that Bailey writes about).
2. **Learners**   Students may also be asked to keep some records of their thoughts on their courses, which are shared in certain ways with their teachers and possibly also each other.

PERSONAL REVIEW 4.1: Reflection Processes

In this 'Personal Review' section, I want you to think about the way that you normally reflect on your teaching (what is sometimes called reflection-on-action). Tick or fill in your response as appropriate.

1. Do you ever reflect on your teaching?
   a) Yes _____
   b) No _____

2. When do you actually do this:
   a) immediately after the lesson? _____
   b) when you go home? _____
   c) at some other time? _____ When? _____

3. Is this:
   a) a private activity? _____
      or
   b) do you share your thoughts/feelings with anyone else? _____
      Who? _____

4. How long does this process last, roughly? _____

5. Do you have any systematic way of reviewing your lessons (e.g. a checklist)? _____
   If yes, describe it. _____
   _____
   _____

6. Would you say that the time you spend in this way is:
   a) productive? _____
   b) unproductive? _____

---

3. **Teachers-as-learners** Sometimes language teachers find it a useful self-development exercise to learn another language and record their thoughts and emotions as they undergo experiences which may parallel those being experienced by their own students. (We shall be looking in some detail at an example of this later.)

4.3 Modes of recording data

There are two commonly used methods of recording data:

1. **Written data**   The person doing the reflecting makes written notes.
2. **Audio data**   The person doing the reflecting dictates his or her thoughts onto a tape recorder.

One advantage of writing one's thoughts down is that, in a classroom setting, it is a less conspicuous and more confidential procedure. Once the writing has been done, if it is filed away properly, it should be easily accessible. The main advantage of using audio tape is that it is much quicker to dictate than to write. On the other hand, once the dictation has been done, it is much less accessible.

Written data can be quickly scanned, but this is usually more difficult with taped data. If we decide to make a *transcription* of the audio-taped data this can be an extremely time-consuming process, unless it is done selectively.

4.4   Time frame

Another variable that will emerge as we discuss different techniques is that of the time frame. So, professional action may be reviewed within the frame of, for example:

- one particular incident
- a lesson
- a working day
- a working week (or longer period)
- a number of incidents over a long period of time (e.g. disciplinary incidents over a term)
- a lifetime's work.

The shifting time frames yield very different kinds of data, affording different perspectives, each valuable in their way, on teaching and training.

4.5   Private or shared?

We have noted how in informal reflection our thoughts can be quite private, or we can share them with others in informal discussion. The same possibilities apply to the techniques that will be discussed here.

It may be that we will have no choice: there is no one that we feel we can or would want to involve in our reflection-on-action. Or we may feel that it is sensible to start collecting data on our own and, when we have become more confident, or when we feel that we are on to something interesting, then to involve others.

If we can find sympathetic and like-minded collaborators (not always easy!), it will probably be the case that the whole data collection and analysis process can be made much more motivating and productive. Sharing our action research is also a way of at least partially overcoming the inevitable subjectivity of the introspective approach. Sometimes we cannot see things properly because we are too close to them.

PERSONAL REVIEW 4.2: Collaboration

Can you think of any colleagues or acquaintances who are potential research collaborators?

If you can, what will be the potential pluses and minuses of collaboration with each one? (You might find it useful to take a sheet of paper and make a list of such pluses and minuses.)

Are there any dangers involved in such collaboration (e.g. within your department, will you be seen as the ringleader of a clique, perhaps)? Are there any ways of averting such dangers (e.g. by raising the issue first 'officially' at a departmental meeting)?

Remember the general issues concerning ethics and protocol that we have previously discussed in Chapter 4. Before embarking on research, or broaching it with colleagues, would it be necessary/helpful/polite to discuss the issue with your line-manager (e.g. Head of Department), or someone else who can give you official support?

If you are working in a group, you might prefer to discuss these issues in more general terms. What are your experiences of collaborating with other teachers on joint projects? What potential advantages would there be in such collaboration in an action research project? What would the dangers/problems be?

Having looked at some general issues, let us now turn to the first of the introspective techniques that we are going to discuss in this chapter.

4.6 Field-notes

In many professions, it is a matter of good practice to make 'field-notes' while actually engaged in professional action. Doctors in General Practice, for example, usually have to make notes as they interview their patients, so that details of symptoms and prescribed medicines, etc. are recorded on the patient's file. Some doctors dictate notes onto audio tape, from which they are typed up later by a secretary.

Making field-notes is not customary among teachers for obvious reasons. Teaching is not usually performed in a one-to-one situation (except sometimes in higher education tutorials, or in certain personalised language courses). The necessity of maintaining discipline and the sheer complexity of interaction with twenty or thirty or more learners leaves little time for taking notes. Yet, if such time can be found, or created by arranging short periods when students are engaged in reading, writing or group activities, etc., the potential benefits are obvious. The complete involvement required by teaching means that many fleeting observations and insights will be lost, and fatigue will play its part in impairing recall. Even simply as an *aide-memoire* to later recall (e.g. in planning the next lesson), the making of field-notes could be a useful practice.

The open notebook or page-a-day diary, etc. is not perhaps as much a feature of teachers' desks as it could be. What sort of information would it contain? At their most basic, field-notes can be in the form of a 'Record of Work', recording such basic information as Date & Time, Class, Number present, Absentees, Work done, Punishments issued, Homework given. This kind of record-keeping may promote efficiency, but does not necessarily form the raw material of reflection-on-action.

The kinds of information that could be useful for later reflection are, for example:

1. general instant self-evaluation of a lesson (minimally this could take the form of an A–E grade: thinking about why we awarded ourselves the grade could take place later; more elaborately, a few quick points under + and − symbols)
2. focus on a particular aspect of teaching and learning, for example:
   - the functioning of group work
   - the performance of an individual student
   - interesting or common errors made by students
   - problematic issues/dilemmas
   - ideas, inspirations, things that worked well
   - amusing incidents, remarks

Apart from increasing efficiency, making field-notes can prevent our hard-won experience ebbing away and being lost in the tide of the pressures caused by 'getting on with the next thing'.

4.7 Teaching logs

Field-notes can be kept in a highly-structured way, following a particular format. We can call such records 'logs' to distinguish them from the more fluid and *ad hoc* field-notes which have just been described. Hancock and Settle (1990) provide an interesting format of this kind (see Figure 4.1). They call it a 'Single lesson time-line record sheet'. You will see that it consists of some administrative details (class, date), followed by some notes made before the lesson on objectives, outcomes and notes/points for attention. This is followed by a time-line (the scale is on the horizontal line in the middle). The vertical axis indicates 'five levels of effectiveness', namely:

A = excellent effective work, objectives and intended outcomes are being achieved

B = good effective work, most objectives and intended outcomes are being achieved

C = reasonable work, some objectives and intended outcomes are being achieved

D = not effective enough, few objectives and intended outcomes are being achieved

E = ineffective work, none of the objectives and intended outcomes is being achieved

(Hancock and Settle, 1990: 103)

Unless there is a video record of the lesson, the time-line would obviously have to be done during or immediately after the lesson. The value of this kind of *log* would come in reflective analysis on why the time-line took the particular changes in direction that it did and what might have been done to keep it in the upper sections of the grid. (This can be also used as an observation technique, and we shall be coming back to that in Chapter 6.)

4.8 Analysis

Once field-notes have been accumulated over a period of time, they can be analysed in two ways:

1. They can be scanned as a source of ideas or issues for further investigation. Are there any recurrent concerns? Are there any common features or events? Are there any ideas that could be followed through? Are there persistent problems or themes that warrant more detailed observation and analysis?
2. The data may already be selective and focused on a particular issue (e.g. questioning techniques, student interaction). Have you got enough data to think your way to a solution?

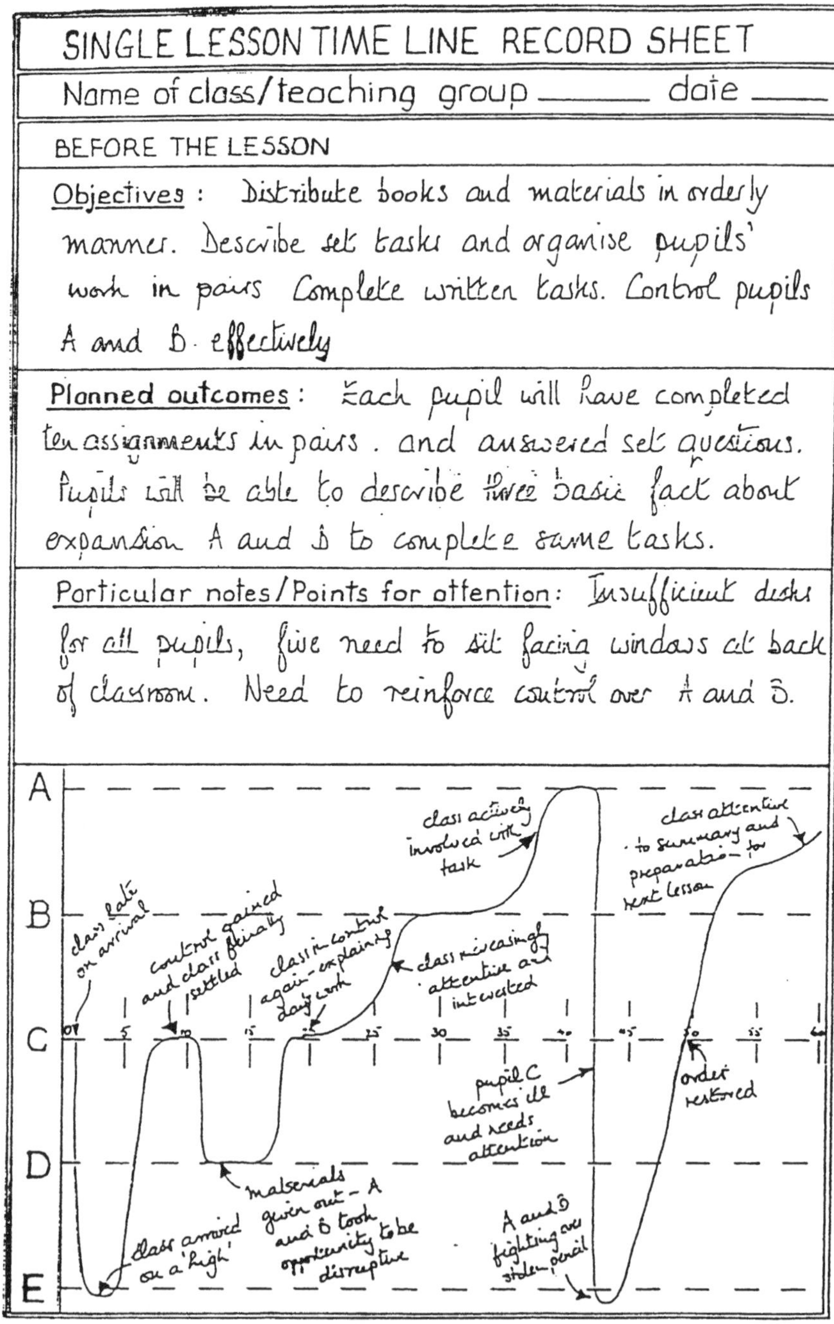

SINGLE LESSON TIME LINE RECORD SHEET

Name of class/teaching group _____ date ____

BEFORE THE LESSON

Objectives : Distribute books and materials in orderly manner. Describe set tasks and organise pupils' work in pairs Complete written tasks. Control pupils A and B. effectively

Planned outcomes : Each pupil will have completed ten assignments in pairs. and answered set questions. Pupils will be able to describe three basic fact about expansion A and B to complete same tasks.

Particular notes/Points for attention: Insufficient desks for all pupils, five need to sit facing windows at back of classroom. Need to reinforce control over A and B.

Figure 4.1

Do you need more data, and if so of what kind? Perhaps the field-notes are not sufficient and you need to complement them with some other kind of investigation.

PERSONAL REVIEW 4.3: Experimenting with Field-Notes/ Logs

1. Decide on one aspect of your teaching that you would like to investigate.

2. Choose a class where you think you might be able to take field-notes on one of the aspects you have decided on. This may well affect your lesson-planning, as you may have to engineer time for taking the notes while the lesson proceeds.

3. Decide on the *format* of your field-notes. Is it just going to be a blank page? (Note: there is nothing wrong with that!)

If you know what you are looking for, is there a page layout which will facilitate the data collection while the lesson is actually proceeding? (For example, in error collection, this may simply mean a page divided into two columns. On the left-hand side, there could be space for recording the error; on the right-hand side, there could be space for a later comment, or categorisation of the error.) Is there a standard format (log) that you would wish to use for all your lessons?

4. After the lesson, think first of all about using field-notes/logs as a technique. How easy/difficult did you find it? Do you think this technique is feasible or not on a regular basis?

5. Look at the data you have collected. Do they seem useful? What if you had more data from other classes?

4.9 Diaries and journals

One of the functions of field-notes might be to act as a prompt or *aide-memoire* for our next technique, which is the keeping of diaries or journals. Professional diaries/journals can take many forms and we shall look at some aspects of diary-keeping now.

4.10 Diaries

Diaries are essentially private documents, and there are essentially no 'rules' about how to keep a diary. Since the diary is private, diary-writers can confide to it whatever thoughts or feelings occur to them. It is therefore especially suitable for exploring *affective data*. Diaries are often kept on a daily basis, and entries can vary from one day to the next, and be either short or long. They can be written immediately after a teaching event, when the details are fresh in the mind, or at the end of the day, when there may be more free time. The main attraction of the diary, as opposed to other ways of articulating reflection, is that the writer can be totally honest and forthright in his or her comments.

We shall be looking at the other advantages of diaries later, but for the moment, let us think about one of their major disadvantages, which is that, by their very nature, they cannot be directly shared or made public. Thus the sharing and joint-analysis of data is impossible. There are several ways of getting round this problem, for example:

1. A teacher may allow a trusted colleague or fellow researcher access to the diary, under the usual rules of confidentiality. Thus, the teacher and his or her collaborator may discuss issues arising from the diary data. Perhaps the 'agenda' for this discussion may be decided by the diary-keeper, or by the collaborator, or both together.
2. There may be a private (original) version of the diary and a public (derived) version. So the diarist may allow others to look at, or listen to, excerpts from the diary, which can then be discussed. This sometimes happens where several colleagues are keeping diaries together, and sharing excerpts from them on a regular basis. Or there may be a one-off meeting where the participants share insights from their diaries. Or the diaries may be written as 'journals', and it is to this technique that we turn next.

4.11 Journals

Journals have many of the attributes of diaries, but the main difference is that they have been written to be read as public documents – albeit, possibly, by a restricted readership of collaborator-researchers. Journals, therefore, have to be, as it were, edited in the process of composition, like any other document that one knows will be read by others. Journals therefore may lose some of the 'truthfulness' of the diary, but what they possibly lose in authenticity they may gain in accessibility.

4.12   Journals: Advantages

What are the advantages of diaries and journals from the point of view of professional development? In their paper on collaborative diary-keeping (for which they have coined the term 'journaling': a pun on the journey of self-discovery that the collaborators make), Brock, Yu and Wong (1992) draw on a number of sources and their own experience to provide the following useful list of the advantages of diary studies. After noting that 'One of the most important of these (benefits) is that this approach can provide access to the hidden affective variables that greatly influence the way teachers teach and students learn', Brock, Yu and Wong then go on as follows:

1. They provide an effective means of identifying variables that are important to individual teachers and learners.
2. They serve as a means of generating questions and hypotheses about teaching and learning processes.
3. They enhance awareness about the way a teacher teaches and a student learns.
4. They are an excellent tool for reflection.
5. They are simple to conduct.
6. They provide a first-hand account of teaching and learning experiences.
7. They are the most natural form of classroom research in that no formal correlations are tested and no outside observer enters the classroom dynamic.
8. They provide an on-going record of classroom events and teacher and learner reflections.
9. They enable the researcher to relate classroom events and examine trends emerging from the diaries.
10 They promote the development of reflective teaching.

(Brock, Yu and Wong, 1992: 295)

4.13   Analysis

Many of the above-mentioned advantages will only be potential advantages until the data generated by the diary or journal is subjected to analysis. Kathleen Bailey (1992: 224), who has written extensively on the use of diaries in action research and teacher development, makes this point:

'. . . I would argue that simply writing diary entries does not yield the maximum potential benefit of the process. In order to really learn from the record, the diarist should reread the journal entries and try to find the patterns therein.'

Bailey illustrates her point with a significant piece of anecdotal evidence (*ibid*: 225):

'When John Schumann (then my professor) first read my French class diary, he asked if I was a competitive learner. I assured him (naively, but quite honestly) that I was a very co-operative group-oriented language learner. John's only comment was, "Look again, Kathi." A subsequent analysis of the diary entries revealed numerous manifestations of competitiveness . . . which I had not noticed in my original review of the entries.'

Apart from exemplifying her point about the importance of careful analysis of the data, this anecdote also illustrates the importance of an outsider's view on the data. Hence, the importance of some form of *collaboration* to get the most out of diary/journal-keeping. This may be, as we have already noted, a one-way process whereby the diary/journal-keeper shares the data with a sympathetic listener. A more promising approach, if it can be arranged, would seem to be the kind of collaborative diary/journal-keeping with a colleague or group of colleagues.

4.14 Problems of diary/journal-keeping

Keeping a diary or journal is for most people not an easy option. First, there is the time factor. During a training programme, time can be set aside for this process. Doing it as a full-time teacher may be another matter. Although they were doing their journal-keeping as part of a training process, Brock, Yu and Wong (1992) still found the process burdensome and fatiguing. Apart from the time factor, there is also the psychological factor. Having survived the traumas of the teaching battlefield, the last thing many of us would wish to do immediately afterwards or even at the end of the teaching day is mentally revisit it.

These problems are to some extent inherent in the technique and have to be accepted as such, or not, as the case might be. However, there are ways of mitigating them. As we have noted, the support of a colleague or of a group of colleagues can help motivation. Brock, Yu and Wong suggest working within a tighter focus: 'We suggest that future teachers undertaking collaborative diary-keeping consider narrowing their focus to a few salient teaching issues during their investigation. Such an approach would allow participants the opportunity to investigate in depth two or three issues of common interest rather than attempting to explore many issues at one time.' (*ibid*: 306)

4.15 Critical incidents

Another way of reducing the burden of diary/journal-keeping and also achieving focus is to concentrate only on *critical incidents*. These are key incidents which you feel have a particular significance for you. They may derive from field-notes or simply from recall, and may be done quite infrequently – perhaps once a week. Writing down the answer to 'What was the most significant event that happened to me this week?' may build up over time a body of data which with analysis could reveal trends and significant concerns in one's professional development. The point is, of course, not simply listing the incidents but also exploring why they were significant to you, how you reacted and why, and what other ways of reacting were open to you, and what the outcomes of those reactions would have been.

PERSONAL REVIEW 4.4: Keeping a Diary/Journal

1. Do you find the idea of keeping a professional diary/journal intriguing or attractive?

2. What for you are the positive/negative aspects of diary/ journal-keeping?

3. If you were ever to keep a teaching diary/journal, how do you think you would organise it? If it was to have a focus, what would it be?

4. What are the factors that would inhibit you from diary/ journal-keeping? Any ideas about how they might be overcome?

4.16 Personal accounts

All the techniques we have been discussing so far assume a commitment to some kind of regular record-keeping, even if it is only for a few weeks or months, or during the course of a training programme. It will readily be admitted, however, that even without such formal record-keeping, many teachers build up a rich store of personal experience which has become part of the mind-sets or 'schemata' which underpin their teaching practice. This experience is sometimes used anecdotally during professional get-togethers, but is seldom investigated systematically and recorded for a wider audience. This seems regrettable since the articulation of highlights of professional experience gained over a period of years, or perhaps even a lifetime, may be not only interesting and valuable for the listener/reader, but also useful to the narrator, in helping him or her to make sense of the experience.

Personal accounts could be done in a purely private way, but it is more usual for them to be 'enhanced by the participation of a *discussant* who lends an interested, informed and sympathetic ear, and who offers help and cues to memory, suggests interpretations, provides like and contrasting experiences . . . and who provides the written account' (Woods, 1987: 131–132). Woods uses the term *life histories* for these accounts; other related terms include: *story, narrative, biography* and *autobiography*. In this form, the technique has much in common with the interview approach (see Chapter 8). It is also possible for accounts to be grouped together by a common focus (e.g. the traumas of first teaching experiences). (Woods, pp. 129–130, notes several accounts that are concerned with this area and the related area of the socialisation of new teachers.) Since we are very much concerned with action research and professional development, it is worth noting that many writers have stressed the importance of the 'teacher's voice' in professional development. (See, for example, Ivor F Goodson's (1992) article on 'Sponsoring the Teacher's Voice: Teachers' lives and teacher development'.)

PERSONAL REVIEW 4.5: Personal Accounts

Get together with a small group of experienced teachers and tape record any anecdotes they may have about their first teaching experiences. Are there any themes that emerge, and any lessons to be learned?

Alternatively, you can 'structure' the anecdotes in some way: for example, the funniest episode, an incident that changed your attitude to teaching, your most rewarding lesson. (Can you think of any more topics?)

4.17 Summary

In this chapter we have been looking at some of the ways in which teachers, by making a record of their professional action and/or of their reflection on that action, can provide themselves with the data for action research.

Many different terms are used to describe the various approaches to this basic process, and an attempt has been made here to distinguish some of those terms. *Field-notes* and *logs* are terms used to describe what has happened during a lesson, and may be written up during the lesson or shortly after. Logs are described here as being more highly structured than field-notes. *Diaries* are personal records, usually written up daily. Diaries are private and confidential, but may be shared with others in some edited or controlled fashion. *Journals* are similar to diaries, but are not written as confidential documents. *Personal accounts* are much more selective and may cover an extended period of time – perhaps even a whole career. They are usually recorded with the help of a 'discussant' (collaborator).

In the next chapter, we will look at another way of reporting on introspective data, namely by using verbal reports.

4.18   Exemplar article

The exemplar article which we are going to look at is concerned with diaries. These are subsequently edited and made public in a seminar setting. As the title of the article indicates, the diaries are kept by teachers-as-learners.

The article is:

TIM LOWE (1987). An experiment in role reversal: teachers as language learners. *ELT Journal* 41/2, April 1987 (89–96).

Read the article with the following questions in mind:

1.   What was the purpose of the 'experiment'?
2.   How was the confidentiality aspect of diary-keeping reconciled with the desire to share the insights derived from keeping diaries?
3.   What, for you, are the most valuable insights into the process of learning foreign languages that can be derived from this study?
4.   What do you think was the main benefit for the teachers-as-learners of participation in this exercise?
5.   a) Can you think of any possible application of an exercise of this or a similar type to your own situation?
     b) If the answer to (a) is 'yes', how would you modify or adapt the procedures adopted here to suit your own professional situation?

An experiment in role reversal:

teachers as language learners

Tim Lowe

This article describes an experiment in which, with the aid of individually kept, confidential diaries, a group of teachers consciously reversed role: they became learners of a foreign language. The article describes the nature of the experiment, and presents an edited compilation of some of its findings, as expressed in a public seminar. Though this was a one-off experiment designed to give individual teachers an opportunity to develop their personal awareness, two important issues emerged. First, many of the issues raised seem to have general relevance to language teachers. Second, the format itself of the experiment seems to provide an accessible model for similar experiments that could be set up by teachers anywhere, as part of a programme of action research.

Introduction

From October 1984 to February 1985 a twelve-week part-time course in Mandarin Chinese (totalling thirty hours) was run by the Teachers' Centre at International House, London. The course was for experienced and inexperienced native-speaker language teachers of English from the London area. The overall objective was to give teachers a chance to renew their connection with language learning, and thereby to become more sensitive to the problems and processes confronting their learners.

The choice of Chinese as an 'exotic' and 'difficult' language was deliberate. Though informal, the experiment was facilitated by the 'diary-study' technique. This provided both the structure and the motivation for continual self-reflection during the course. The keeping of a diary by all participants (course teacher, course students, and researcher/observer) enabled them to talk about their experiences in a follow-up public seminar. The extracts in this article are quotations from this seminar: the diaries themselves, as is always the case in such studies, are confidential. The extracts are taken from contributions by the following:

Felicity Henderson (FH): Seminar Chairperson
Martin Parrott (MP): 'Teacher'
Livy Thorne (LT): 'Student'
Benita Cruickshank (BC): 'Student'
Lesley Lofstrand (LL): 'Student'
Lynette Murphy-O'Dwyer (LOD): Researcher/observer

The role of the diary study

The diary study is one of a number of methods designed to encourage self-reflection. (Others include structured interviews, questionnaires, 'self-reports', and personal construct grids elicited by researchers.) In this case, diaries were kept by all the participants: teacher, students, and researcher/observer. Periodically, the diaries were given to the observer, who as an 'objective' witness was in a better position to detect the salient features of each diarist's experience—thus, in principle, helping each one to make sense of the whole experience, and to draw conclusions from it. To give the diaries spontaneity and immediacy, and to prevent the intervention of memory and recall, experiences were recorded immediately, and in any form favoured by the diarists. As one participant said: 'I probably wouldn't have been able to remember any of these things, or even been able to believe them, if I hadn't kept a diary.'

The observer's role enabled the study to form a 'triangulated' picture of what was going on. She was thus able to compare her own 'outsider' viewpoint with the subjective viewpoints of the teacher and students. But since confidentiality is one of the conditions of triangulated studies, at no point in the experiment did the teacher or students see each other's diaries.

Participants' reflections

At a public seminar held about two months after the course had finished, three of the twelve students, the teacher, and the observer presented accounts that provoked a debate from which emerged a number of themes. Notwithstanding the temptation to make generalizations from such a limited experiment, and despite the high motivation and relatively sophisticated and self-conscious perspective of those taking part, some of these themes are probably of interest and relevance to a great number of teachers. What follows is a short, much reduced compilation of comments at the seminar, under headings that I have felt important and useful.

Affective, social, and attitudinal factors

Anxiety

A considerable degree of anxiety had been felt by all participants. In particular, this related to a fear of oral production early in the course, and the distorting effect this had on different individuals' personalities and behaviour. As LT said:

> I think what surprised me most was how much I needed to be passive in the class, because I've always considered myself very outgoing, bossy, and domineering, and to suddenly find that I wanted to sit quiet and not be noticed at all was a great surprise.
>
> I really did have a horror of speaking, particularly when I was asked a question. Perhaps Martin would ask somebody else, and I'd think, 'Oh yes, the answer's so-and-so', and then when he asked me, I was dumbstruck, I blushed scarlet, and I covered my face. And I was surprised by that, because I don't think of myself as timid or easily embarrassed, and yet I was. And it made me aware of the problems of the Vietnamese refugees whom I used to teach on an ESL programme: they were completely dominated, culturally, by being here in the UK, and having to do pairwork must have been very threatening for them.

And LL endorsed this:

Right from the first moment, I was terrified that Martin might call on me to speak. For the first two or three lessons, my diary's full of references to the sheer terror of being put in a position where I might have to say something when I wasn't terribly sure of my ground. It was terribly powerful, far more so than I would have dreamt it could have been. However, after a little bit I did bite the bullet and try to say something, and the result was that I got a terrific response from Martin.

Motivation

Various factors were identified as improving individuals' motivation, many of them stemming from the need to feel confident. There was general agreement that this confidence derived mostly from some sort of approval or encouragement by the teacher. LL commented:

He was very encouraging, and seemed a benevolent figure, and immediately my nervousness started to slip away and I got obsessed with a 'teacher-approval' thing. [laughter] Really for the first few classes, I haven't got a lot to say about learning Chinese, I was just going through this tremendous experience of see-sawing between real terror on the one hand and tremendous gratitude and excitement if I did manage to say something right and Martin said 'Well done'.

This theme was explored in more depth among the audience, and extended to questions such as: Does encouragement always have positive results? What kind of encouragement works best? MP (the 'teacher' in this experiment) observed:

I wonder how much people from certain other parts of the world would feel the same, or whether they might find it, say, patronizing, for the teacher to show approval. I have watched teachers from certain countries, some of whom taught in what seemed to me, a Westerner, a very abrupt, ungiving way. And maybe, in their culture, the expectations of the students are quite different. And if these students then found a teacher saying 'Good' and smiling and so on, they might find that was a negative experience.

There's even a whole approach to teaching which calls itself humanistic, which seems a bit of a contradiction, which says that the teacher shouldn't show any kind of approval at all—the Silent Way. And the idea is that you build up the learners' confidence to rely on their own judgement of whether it was good or not.

One of the other students added:

I think we would all agree that there is a basic need to be approved of . . . But how do you show approval? . . . When I taught the Chinese in China, I used to get ticked off by my students for saying, 'Oh, that's wonderful' . . . and they'd say, 'Shut up. It's not wonderful.' They liked a certain amount, but they didn't like the amount I was giving them.

The personal experiences of members of the audience further enhanced the discussion:

Outside the classroom as a foreigner, in a particular country, you're always getting complimentary feed-back. Every time you speak the language, the native-speaker who hears you, however bad you are, is always telling you how good you are. They say to you, 'Great, don't you speak good French', for instance, as you're cobbling three words together. And I think that encouragement is part of it'; if you don't get that, you probably can't progress.

A different view of encouragement and its effect on motivation was offered by another member of the audience—the encouragement gained from communicative success:

I did a brief Italian course with the BBC—a very basic travellers' course of five lessons. I went to Italy for a holiday, and I was amazed at how I was able to get around with basic numbers and asking for things in cafés, and I was so pleased with my progress that I actually did a full course. The fact that I went to the station and asked the time of the train in Italian and that the person answered me and I could understand the reply—I think that was encouragement, though it wasn't somebody saying, 'Yes, you speak very good Italian.'

FH summed this up effectively: 'Yes, it's reinforcement in the true behaviourist sense.'

Position in the classroom

The idea that a learner's position in the classroom has some importance to that individual is not likely to occur to many teachers who are used to the fluid seating arrangements of modern EFL classrooms. However, LL was very clear about it:

My position in the classroom became quite important to me. I settled in a particular position in the semi-circle in the first lesson, and I always gravitated back to it ... I also noticed what a difference it made who I sat next to. For instance, one week I sat next to somebody just once who wanted to talk in English much more than I did, and when we were doing pairwork, they'd say the sentence in Chinese and then say 'Did that sound right?', or something. And that interference from English when we were trying to practise in pair work was very disturbing. ... Whereas about three times I sat next to somebody who was terribly good and terribly enthusiastic; she was enjoying doing it and very good at it, and she really lifted me. I mean, I did much better in that class than I would have done if I hadn't been sitting next to her.

In drawing conclusions from participants' contributions about affective factors, it was salutary to hear MP, a sensitive and experienced teacher, admit that:

I've been teaching for ten years, making assumptions about how my students felt, which ones were nervous and which ones weren't, and it's really rather frightening for me to realize how much was going on, important things that were happening to people in the class, that I really didn't know about.

Cognitive factors

The need for diversity

LT expressed her feelings thus:

The most surprising thing to me was how contradictory I was as a learner ... that at the end of the day I couldn't say, 'Well, I know that I want a particular approach or methodology'. I was constantly wanting different things at different moments, which must have made me a very difficult person to teach.

The implication here is that not only do different learners have different *general* learning styles, but also that individual learners have within them a range of learning needs at different stages. This underlines even more emphatically the need for diversity of teaching approach in any one classroom.

Responses to specific classroom activities

Various classroom techniques were identified as being significant for the students. LT cited, for instance, listening to her fellow learners' mistakes:

> I realized how valuable it is to listen, and to listen to other people making mistakes, because that allows your own monitoring system to operate, and you can say, 'Ah yes, that's not quite right. I can't remember exactly what he said, but I know it wasn't quite like that.'

She then commented on her delight at grammar-based activities:

> I really loved it when we did anything that was grammatical, and I had a dreadful sort of 'Teach Yourself Chinese' book, where I used to read all those sentences like 'It's a book. Is it a book? Yes, it's a book. No, it isn't a book', and I used to read this with great pleasure. And it was quite separate from the wanting to communicate. It was feeling 'This is what it's all about. This is the structure. I really need this.' And when we learnt some sort of classroom expression like 'Can you say that again?', I really did get a pleasure from being able to make connections between what I knew grammatically and these classroom expressions, and to be able to extract out the structure, and think about it, and then put it back into the phrase, and feel: Yes, I had something that was communicative, but at the same time I had something that fitted into a structure that I could build on.

MP was then asked about practice activities that were repeated the following week, and whether this affected the amount of new language he was able to introduce in the time available. An answer came, in fact, from LT:

> I certainly felt that we went as fast as we reasonably could have done. I don't know about anybody else, but I felt that even though we were doing a lot of revision, we were getting an enormous input.

And this view was supported by a member of the audience, who said:

> When I was learning Arabic in Egypt, I remember that in my class we were mainly teachers, and we all went out of the lesson saying, 'What an enormous workload', and then we compared it with the very things we were teaching our own students, who weren't in the target-language environment, and we were giving them *twice* as much.

On the issue of communicative approaches, some doubt was expressed by LT:

> In our first lesson, what we did was supposedly very useful. It was saying to people, 'Hello. What's your name? What's your job?', etc. But I had an instinctive reaction against this, because it's the last thing I ever do when I meet people in social gatherings. In a sense it wasn't meeting my communicative needs.

However, things improved when we did likes and dislikes, because I really wanted to know about Graham's love of American films and Sheila's preference for Italian food. What's more, by this stage I had enough vocabulary not just to repeat the model sentence, but to create my own questions. So I could be really independent.

A final point on the theme of responses to method was proffered by LL, who was surprised by the need she felt for pauses in class activity:

I used to think, when there was a pause in my teaching, 'Oh Lord, they're not getting their money's worth. They're getting bored.' But I noticed in the Chinese class that when we did have a pause, when, say, Martin was handing out things for a game, I was very relieved to have a little break, and didn't feel that time was being wasted. If I hadn't noticed that, I would have carried on worrying about pauses in my own teaching.

In summary, MP identified once again the teacher's dilemma:

Different people liked different things. Yet there seemed to be no rationale. The student I thought would like X didn't like it, and the student I thought would hate it actually liked it.

The role of hard work

Several people mentioned homework and the significance of personal effort by the learner. MP went so far as to state:

I think that maybe ninety per cent of what people learn is outside the classroom. I think the most important thing in language learning is hard work. And I think it's a myth that gifted language learners go into the classroom and walk out with the language ... they're the ones who very quietly sit down and try and memorize everything that's gone on in the classroom.

Developing personal learning strategies

This was a particularly enlightening aspect of the discussion in terms of the specific strategies identified. BC spoke almost entirely about how she had spent the course trying to 'make sense' of what this (to her) very difficult language was like—to organize her learning and 'get hold of' the language:

First of all, I needed to know what something meant. Half the time I didn't know what things meant, and I couldn't guess. Secondly, I needed to know what its 'sound-shape' was. But I couldn't say, 'Oh, that word sounds like an English or French word'. So I needed to hear the word many more times, and then I needed to say it just as many times. Thirdly, I could not manage to learn it if I hadn't seen it written in 'pinyin' [a romanized form of phonetically-based script used as an alternative to Chinese characters]. Fourthly, I needed to know that it went in this or that place in a sentence, not technically what part of speech it was necessarily, but where it went. What threw me a lot of the time was that an identical word could go in different parts of the sentence. So I spent the whole twelve weeks cognitively trying to 'organize' the language internally before I could start to get hold of it to *use* it.

LL hit upon a strategy that was for her very successful:

> One night I was trying to get myself going on some homework and I started to write vocabulary on index cards. And I thought I'll write the English on one side and the Chinese on the other. From then on I had this little stack of flashcards which I kept in my pocket with my car-keys and my tube-pass, and every time I had a spare moment, I pulled them out and flipped through them. And I played games with them, on the tube for instance. I would say, 'Right, before we get to Piccadilly Circus, I'm going to know these two cards.' It made a tremendous difference to my confidence and how much I was learning.

This and other points led the teacher to observe what a radical transformation he had noticed in LL's approach and presence in the class.

LT then recounted an interesting discovery she had made:

> I found that I wasn't doing my set homework, but what I was doing was writing stories. I actually tried to write in Chinese, after about five lessons, the dialogue between Little Red Riding Hood and the Wolf. I looked up nearly every word in the dictionary, and I'm not sure how much I learnt from this exercise, but it became terribly important to be able to do it. I knew it wasn't a 'good' learning strategy. There I was with my Penguin dictionary, looking up all the wrong words, and I realized that as a teacher if I saw somebody trying to do the same, my reaction would be to say, 'No dear, don't do that. Go and do something more useful.' But for me as a learner I would have been furious if that had been Martin's attitude. In fact he was very encouraging and marked all my efforts.

To summarize the comments here, what is clearly important is not that these strategies, however original they may be, should be adopted by other learners, but that all learners should be encouraged to discover and develop the strategies that they, as individuals, find effective.

Evaluation of the experiment

LOD was asked to sum up her reactions, as the outside observer, to the success of the 'diary' technique. She said:

> Perhaps the most interesting general point is that people suddenly realize they're learners again, and whether they are experienced or new teachers, the diary makes them realize how essential it is to remember what it was like to learn. At least once in every diary somebody said something like, 'I had quite forgotten it was so difficult to do so-and-so', or 'My poor students. I must try and remember that I hate this, and yet I force people to do it all the time.'

She added that, by demonstrating the variety of experience among the contributors, the diaries helped us to remember the variety of response among our students to our teaching approaches. Furthermore, some course students had not written diaries, she said, and this highlighted an important aspect of learners as real people, namely 'that there were other things that took priority in their lives'.

She concluded by saying:

I think the diary acts as a self-awareness instrument: if you know what's going on in your own learning, it makes you aware of what's possibly going on in the learners in your classroom.

Summary and conclusions

I do not claim that the 'findings' as expressed here are particularly surprising. But, like the participants in the experiment, I do think that in their roles as students, the teachers were able to look again at some of their professional preconceptions. In particular, they were able to reconsider the roles of praise, grammar, repetition, revision, and communicative teaching, at least as they understand and practise them. I think too that the process of developing self-awareness and through the technique of a carefully structured diary-related setting is a useful and telling one, and one that other teachers might wish to try. It would be interesting to hear their reactions to this, and to their own experiments of a similar kind.

Finally, I would like to thank my colleagues Felicity Henderson for her part in setting up the experiment, Martin Parrott for being the teacher, and the three 'students', Livy Thorne, Benita Cruickshank, and Lesley Lofstrand, for permission to include short extracts from their contributions to the seminar. I am grateful too to Lynette Murphy-O'Dwyer, of the Royal Society of Arts, for carrying out the diary study itself. □

Received July 1986

Bibliography

Bailey, K. M. 1979. 'An introspective analysis of an individual's language learning experience' in S. Krashen and R. Scarcella (eds.): *Research in Second Language Acquisition: Selected Papers of the Los Angeles Second Language Research Forum.* Rowley, MA: Newbury House.

Murphy-O'Dwyer, L. 1983. 'Teachers in Training: a Diary Study during an In-Service Course.' University of Lancaster: MA thesis.

Rivers, W. M. 1983. 'Learning a sixth language: an adult learner's diary' in *Communicating Naturally in a Second Language.* Cambridge: Cambridge University Press.

Schumann, F. M. and **J. H. Schumann.** 1977. 'Diary of a language learner: an introspective study of second language learning' in Brown *et al.* (eds.): *On TESOL '77.* Washington DC: TESOL.

The author

Tim Lowe has taught EFL since 1975, and worked in The Sudan, Poland, and England. He is currently the International House visiting fellow in the ESOL Department at the Institute of Education at the University of London. In 1981 he established at International House in London the Distance Training Programme for the Royal Society of Arts Diploma in the Teaching of English as a Foreign Language to Adults, for which in 1986 he was awarded first prize in the English Speaking Union's English Language Competition (unpublished material category).

An experiment in role reversal

5 Verbal reports

5.1 Introduction

In this chapter, we will be looking at another range of introspective techniques which can sometimes yield rather different kinds of data from *diaries*, *journals* and so on, that we discussed in Chapter 4. This range of techniques is sometimes given the generic title of *verbal reports*, which includes the techniques of *self-report*, *self-observation* and *think-aloud*. The written data resulting from verbal reports are sometimes called *protocols*, and so these techniques are sometimes described as *protocol analysis*. The main focus of these techniques is usually to afford insights into the *processes* of learning and teaching.

5.2 What do we mean by 'verbal reports'?

The assumption underlying this approach is that at least some of an individual's thought processes are either immediately available to conscious self-examination and self-analysis, or can readily be made available by telling or writing about them. (Not everyone would be willing to go along with this line of thought, of course: we will be looking at some objections to this approach later in the section entitled 'Problematic aspects of verbal reports'.)

Let us take a question that is of interest to most language teachers: how do our students handle new vocabulary when they come across it in, let us say, a text for reading comprehension? We could observe the students' behaviour, but this would not necessarily tell us much. One student may occasionally frown or scratch his or her head, while another reads on impassively: but what does this tell us about their thought processes? Admittedly, there do exist some sophisticated machines which can track eye movements across a text, but such equipment is not usually a feature of language classrooms! As an alternative to observation, we can give the students a comprehension test on the passage or a vocabulary test. Such *learner product* data may yield valuable insights. But it is still data on *product* rather than *process*, which has to be inferred.

Another method that we can use is one which we will be discussing in the next chapter: the audio taping of group discussion. This would involve turning the process of silent reading into some kind of group task. Perhaps we could ask the group, as a group, to identify the words they don't understand and then to see if they can discover, through group discussion, the meanings of the unknown words. Variants of this technique have been used very successfully by language researchers to come up with all sorts of interesting findings, as indeed you will see when you come to read the exemplar extract at the end of the next chapter. It is also clear that, as a research technique, this comes very close to the 'verbal report', since it involves individuals sharing their thoughts with the rest of the group, and thereby revealing them to outside scrutiny.

However, in the case of handling new vocabulary, there may be reasons why we could be less than satisfied with the resulting data. For one thing, the data will undoubtedly be affected by the composition and dynamics of the particular group. There may be individuals who have vocabulary problems which they are too shy or intimidated to reveal. One individual with a very good command of vocabulary may short-circuit, as it were, a lot of interesting discussion. As before, much of the data may be in the form of product rather than process, since members of the group may share their guesses at the meanings of words, but not necessarily the thought processes that led them to making those guesses.

In these circumstances, you might decide that you would like to acquire data, or complement data from other sources, by getting the learners to introspect on their own individual thought processes, and making a verbal report on them. By doing this, we may be able to get learners or teachers (or ourselves) to reveal aspects of their teaching or learning that would otherwise be 'hidden'. To explore this, do PERSONAL REVIEW 5.1.

5.3 Commentary

You might have found PERSONAL REVIEW 5.1 difficult to do, but I hope you may now have a clearer idea of what is at issue here.

First of all, there are certain processes which are 'open' in the sense that everyone can observe them (e.g. learners' language practice, learners' language production, the teacher's teaching methods, how the teacher uses the textbook, etc.). There may be some things open to the learner but hidden from the teacher (e.g. their feelings about the teacher

PERSONAL REVIEW 5.1: 'Hidden Areas' of Teaching and Learning

We have been discussing how the actual process whereby a learner infers the meaning of an unknown word is very difficult to ascertain from external evidence: it is, in fact, a type of 'hidden area'. This 'Personal review' section invites you to explore this topic by thinking of areas of teaching and learning which are 'hidden' in this way, and to contrast them with others which are more 'open' to outside scrutiny in the sense that they can be observed. Take a blank sheet of paper and divide it the same way as the table on the opposite page is divided. (This table is ultimately derived from the 'Johari Window', Luft, 1969; see also Sergeovanni and Starratt, 1983.)

You will see that the table is arranged in four sections: *Learner, Teacher, Open* and *Hidden*.

1. First of all, think of your learners. Which aspects of their learning processes are 'open' to you, and which aspects are 'hidden'? Put down, say, four examples of each. Just to make this clear, an 'open' aspect would be answering questions in class, or performance in a group talk. 'Hidden' aspects might include doing an individual cloze test, or silent reading. Then think of yourself as a teacher. Which aspects of your teaching processes would be 'open' to observation by an outside observer, inspector, or whatever, and which would be 'hidden'?

2. When you have done that, see if you can think of ways in which your students' hidden processes could be made open. Then do the same for your own hidden teaching processes. For example, after the students had completed a cloze test, you could ask them how they went about identifying the missing words.

3. Finally, *but very importantly*, ask yourself these questions:
   - Are there any aspects of the learners' own learning processes that might well be hidden *even from the learners themselves*?
   - Similarly, are there any aspects of your own teaching processes that might well be hidden, or at least obscure, to yourself?
   - If there are any such aspects, what if anything could be done to open them up to scrutiny by oneself or by others?

	Open	Hidden
Learner	to teacher:	from teacher:
	to self:	from self:
Teacher	to outsider:	from outsider:
	to self:	from self:

or the subject). Some things may even be hidden from the learners (e.g. their own reading processes).

Similarly with the teacher. There may be some things which are open to the teacher but closed to an outsider (e.g. teaching objectives [these cannot always be inferred from observation!]). Again, there may be certain processes of which the teacher is not consciously aware (e.g. his or her decision-making procedures when preparing a lesson).

5.4 Varieties of verbal report

In doing PERSONAL REVIEW 5.1 you probably came up with a number of different suggestions for ways of making hidden processes more open to scrutiny. Some of them might have been techniques which are described elsewhere in this book, such as interviewing, keeping a diary or journal, and so on. What I would like to suggest here is that, through using verbal reports, we have another way of tapping into introspective processes, which may well be in certain cases more direct and immediate in their application. Indeed you may well have anticipated some of the approaches to be described here, when you did the 'Personal review' section.

There are various ways of categorising what we have called here 'verbal reports'. (For a useful survey and discussion of verbal reports of introspection, you could read Kazuko Matsumoto's 1993 state-of-the-art article. Especially relevant in the present context is the note on page 52, where Matsumoto summarises the different terms that have been used by various writers on this topic.) In the rest of this chapter, we shall mainly be using the terms that are suggested in Cohen (1987). The terms that will be used here are: self-report; self-observation; think-aloud. Let us now look briefly at each of these in more detail.

5.5 Self-report

A self-report is the process by which we report to others, usually through an interview, how we go about teaching or learning. Let us take the example we have been using, of learning vocabulary. If someone were to be asked how he or she went about learning vocabulary in a foreign language, the response might be: 'Well, I start by making a list of the new words that I have still to learn, with the new words in one column and the translation in another column. Then I simply memorise them by repeating them over and over again. From time to time, I cover up the translation to see how much I've learned.' Self-reports are obviously highly conscious, considered responses. They may also be well-removed in time from the events they are reporting on. For example, we can ask *informants* how they learned languages when they were at school. Clearly, though, the greater the time-lapse, the greater risk there is of the data not being reliable: the learner in question may have been using this method of studying new vocabulary over a period of many years.

5.6 Self-observation

Whereas the self-report is a generalised report on some aspect of learning or teaching behaviour drawn from many instances, self-observation relates to one particular instance or occasion. Also, we have seen that a self-report may be quite removed in time from some of the incidents being reported on; it is usual for a self-observation, on the other hand, to be much closer in time to the particular episode being discussed, and indeed it is possible that self-observation can take place during the event itself. As before, let us try to make this process more concrete by looking at an example: this time, in the area of reading. How could I get my students to make a self-observation on reading? There are many possible stratagems, but one procedure could work like this:

1. You give the class a short text and allow them, say, five minutes to read it silently.
2. At the end of the five minutes, you get the class to make self-observations on their reading processes by asking questions, such as:
   - Did you read the passage straight through from beginning to end? Or did you pause from time to time and go back to read things again? If that happened, how many times did it happen?
   - What happened when you came to a word you didn't know? Did you:
     a) skip it?
     b) use a dictionary?
     c) try to figure out its meaning for yourself?
   - How many times did these things happen, as far as you can remember?
   - How many of you found five minutes plenty of time? How many found it just about right? How many were not able to finish reading the passage?
   - There is a picture that goes with the text. Did you pay any attention to the picture at all? If you did, when did that happen: before/while/after reading?
   - Did the picture add anything to your understanding of the passage?

Questions could be answered orally, or by writing down the answers. No doubt you could think of other questions that you would like to ask your own learners. They could also be asked to volunteer their own comments.

You may have noticed in one of the questions that the phrase 'as far as you can remember' was used. Since self-observation relates to a particular learning or teaching event, it is important that the reflection process takes place as close as possible in time to the event being analysed. Otherwise, there is a real possibility that the self-observation data may become 'contaminated' as it were by self-report data. In other words, there is a natural human tendency to remember our actions on a given occasion in the past in terms of what we would generally do in those circumstances, or what we think we generally do. Obviously, the further we are removed from the actual event, the more likely this is to happen. As I have said before, we might even decide to interrupt the learning event in order to access self-observation data while it is still fresh in the memory.

PERSONAL REVIEW 5.2: Questions to Generate Self-Observation Data

Take any aspect of teaching or learning that interests you and imagine it taking place in a specific typical context. Then see if you can generate a series of questions, along the lines of the example we have been looking at for reading.

Some examples would be:
- writing a composition
- writing a summary
- doing a group task
- trying to infer vocabulary learning
- doing a test

The questions could be asked either immediately or very shortly after the learning/teaching event, or at some point during the event, or perhaps a combination of the two.

Once you have got a list of questions, you might think of trying them out.

5.7 Think-aloud

This is the most immediate of the three verbal report techniques that we will be looking at, and therefore potentially the one that is closest to revealing the processes involved in a particular teaching/learning situation. It may also be, however, the one that is most problematic to manage. What we are asking the teacher or learner to do in this case is to think aloud while he or she is performing a given teaching or learning task. Sometimes this thinking aloud occurs spontaneously when we are working on a task alone. We may mutter to ourselves, 'How on earth am I going to do this? . . .Oh, I've got it. I'll try . . .' The think-aloud technique is the result of a conscious decision to behave like this during the whole period of the investigative task.

Let us take an example of this, this time from teaching. Let us say the question you are investigating is this: what are the processes that go through a teacher's mind when he or she is preparing, say, a reading comprehension lesson? You could easily generate data on your own practice using think-aloud. (You could also do so by using self-report or self-observation. Self-report would not be very informative, since you would only be reporting to yourself what you know already! Self-report usually only becomes interesting when the reporting is being done by someone else. Self-observation might be more interesting, especially if it were done on a regular basis [e.g. whenever you prepare a lesson, to note how you actually went about the process of preparation]. But the most informative of all is likely to be think-aloud.)

You would have to have some method of being able to gain access to the data generated by your thinking aloud. The simplest method of doing this would be by audio recording, using a small cassette recorder. The technique would then be to simply speak aloud the thoughts that go through your mind as you prepare the lesson. Perhaps you might like to consider the possible uses or benefits of such data.

As we have noted, the think-aloud technique can equally well be used to investigate learning processes. For example, much think-aloud research has been done in the area of reading. Various possibilities here include:

- actually intervening in the reading process from time to time to elicit data;
- marking pause marks in the text, where the reader has to stop and, perhaps, share his or her understanding of the text so far, or to make a prediction as to what he or she thinks is coming next;
- doing likewise at the end of each paragraph;
- starting to think aloud whenever he or she is conscious of a pause in his or her reading (pauses are usually related to problems in reading).

You could now try PERSONAL REVIEW 5.3.

5.8 Verbal reports: The seven questions

Now that you have a clearer idea of what is meant by this term 'verbal reports', also what the main kinds of verbal reports are, the next issue is how you could go about getting data in this way. In fact, some of this ground has also been covered through the examples that we have been using.

One way of approaching this issue is by using seven key question-words. The first of these is: *What?* What is it that we want to investigate? The work you have done in previous 'Personal review' sections in this chapter, may have helped you to consider some of the possibilities in this area.

As far as self-report and self-observation are concerned, the possibilities are almost limitless: any aspect of teaching or learning is open to self-report or self-observation. The uses of think-aloud are clearly more limited, since not every context allows us to think aloud, either as teachers or learners: it is clearly impossible for teachers to think aloud while they are engaged in talking to their students! But there are

PERSONAL REVIEW 5.3: An Experiment with Think-Aloud

This 'experiment' can be done either as a teacher or as a learner.

Teacher   Think of a professional task that you do which will not take longer than 5–15 minutes. Examples might be: preparing an exercise for your students, or even part of a lesson; correcting a composition or other written work; reading and reacting to a short article written in a journal; and so on.

Learner   Think of a short learning task that you can do which will take you around 5–15 minutes. This could be, for example: memorising new vocabulary; doing a cloze test; reading a short passage for comprehension; and so on.

In either case, what you have to do is think aloud during the selected task from beginning to end, and audio record your thoughts as you express them. Then play back the recording and make notes on what the recording reveals about how you went about this particular task. Probably you will find equally interesting data if you can persuade a colleague/fellow learner to go through the same process performing a similar task. You could then compare the data.

As far as learners are concerned, this process could be part of a learner-training or learner-awareness programme.

contexts in which it is possible, and some of them may already have occurred to you as you have been working your way through the present chapter.

The next question follows on naturally: *Why?* This question is important because our purpose in collecting data will determine the kind of data we collect, and that in turn will determine the kind of technique or techniques that we will use. For example, we may have decided that the issue under investigation is our students' vocabulary learning. This gives rise to other questions. Have we chosen this because we want to raise our students' self-awareness of their vocabulary learning? In that case, we might decide to proceed by concentrating on self-observation or self-report, using perhaps questionnaires, interviews or class discussion. However, instead of this (or in addition to this), we may wish to investigate the vocabulary learning process itself. In this case, we will have to think up ways in which our students will have to learn new vocabulary in conditions where they will have to think aloud. Our students may help us to think this through. We could do this, for example, by giving a few students texts in which unknown words (perhaps even nonsense words, or words from a language not known to the students) have been inserted, and ask them to think aloud into a tape recorder as they try to puzzle out the meaning of the target words.

The next question is *Who?* Who is going to collect the data? Teachers can collect data on themselves, simply by recording themselves. Or they can enlist the help of colleagues who observe them and make notes. Learners can also record themselves, or they can be observed and/or recorded by their teachers or by fellow learners.

Another question is *Whom?* Whose thinking processes are going to be investigated? As we have just seen, the research can be conducted on either teachers or learners. Also, the number of people being investigated can vary from one upwards. One teacher can collect data on aspects of his or her own teaching, or he or she may decide to take a student as a kind of case study, in terms of some selected aspect of his or her learning. Or, indeed, the teacher might decide to collect data from the class as a whole, perhaps by giving them a questionnaire to fill in, or simply by having a discussion in class where students reflect on their habitual learning techniques, perhaps as part of a learner-training programme.

We also have to know *When?* The data can be generated when, say, reading or writing is actually in process, using the think-aloud technique. Or the process may be interrupted, by asking questions. Or it may take place after the event. But not too long after, if you need reliable self-observation. Of course, if you are interested in self-report (i.e. people telling you what they usually do when learning or teaching), then the timing is not so crucial.

Now we come to *Where?* If you want to elicit data from your class, then the most convenient place will probably be the classroom. If you are investigating your own thinking processes, then the most convenient place will probably be your own private work-space. Some researchers have obtained data from a number of students thinking aloud simultaneously by using a language laboratory, which has obvious advantages, although is not available to everyone. One of the main advantages of using the language laboratory is that several 'think-alouds' can be done at the same time. Audio or video recordings may need special venues, or could be done quite informally, perhaps using a camcorder.

A vital question is *How?* We have already touched upon many of the techniques that can be used. We can elicit data from others by questionnaires and interviews – techniques that we shall be discussing in more detail in a later chapter. We can have class or group discussions where people share information on their learning or teaching processes, and these may or may not be recorded. We can ask people to think aloud, or we can do the thinking aloud ourselves, and during this process there may be an observer taking notes, or it may be recorded, or both.

Very often, we will feel that it is difficult or perhaps impossible to analyse the data we have recorded on audio or video tape unless we actually write it down (i.e. transcribe it). Transcriptions of verbal reports, often (as I have already mentioned) called *protocols*, can reveal patterns of learning or teaching behaviour. These patterns can be named or categorised, thus giving us new ways of talking or reflecting on teaching or learning processes. The article that will be presented at the end of this chapter will give you an idea of how this can work out in practice.

Before going on to that, let us take a little time to give more thought to the seven questions we have just been considering. See PERSONAL REVIEW 5.4.

5.9 Problematic aspects of verbal reports

If you are considering using verbal reports, it might be useful at this point to consider some problematic, or even controversial aspects of this approach to investigating teaching or learning processes.

At one time, particularly in the last century and the earlier part of this century, techniques similar to those we have been discussing were widely used by psychologists. Then they fell out of favour. Why did this happen?

We discussed this issue in Chapter 3, when we were discussing reliability and validity.

1. **Reliability** Since the processes being described were 'hidden', how could the data be checked? If self-reports by different informants were contradictory, how could they be evaluated? This led many psychologists to concentrate on recording observable behaviour. Such behaviour could be observed by more than one observer and could even be recorded for checking by anyone who wished to do so.
2. **Validity** Other psychologists had problems with the actual validity of the data. Were people reporting on the targeted thought processes or were they actually reporting on something else? For example, if I ask students to think aloud while they are attempting to write an English essay, is it not possible that the very process of thinking aloud will change the nature of the thought processes themselves?

PERSONAL REVIEW 5.4: The Seven Questions

Using the kind of layout given in the table below, try to develop
some ideas for research into teaching and/or learning
processes using verbal report techniques. Try to make your
suggestions as varied as possible. You can, of course, further
develop some of the ideas that you have already considered in
earlier 'Personal review' sections in this chapter. The first has
been done for you as an example.

	Idea 1	Idea 2	Idea 3
What?	vocabulary inferencing		
Why?	to discover inferencing processes currently being used by students		
Who?	teacher (myself)		
Whom?	students (and also myself, for comparison)		
When?	during event		
Where?	language lab		
How?	think-aloud		

Since the whole point of the scientific credibility of research methods, at least in the empirical tradition, is that they should be both reliable and valid, these are serious criticisms. (Remember that we have already noted that, for action research, it is local reference that is important, so generalisability to other contexts may not be such a major issue.)

5.10 Reasons for using verbal reports

If there are sound reasons to be suspicious of the reliability and validity of verbal reports, why have they once again become quite widely used?

One reason often put forward is that, if verbal reports are not used, significant areas of interest will be closed to investigation. Some of the things that interest us most are not available to straightforward observation. The choice for most teachers or unfunded researchers is either to give up on whole areas of professional interest, or else to glean what they can, while remaining aware of the limitations of whatever techniques they use.

As we saw in Chapter 3, when discussing the issue of reliability it is sometimes also the case that the findings of introspective research can be cross-checked against other sources of data. For example, if we are interested in the decision-making processes of teachers while they are marking assignments, we can have access not only to the *process* through think-aloud, but also to the *product* in terms of the marked scripts. These data could be further complemented by interviews with the teachers, perhaps, using a marked script as the basis for discussion.

When we accept or reject evidence of any kind, even in a court of law, it is almost always a matter of *judgement*. If we ask someone to self-report on how he or she learns vocabulary, for example, it seems reasonable to accept his or her evidence, unless we have good reason for not doing so. Many of the findings using verbal reports are convincing, both in terms of their own merits, and also because they correspond with one's own intuitions as a teacher. Two examples can be given from Cohen and Hosenfeld's (1981) paper on 'Some uses of mentalistic data in second language research':

1. The first example is in the area of error analysis. Error analysis is often done by working backwards from the product. In other words a mistake is noted, and the researcher (teacher) uses his or her knowledge of the L1 and L2 to work out a plausible *hypothesis* as to how the error occurred. The writers give instances to show how such plausible hypotheses can be shown to be sometimes incorrect by getting feedback from the learners very shortly after the error has been made (i.e. through self-observation). Sometimes the

learner's reasoning was quite idiosyncratic, and it seems safe to assume that someone using observation alone would never have worked out the true source of the incorrect form.

2. The second example relates to language exercises. Cohen and Hosenfeld show that learners sometimes work out fairly elaborate ways of avoiding the intended task and finding short-cuts to the correct or desired response. This finding will not come as a surprise to most experienced teachers, but it is still a factor easily over-looked in devising or selecting learning tasks. As the authors point out (p. 293): 'Students' strategies are often quite different from (the) strategies teachers assume they are using.'

There is perhaps another reason for the renewed interest in introspective methods generally, and it has to do with the enhanced status of the experiential knowledge of the teacher (Wallace, 1991), and indeed of the learner too (Ellis and Sinclair, 1989). At one time it seemed to be assumed that the only knowledge worth bothering about resided with the 'experts' who were often academics spending most or all of their time engaged in funded research projects located in universities. In more recent times it has come to be recognised that this kind of 'received knowledge' is only part of the story. The beliefs, attitudes and experiential knowledge of both teachers and learners are also important factors in the learning/teaching equation. Verbal reports, and other introspective techniques, are ways in which these factors can be articulated and given their due weight.

5.11 Learner training and professional development

Quite apart from arguments relating to research considerations, in a narrow sense, there are other reasons why we might wish to use verbal reports, and these relate to the very important issues of learner training and professional development.

Learner training

In EFL/ESL methodology over recent years, there has been an increasing consciousness of the role of learner training in promoting efficient and effective language learning. Very often, the first step in developing more effective learning strategies is to bring about situations through which students can become more aware of their present learning strategies, perhaps also comparing them with those used by their fellow learners.

The techniques we have been discussing (namely, self-report, self-observation and think-aloud) could well have a part to play in this process, as well as other introspective techniques, such as journals and diaries, as we saw in the previous chapter.

Professional development

The role of action research in professional development has been a key theme throughout this book, and in that context verbal report commends itself as potentially one of the most 'user-friendly' techniques available to teachers. The vast majority of teachers are well aware of the significant proportion of their time that is devoted to professional duties outside the confines of the classroom, notably in relation to preparation and correction. For teachers interested in developing self-awareness in such areas, self-observation and think-aloud might well yield informative and productive data.

5.12 Summary

In this chapter we have been looking at ways of generating verbal reports (often transcribed into protocols), which can hopefully be analysed to give insights into certain 'internal' or private processes of teaching and/or learning.

The three techniques that have been featured are:

- self-report
- self-observation
- think-aloud

We have noted that there are some problematic aspects to these techniques, but that there is still much to commend them, particularly from the perspectives of learner training and professional development. We will now conclude with a report of the approach in action, in the area of second language written work.

5.13 Exemplar article

The exemplar article is a study of writing processes using introspective techniques.

The article is:

Valerie Arndt. Six writers in search of texts: a protocol based study of L1 and L2 writing. *ELT Journal* 41/4, October 1987, 257–267.

Read the article with the following questions in mind:

1. What would you say is the main research question that Arndt is focusing on in this paper?
2. Make up a 'seven question' chart for the research reported in this article, as you did for your own ideas in PERSONAL REVIEW 5.4.
3. What are the reasons Arndt gives for deciding to use the think-aloud technique?
4. Explain how her coding system for the analysis of protocols worked. Why did she decide to use this system?
5. Has the researcher triangulated data (i.e. corroborated it with other data) in any way?
6. What, in your view, are the most important findings of this study?
7. Is L2 composition an area that you are interested in? Is there a particular aspect of it that you would like to investigate? How would you go about conducting your investigation?

Note: if you would like to find out a bit more about coding protocols, there is a very helpful appendix in the article cited below. But remember that you don't always *have to* code transcriptions, or even transcribe recorded data at all, in order to be able to use it to further your development as a teacher or learner.

Ann Raimes. What unskilled ESL students do as they write: a classroom study of composing. *TESOL Quarterly*, 19/2, June 1985, 229–258.

Six writers in search of texts:

A protocol-based study of L1 and L2 writing

Valerie Arndt

Following the change of focus in much recent writing research from composition to composing, a number of studies have attempted to probe the second-language writing processes of EFL/ESL students. However, few comparative investigations of writing processes in the first and second languages have been published to date. This article reports one such exploratory study of the composing activities of six Chinese postgraduate EFL students as they produced academic written texts in both their first (Chinese) and foreign (English) languages.

Two findings are discussed. First, while the composing activities of each individual writer were found to remain consistent across languages, there was considerable variation among the writers in their approach to the task of producing written text. Second, a limited awareness of the nature of the task was a common source of difficulty in both languages: there was neither adequate awareness of the nature of written language and the demands its production makes upon the writer, nor was there sufficient exploitation of the creative nature of the activity of writing itself. Finally, some implications of these findings for the teaching of writing at this level are considered.

Writing: text and activity

When we talk about the teaching of 'writing', what do we refer to: the composition, or the composing? The text, or the activity? Or both? And what is our answer if we ask ourselves which aspect we *should* be concentrating on? Indeed, the very fact that the term 'writing' can refer both to finished products and to the processes underlying their production mirrors rather neatly the choice of focus available to those who are involved with the teaching of this highly specialized type of communicative competence.

Over the last decade or so, the change of emphasis in writing research from product to process has centred attention on the composing activities through which initial ideas and meaning evolve into written texts. Yet it may be ill-advised, and perhaps even impossible, to divorce the processes and products from each other, either in teaching or research. For at the heart of effective writing lie the techniques for successful *fusion* of thought and language to fit the rhetorical context—rhetorical, that is, in the fundamental sense of gearing message to audience. Such techniques are responsible for matching content with form, and for ensuring that the writing is under the control of a purpose whereby an intended meaning is successfully conveyed to an intended reader. The tantalizing question, however, is whether these matching techniques are actually accessible to consciousness, and hence to observation, and hence, perhaps, to being taught. For writing-as-activity is one form of language production, and as Martlew remarks: 'examining the process of language production is notoriously difficult' (Martlew, 1983:313). Though it may be possible to probe certain superficial aspects of the activities which result in a finished text, the underlying processes of what has been called 'the dialectical interpenetration of language and thought' (Britton *et al.*, 1975:47) remain elusive and inaccessible.

Nevertheless, many researchers have still felt it worthwhile to investigate those aspects of writing processes which *are* available to observation, in the hope that this will illuminate some of the complexities involved in creating written texts—the task which is for many people the surprisingly difficult one of 'putting together form and content of language to achieve extended sequences of text that are coherent' (Bracewell 1981:412).

Background to the study

Interest in probing the activities of writers while they are in the process of producing written text in a second language (L2) has been stimulated by the growing body of first-language (L1) process-centred research. Although many fewer studies of L2 writing processes have been made than of L1 writing, those patterns which are emerging seem to suggest that L2 composing is, despite the additional linguistic burdens involved, very similar to L1 composing. It is the constraints of the composing activity, or of discourse type, which create problems for students writing in L2, not simply difficulties with the mechanics of the foreign language. Whereas problems of poor L2 writers have been found to stem from inefficient writing strategies, successes of proficient L2 writers result from effective strategies of evaluation and text generation, although, naturally, language proficiency is a factor in the efficacy of the total process.

However, though studies have been made of EFL/ESL students composing in L2 (Jacobs 1982; Jones 1982; Lay 1982; Raimes 1985; Zamel 1982, 1983), there seems to be a dearth of comparative studies. Edelsky's (1982) comparison of the L1 and L2 writing of bilingual children is one of the few published ones, supporting the notion that the knowledge writers already have about writing processes in their mother tongue 'is applied to rather than interferes with writing in another language' (Edelsky 1982:214). The study reported here, of the L1 and L2 writing of EFL students at postgraduate level, suggests that the language of composition and the writer's proficiency in it seem to be less significant as factors governing *how* the writing comes into being than is the individual cognitive capacity brought to bear upon the task by the writer.

One overall conclusion to be drawn from research to date in L2 composing is that the composing skills of proficient L2 writers are very similar to those of proficient L1 writers. The present study suggests as a corollary of this that, in the case of individual writers, where composing skills are efficient and effective—or otherwise— in their L1 writing, they are likely to be so too in their L2 writing.

Design and procedure

In line with procedures used in much recent writing research, I decided upon a case-study approach, and used the technique of 'protocol analysis' as the major source of data, despite the many reservations which have been expressed about its validity and reliability as a means of investigating composing processes. 'Protocols' are produced by asking writers to compose aloud into tape recorders, verbalizing as much as possible of their thoughts as they write. The tapes are later transcribed, so that different kinds of composing activities can be categorized and coded; these coded 'protocols' are then analysed in conjunction with the written texts produced during the writing sessions.

Although there can be no doubt that the task of composing aloud into a tape recorder is not at all the same as that of composing silently, and quite conceivably interferes with normal composing processes (Faigley and Witte 1981), protocol analysis has still been felt by many investigators to be 'too good a tool not to be used' (Raimes 1985:234), despite its limitations, and despite the necessarily inferential nature of some of the judgements made in the analysis. Moreover, though the accounts they yield may be incomplete, think-aloud procedures are none the less acknowledged to be a useful means of tracing cognitive processes, especially if the verbalization involves 'direct articulation of information stored in a language (verbal) code' (Ericsson and Simon 1980:227), as is of course the case with writing.

The six writers who took part in the study (three male, three female) were all Chinese-native-speaking students at Nankai University in the large industrial city of Tianjin in north-east China. As post-graduate EFL students in their final year of study, they found that not only were they doing much of their writing, both academic and non-academic, in their second language, but that their written L2 performance was frequently used as a basis for judging their academic competence. Obviously, therefore, an ability to write competently in L2 was of great importance to them.

There were two writing sessions of approximately one hour each, separated by a short break.[1] They took place in the individual booths of the language laboratory, the L1 text and protocol being produced first. In both tasks, the students were told that they could verbalize their thoughts in whichever language they preferred—Chinese or English—but that the *text* in the first task should be written in Chinese, and that in the second task in English. To enable comparisons to be made, the texts were intended to be similar with regard to discourse type, purpose, and audience. Accordingly, the Chinese task was to write an article for a Nankai University magazine on the place of tradition in modern Chinese life; in the English task, the writers were asked to write about an aspect of life in modern China (which they had not already covered in the first task) for an article in an English university magazine. In addition, open-ended interviews were conducted with the students in order to develop a 'writing profile' (Perl 1979) of each writer, including feelings and perceptions about writing, to be used together with the data from the protocols and texts.

The composing activities recorded on the tapes were coded according to a modified version of the coding scheme developed by Perl (1979, 1981). Twenty-one major categories were adopted, such as *planning* (finding a focus, deciding what to write about); *global planning* (deciding how to organize the text as a whole); *rehearsing* (trying out ideas and the language in which to express them); *repeating* (of key words and phrases—an activity which often seemed to provide impetus to continue composing); *re-reading* (of what had already been written down); *questioning* (as a means of classifying ideas, or evaluating what had been written); *revising* (making changes to the written text in order to clarify meaning); *editing* (making changes to the written text in order to correct the syntax or spelling, and so on). In order to provide as detailed an analysis as possible, a further thirty-three 'subscript' categories were used to qualify the major ones. Thus, for example, it would be clear whether a 'rehearsing' activity was concerned with developing a new idea, or elaborating upon a previous one; or whether a 'revising' activity involved a change of lexis, or a re-ordering of words.

These coded activities were then entered upon a 'composing-style' sheet, one for each protocol. In this way, the activities could be seen in relation both to the amounts of time spent upon them and where they occurred in the course of the composing, and to the written text which resulted from them. Let us imagine that a text is being written in a writer's L2, and look at two minutes' worth of hypothetical coded composing activity as it might appear on a composing-style sheet (each segment of broken line in Figure 1 represents one minute's worth of composing time; the horizontal brackets *above* the time-line indicate that a certain sentence or segment of text is being written down; and the horizontal brackets *beneath* the time-line indicate verbalization in a language different from that being used for the written text):

Figure 1

Thus, we can see that the fifth sentence of this hypothetical L2 text takes just less than one minute to compose and transcribe, the words being spoken as they are written; it is interrupted by one instance of rehearsal, in which a previous idea is elaborated, and which leads directly to the completion of the sentence. The writer switches to L1 to verbalize this rehearsal. Then follows a brief period of silence, after which the writer reads over what has just been written. This re-reading leads directly to the simultaneous composing and writing down of the next sentence in less than one minute.

Reducing the information on the tapes to charts in this way provides a basis for generalizing about the patterns and styles of each writer's composing process; it enables parts of the process to be seen in relation to the whole; it shows the frequency and sequencing of various types of composing operations; and it facilitates comparisons, both between writers, and between an individual writer's approaches to different tasks.

The individuality of the writers

In many previous studies of writing processes, writers have been classified according to the degree of their writing proficiency, so that conclusions may be drawn about what constitutes skill in writing, and how methods of more proficient writers differ from those of the less skilful. Perhaps the most striking finding of the present study, however, was the *lack* of similarity in writing behaviour among members of a group assumed to be relatively homogeneous with regard to academic achievement and language proficiency.[2] Bearing in mind the findings of previous studies of L2 writing, it was expected that there would be considerable similarity between the L1 and L2 writing processes of the writers. And indeed there was—but only as far as the individual writers were concerned. What emerged unexpectedly forcefully across the group were the *differences* among the writers in their approach to the same tasks. A brief look at their composing styles will make these differences clear.

Bao was the 'planner'. His overwhelming need was to impose a complex super-structural framework on his texts from the very beginning and throughout the two tasks, frameworks complete with outline, introduction, main points in order, examples to support each point, and conclusion. But, as he wrote, it emerged that these preconceived frameworks did not fit the text he was generating, nor did they help him to perceive how his ideas related to each other.

Chun, on the other hand, felt no need at all for any outline or plan. He was the 'thinker', in that his great need was to get to the *logical* heart of the idea being expressed. His approach was rational and careful, with constant monitoring of whether his writing was evolving in such a way that his ideas made logical sense.

Dai was also a very careful writer, but for her the process of writing seemed to be particularly painful. The 'struggler', she was constantly wrestling with words and meaning, questioning and requestioning herself to find out if she was making sense, not in Chun's logical way, but rather to make sure *to herself* that what she was writing was what she really had in mind to say.

Lin, by contrast with Dai, seemed to find the writing process enviably painless. Spontaneously, and seemingly without effort, she produced fluent and coherent text in considerable quantities in both languages. What distinguished her from the group, and hence earned her the title 'reviser', were her strategies for revision. Not only did she revise the most often, but her revisions were made most frequently as a result of reading over what she had already written, and not, as was the case with most of the others, only as she was composing individual sentences. She showed the most concern with the evolution of the *total* text, scanning back over the whole of what she had written so far, and revising if she felt it necessary.

Zhou's writing offered a most interesting contrast with that of Lin, as it was superficially similar in terms of quantity produced and spontaneous manner of text-generation; but fundamentally it was very different. For Zhou, the 'lister', the activity of writing seemed to be nothing more than a process of listing thoughts and ideas as they occurred, an activity which resulted in rambling, incoherent texts. What his protocols revealed, however, was that much of the coherence missing from the texts was there in this thoughts—logical connections between propositions and paragraphs, textual cohesive ties, explanations and elaborations of ideas and concepts. Interestingly, he was the writer who revised least often.

Finally, *Liao*, the 'outliner', seemed torn between her natural instinct to let the activity of writing itself generate her text, and her consciously learned procedures of outlining, listing main points, and producing 'topic sentences'. Her preoccupation with what she thought she *ought* to be doing prevented her from getting to grips with many of the interesting ideas she had, so much so, that in one task (L1) the entire session was taken up with producing a succession of outlines, but no text proper.

Task awareness

Besides revealing the very different cognitive styles and capacities of the individual writers, the study also suggested that certain problems faced by all of them, regardless of whether they were writing in L1 or L2, related neither to inefficient composing strategies, nor to lack of language resources, but rather to an inadequate awareness of the properties of what Ludwig terms 'language in writing' (Ludwig 1983:35) and of the demands its production makes upon the writer, particularly in its function of academic exposition. Let us look first at some of the characteristics of this type of written language and how they affect the writer, and then consider what the protocols revealed about our six writers' awareness of the task of producing it.

Writing-as-text and the writer

A written text, as completed product, is irreversible (although the activities of production are, as Nystrand (1982) puts it, 'thoroughly reversible'). It is also potentially permanent, and this possibility that the language will be preserved ought to entail activities of critical appraisal and judgement on the part of the writer, not only because by translating private thought into public text writers lay themselves open to the evaluation of their texts by readers, but also because the act of writing is by its very nature one of commitment. Writers must constantly assess how successfully the language they have chosen to commit their ideas to paper conveys their intended meaning. The protocols suggested that such a capacity for critical self-evaluation was insufficiently developed, or at least under-exploited by the writers in this study.

Another feature of written language is its abstract nature. A written text uses language in a most decontextualized form, produced in isolation from its intended audience and without recourse to shared context. One of the most essential activities of writers, therefore, is to provide a context for what they write, so that the preserved language will be understood when it is eventually read. Again, the protocols revealed that none of our writers dealt with the problems of gearing message to intended audience with sufficient thoroughness or effectiveness—if indeed they considered them at all. They did not, in general, get to grips with the difficulties of 're-viewing' the emerging text with the eyes of potential readers; neither did they use their audience as a force for generating their texts.[3]

This brings us to what is conceivably the most challenging characteristic of written language: what Olson (1977) terms the 'intrinsic' relation of meaning to language, whereby *the whole of the meaning* intended by the writer must reside in the text itself. The construction of such explicit, coherent meaning is perhaps the most difficult part of the writing task, and yet the most essential part of the written text. It requires conscious and deliberate intellectual effort sustained over a considerable period of time; and it demands not only *knowledge* of the resources of the written language, but also *conscious manipulation* of them. Those glimpses of the writers' activities afforded by the protocols suggest that their strategies in this respect were not adequate. In general, there was too little evaluation of the developing text in terms of whether the meaning underpinning its superficial structure had been made sufficiently explicit and coherent.

Turning now to the nature of the activity of writing, as opposed to the characteristics of written texts, we find that an interesting paradox highlighted by the study was how over-zealous planning and over-strict adherence to precise 'rules' for writing was often more of a hindrance than a help in the actual generation of text (a finding paralleled in a previous study by Rose (1980)). The students had been exposed in their L2 writing programmes to what we might term the traditional 'Freshman Composition' approach to teaching academic writing, based on a linear, pre-writing/ writing/re-writing model of the writing process, with its precepts of outlining, pre-planning, and constructing paragraphs around previously created 'topic sentences'. But, it seems, we may be better off helping students with *post-planning* rather than pre-planning, for the protocols of our writers confirmed time and again not only the recursive, *non*-linear nature of the writing process, but also the enormous generative power of the actual activity of writing itself. Writers cannot plan for what they do not yet know they are going to write.

That writers frequently discover their meaning only in the actual process of writing is a commonplace enough observation. But what is not so often noted, and what the protocols made abundantly plain, is how much of what is generated by the activity often fails to be incorporated into the text. For example, here is Dai, in the L2 task, finding the true *focus* of her meaning. Her original topic was 'Pop Songs in Modern China', but as she wrote, she found she was writing about something else (italicized words in this and all following quotations from the protocols are those which were written down as they were verbalized):

> ... *on young* people's life young people ... then my title should be changed, it's not in China, but among Chinese young people, let me see, pop songs in China, pop songs and young people, would that be better? with, ya, with young people, Pop Songs *and*, with, *Chinese*, Chinese Young People, and *Young Chinese* ...

And Liao discovered the key to the *organization* of her L2 text when she found that her writing was revolving itself around the differences between graduate and undergraduate life (her chosen topic was 'Campus Life in China'). In her L2 task, she found a new *aspect* of her theme as she was writing:

> ... *the story my roommate told me—a man who has no feeling for his wife but doesn't want to have a divorce because he was afraid of public* opinion, oh ya, public opinion would be a good, a very good *opinion*, public opinion would be a very good example of how traditional ideas influence people's thoughts ...

Chun discovered a *thesis* for his L1 text when he elaborated the criterion which he thought should be used to evaluate tradition; Lin's writing generated a whole *section* in the L1 task on cultural traditions, which she had not previously thought of; Dai's writing clarified for her the *conceptual relationship* between two ideas—'zhongxiao' (filial piety) and 'fucong' (absolute obedience); and, most dramatic of all, Bao discovered a good *example*—marriage advertisements—to illustrate his theme of traditional attitudes, an example which eventually took over his text and became its *theme*.

All these realizations *were* subsequently included by the writers in their texts. But a disconcerting proportion were not. Connections, for example, between ideas or paragraphs, which would have made for more cohesive texture, were verbalized, but not written—and this applied even to the more coherent of the texts. Lin's L1 text, for instance, began in a very abrupt manner—simply a heading 'Political Life'; but in her protocol she introduced it more satisfactorily with the following question (in rough translation):

> Where can the effects of traditional outlooks be seen most clearly in modern life? In the political sphere, yes, political life, *Political Life* . . .

Elaborations and clarifications which would have illuminated the written text were frequently verbalized, but not included. Here is a sentence from Zhou's L1 text (in translation), where the coherence of meaning is lost:

> (as far as) the open-door policy, and being open to the influence of the new technological revolution (is concerned), we need large numbers of reformers with the pioneering spirit, who have the daring and the ability to adjust their own production according to whatever the market changes may be,* this is mainly because of the bondage of tradition.

In the protocol, his intended meaning was clear: after writing about the need for people with pioneering spirit and adaptability, he *said*, at the point marked by the asterisk (in rough translation):

> but we really have few of such kinds of people in modern China. If we speak of the present situation, of course we can't say there aren't ANY, but . . . why should this be so? Most important is because of the 'Doctrine of the Mean', the traditional outlook, *this is mainly because of the bondage of tradition* . . .

but all this clarification was omitted from the written text, which contains only the latter conclusion of this train of thought. Moreover, in the text, since the referent of 'this' is unclear, a wrong interpretation of his intended meaning arises: that the *need* for large numbers of people with pioneering spirit results from the bondage of tradition, and not, as he intended, that the bondage of tradition is the *reason* why there are so few.

Perhaps most disconcerting of all, however, was the omission from the texts of verbalized judgements and opinions which might have helped to bring them to life. Dai, for instance, *thinks* about the power of pop songs over young people, but she *writes* merely about their themes and types. Liao, in contrasting city life with rural life, focuses her underlying meaning on the judgement that urban existence is 'more enlightened' than rural existence, but, although her protocol makes it clear that she *thinks* about 'the higher degree of enlightenment', she *writes* about 'the low degree of influence of tradition' in the city. Zhou *thinks* about the 'great significance' of current reform in the countryside for China's development, but merely *writes* a flat description of some of its manifestations.

In a limited study such as this, it is impossible to predict how subsequent revision and re-drafting might have altered the writers' present focus on the struggle for expression of immediate meaning, and led them to give priority to 'finding the form or shape of their argument', which Sommers (1980) found to be the primary revision objective of experienced writers. The protocols *do* suggest, though, that potential cues for finding this form are there, even as a first draft is evolving, if only they could somehow be 'captured'. This might also partially explain the perplexing phenomenon noted by Galbraith (1981) as a major source of writing difficulties: that written thought so often appears 'impoverished' in comparison with the reflective thought which created it. Here, perhaps, is one area where protocol analysis could make a significant contribution to writing pedagogy.

Implications for teaching

The belief that certain aspects of the creative process of writing can be examined and taught to help students produce effective written language is what has led to the current emphasis on *process* in the literature on L1 and L2 writing. But just as 'it would be wrong to suppose that there is one best way to understand how people write' (Wason 1981a:340), so it seems unreasonable to propose that there should be one best way to teach writing in view of the greatly different needs of individual writers, even in such a small and supposedly homogeneous group as in the study reported here. Whilst those L2 writers with inadequate composing skills would certainly benefit from the incorporation of a 'process-centred' approach into EFL writing pedagogy, one implication of the study's findings is that all L2 writers, proficient or otherwise in terms of writing-as-activity, need more help with the demands of writing-as-text.

This means, then, that the teaching of L2 writing must always have a two-fold aim: not only must it help inefficient writers become more efficient in regard to their writing strategies; at the same time, it must help all writers produce more effective L2 texts by enriching knowledge of linguistic resources in the foreign language and fostering awareness of how they can be effectively utilized for the specific demands of language-in-writing—including those relating to formality and coherence at the discourse level. Such expansion of an adequate basic knowledge of the language is of vital importance for students such as those in the study, whose chances for acquisition of the language through a variety of media—films, radio, television, contact with native speakers—are very limited, according to their interview reports, and whose reading activities in English are restricted, by and large, to the narrow confines of academic textbooks. They all felt, for example, that their ability to discriminate between varying levels of formality, and their capacity to exploit such differences in their own writing in English, was far from adequate. Also, where breadth of lexical knowledge was concerned, they *revised* for word-choice more in the L2 task than in the L1 task, but *rehearsed* for word-choice more in L1 than L2. This suggests that they felt less able to try out alternatives and less happy with their decisions in L2 than in L1, not only because they had more limited resources to draw on, but also because they felt less secure about whether they had chosen appropriately.

A second implication relates to seeing writing as a sophisticated kind of problem-solving activity. Flower and Hayes (1980a) include among the characteristics of good writers the ability to 'solve problems they represent to themselves'. But the study suggests that one problem might be to create the right problem to solve, and this is perhaps where teaching could help. Students could be encouraged to enlarge the scope of the problems they set themselves; they could be pushed beyond their concern with the immediate problems of translating thought into words and helped to distance themselves from their creations, so as to appreciate the evolving meaning structure. For this, writers need that creative self-criticism which would also help them to deal with the explicitness required of written language. The writers in the study, for instance, often failed to translate meanings conveyed prosodically in the protocols into conventions of written language; they failed to provide adequate connections between, or clarifications of, their ideas; they failed to anticipate that their readers might not share their own 'knowledge of the world'.

Most of the writers in the study expressed open hostility to the artificiality of the 'school-set assignment', yet stressed that if they really had something to say through their writing, then the task became less burdensome, and even, on occasion, enjoyable. This suggests two further important implications for teaching, the first of which concerns evaluation, and the second, involvement. Writers inevitably lay themselves open to criticism and judgement when they write. If the writing teacher's task is to convince students that this risk is worth taking, and not just an ordeal to be endured for the sake of a grade, then assignments set must be worthwhile, and they must be responded to as communications of meaning, not merely assessed as exercises in correct verbal behaviour.

As for involvement, I have stressed that writing is, by nature, an act of public commitment. But *effective* writing is a matter of personal commitment. On the evidence of the texts in the study, produced as they were in the artificial rhetorical context of 'essay-making' (Nystrand 1982:5), little serious effort was made by the writers to struggle towards what Galbraith (1981) calls a 'private conception' of what they were writing about. Yet, on the evidence of the protocols, the opinions and judgements necessary for this *were* often voiced. This suggests that an important teaching task may be to convince students of the vital importance of personal involvement in effective writing. For even in academic writing—that ostensibly most sober of genres—the commitment to 'a particular attitude to what you want to say', and ability to say it in your own voice, is an important measure of quality (Wason 1981b).

One final implication concerns protocol analysis as a teaching tool. If conscious consideration of a process can enhance it (Squire 1983), and if the ability to monitor the process of one's writing is indeed a major component of writing skill, as Flower and Hayes (1980b) contend, then protocol analysis could be a valuable aid for writers to diagnose their own deficiencies and develop the evaluative capacities necessary to oversee the evolution of a successful text. Furthermore, since it is so far the only method of looking into the process of composing *as it is happening* which is relatively easily replicable in all kinds of classroom settings, it could be invaluable as a means of demonstrating to writers the truth about the composing activity, dispelling the notion of linearity, and revealing the essentially generative nature of the act of writing. □

Received January 1987

Notes

1 It would have been preferable had the tasks been performed with a much longer time interval between them, but unfortunately, restrictions on time and laboratory facilities precluded this.

2 Objective measures were unavailable, but the writers were assumed to have considerable academic and linguistic proficiency by virtue of having been accepted for postgraduate study at one of China's 'key' universities.

3 One possible explanation for this is that, consciously or unconsciously, they perceived the 'real' audience of their texts to be myself.

References

Bracewell, R. J. 1981. 'Writing as a cognitive activity.' *Visible Language* XIV/4:400–22.

Britton, J. L., T. Burgess, N. Martin, A. Mcleod and **H. Rosen.** 1975. *The Development of Writing Abilities (11–18)*. London: Macmillan Education.

Edelsky, C. 1982. 'Writing in a bilingual program: the relation of L1 and L2 texts.' *TESOL Quarterly* 16/2:211–28.

Ericsson, K. A. and **H. A. Simon.** 1980. 'Verbal reports as data.' *Psychological Review* 87/3:215–51.

Faigley, L. and **S. Witte.** 1981. 'Analysing revision.' *College Composition and Communication* 32/4:400–15.

Flower, L. S. and **J. R. Hayes.** 1980a. 'The cognition of discovery: defining a rhetorical problem.' *College Composition and Communication* 31/1:21–32.

Flower, L. S. and **J. R. Hayes.** 1980b. 'The dynamics of composing: making plans and juggling constraints' in L. W. Gregg and E. R. Steinberg (eds.): *Cognitive Processes in Writing*. Hillsdale, N.J.: Lawrence Erlbaum Associates.

Galbraith, D. 1981. 'The effect of conflicting goals on writing: a case study.' *Visible Language* XIV/4:364–75.

Jacobs, S. E. 1982. 'Composing and coherence: the writing of eleven pre-medical students.' *Linguistics and Literacy Series*. Washington, D.C.: Center for Applied Linguistics.

Jones, C. S. 1982. 'Composing in a Second Language: A Process Study.' Paper presented at the 16th Annual TESOL Convention, Honolulu, May 1982.

Lay, N. D. S. 1982. 'Composing processes of adult ESL learners: a case study,' (Research note), *TESOL Quarterly* 16/3:406.

Ludwig, O. 1983. 'Writing systems and written language' in F. Coulmas and K. Ehlich (eds.): *Writing in Focus*, Trends in Linguistics Studies and Monographs 24. Berlin: Mouton.

Martlew, M. 1983. 'Problems and difficulties: cognitive and communicative aspects of writing' in M. Martlew (ed.). *The Psychology of Written Language: Developmental and Educational Perspectives*. Chichester: John Wiley and Sons.

Nystrand, M. (ed.). 1982. *What Writers Know: the Language, Process and Structure of Written Discourse*. New York: Academic Press.

Olson, D. R. 1977. 'From utterance to text: the bias of language in speech and writing.' *Harvard Educational Review* 47/3:257–81.

Perl, S. 1979. 'The composing processes of unskilled college writers.' *Research in the Teaching of English* 13/4:317–36.

Perl, S. 1981. 'Coding the Composing Process: a Guide for Teachers and Researchers.' MS written for the National Institute of Education, Washington, D.C.

Raimes, A. 1985. 'What unskilled ESL students do as they write: a classroom study of composing.' *TESOL Quarterly* 19/2:229–58.

Rose, M. 1980. 'Rigid rules, inflexible plans, and the stifling of language: a cognitivist analysis of writer's block.' *College Composition and Communication* 31/4:389–401.

Sommers, N. 1980. 'Revision strategies of student writers and experienced adult writers.' *College Composition and Communication* 31/4:378–88.

Squire, J. R. 1983. 'Composing and comprehending: two sides of the same basic process.' *Language Arts* 60/5:581–9.

Wason, P. C. 1981a. Introduction to *Visible Language* XIV/4 (Special Issue: 'Dynamics of Writing').

Wason, P. C. 1981b. 'Conformity and commitment in writing.' *Visible Language* XIV/4:351–63.

Zamel, V. 1982. 'Writing: the process of discovering meaning.' *TESOL Quarterly* 16/2:195–209.

Zamel, V. 1983. 'The composing process of advanced ESL students: six case studies.' *TESOL Quarterly* 17/2:165–87.

The author

Valerie Arndt has taught in a wide variety of EFL/ESL situations over the last twenty years, both in England and overseas. Much of her experience abroad has been in East Asia, and most recently she has been teaching for four years in China, where she has been specifically involved with the teaching of writing. She has recently returned to England and completed her MA in TEFL at the University of Reading.

6 Observation techniques: recording and analysing classroom skills

6.1 Overview

In Chapters 4 and 5 we were concentrating on techniques which 'look inward': diaries, journals, thinking aloud, and so on. Now, we will 'look outward' on the classroom by considering some techniques for observing classroom life.

I will begin by discussing the possible aims of observation techniques, and then go on to consider what the research focus of the observation might be. I will review various methods of recording data, with their advantages and disadvantages. Finally, there will be some examples of teaching/learning areas that might be usefully investigated using these techniques.

6.2 Aims of observation

Most teachers have first come across classroom observation in the context of the assessment of our teaching practice during teacher training. We therefore tend to equate being observed with being assessed. This may be one of the reasons why as teachers we are resistant to the presence of others in our classrooms. This is linked, of course, to the nagging sense of anxiety that most of us have about our performance as teachers. Even experienced and competent teachers may feel that they are not teaching to their potential. Yet another reason might be that, unlike some other professions (e.g. medicine, law), we are not used to performing our craft in the presence of our peers, or even (if we teach in a school) other adults. Being observed is an unusual event, and makes teaching under observation an even more stressful experience than usual.

So it must be made clear that when we speak of observation here, we are making no immediate reference to the observation associated with supervision, inspection or teacher-training (although action research could, of course, be a part of all these activities). There is also another use to which observation is put, namely to establish objective data concerning what goes on in most classrooms, or in a range of classrooms. I am thinking here of, for example, the research done by Arno Bellack and his colleagues (Bellack et al, 1966). This research was done using very rigorous procedures across a range of teachers (15 high school teachers) teaching one particular subject (international trade). From this investigation the researchers came to certain conclusions about the various kinds of 'moves' (e.g. structuring classroom activity, soliciting responses, etc.) which teachers used in their teaching, and the way in which these moves were combined into what they called teaching 'cycles'. Using these data, Bellack and his colleagues, therefore, felt able to make generalisations about the nature of teaching behaviour which have been very influential on subsequent work in this area. (See, for example, Sinclair and Coulthard, 1975; Fanselow, 1987.)

This sort of activity is clearly much closer to what concerns us here, although the emphasis is still too general for the needs of action research. What does concern us here is, of course, our own professional development and the improvement of teaching and learning in our own classrooms. From an action research perspective, our aim is not concerned with assessment, nor (in the first place) with generalisable findings, but with exploring through observation aspects of what goes on in our classrooms for the benefit of our own development. The rest of this chapter will therefore be concerned with ways in which this aim might be achieved, and in the next sections, I will discuss how systematic observation can be implemented.

6.3   Who and what is to be observed?

There are several possible answers to this question:

1. The focus of the observation can be *ourselves as teachers*: the techniques we use, our physical presence, voice projection and quality, use of gesture, management procedures, and so on.
2. The focus can be on *our students*: the way they work, the way they interact, the way they respond to our teaching, their on-task and off-task behaviour, and so on.
3. The focus can be on *the context* in which we teach: the classroom layout, the teaching aids available and how they are used, and the use of posters and visual aids [if any] in the classroom, and so on. Observation of the context may occasionally extend outwards to include the *institutional context*. These contexts can obviously be linked to self-observation and/or observation of our students.

6.4 Who does the observing?

Again, there are several possibilities:

1. The observation can be done by *the teacher concerned*. This is easiest to handle if the focus of the observation is our students or some aspect of the context that we teach in. It is less easy to organise if the focus is ourselves as teachers, although it is still possible, for example by using audio tape or setting up a video camera to record ourselves.
2. We may work with other colleagues to observe *one another's teaching* (reciprocal observation or peer observation). In this case, we are benefiting from other colleagues' perceptions and they from ours. Such co-operation greatly extends the scope of what can be observed, of course.
3. Alternatively, we may wish to be observed by someone on a *non-reciprocal basis* (i.e. they observe us but we don't observe them). Observers who are used to working in this way are often academic researchers, working on their own research projects, but it could be, perhaps, one of the management team in our own school. It should be noted that this is still very different from the supervision/appraisal situation, since it is the teacher who is initiating the process, and ultimately the evaluation that matters is the teacher's personal self-evaluation.
4. Finally, it is possible to use our *students as observers*. For example, a few students may be given checklists to either categorise our teaching behaviour, or to analyse the interaction of their fellow students.

6.5 Methods of recording

The following methods of gathering observed data will be discussed here: real-time observation; audio taping; video taping and transcription.

1. **Real time observation** This means that the observation is observed and analysed as the teaching/learning actually happens without using any electronic means of recalling the data. This can be done by marking checklists or simply taking notes.
2. **Audio taping** It is worth remembering that much interaction can be recorded using a small portable cassette recorder. Sometimes cheap recording machines are more appropriate than more sensitive advanced machines, as several can be used at a time, and also more sophisticated machines are sometimes more difficult to operate.

Using a small cassette recorder is, of course, most effective in one-to-one teaching situations, or with small group work.

This approach is more intrusive than real-time observation, but it is often the case that after ten or fifteen minutes learners forget the presence of the tape recorder, and interact normally and unself-consciously. In certain lessons, the taped interaction may be exploited for teaching purposes (e.g. by playing it back and asking the group to spot any errors that they have made).

3. **Video taping** This is the most intrusive technique, but with the development of 'palmcorders' and similar hand-held video recorders, it has become much less so. The justification of the extra expense and inconvenience of video recording is that it can make a permanent record of contextual and paralinguistic data, such as chalkboard work, the layout of the classroom, movement, gestures, facial expressions, and so on. Whether such data are relevant will depend on the nature of the action research being done, and what aspects of the teaching/learning process you are interested in. Remember, also, that all video taping is selective: you can't capture everything.

4. **Transcription** The problem with both audio-recorded and video-recorded data is that, although they provide rich data on a permanent-recall basis, specific items of data may not be very accessible. For example, if you are interested in how you corrected errors, you will probably find it much quicker to locate examples in a transcript, than by going backwards and forwards on a tape. Also data only on tape are not amenable to certain kinds of analysis (e.g. detailed discourse analysis). It is very often the case, therefore, that material which has been recorded then has to be transcribed. This is a very time-consuming business. Before committing yourself to a research design that involves a lot of transcription, it would be wise to do a short piece of recording, say ten minutes, and then see just how long it takes you to transcribe that amount. This should give you a useful rule-of-thumb for the ratio of recording time to transcription time for your project. You may decide that you only want to transcribe on a selective basis, not the whole thing. Go to PERSONAL REVIEW 6.1.

6.6 Commentary (Personal Review 6.1)

There are many possibilities. I'll just discuss a few of them here:

1. **Self as teacher** If you wanted to self-observe your use of expression and gesture, then audio taping is clearly out: you would either have to set up a video camera at the back (which might or might

PERSONAL REVIEW 6.1: Observation Topics

Using the table below, you are invited to think of a topic that interests you within each of the three main areas of focus (yourself as a teacher, your students, or your class/institutional context). Decide who would be responsible for the observation and which method of recording you would like to use.

Focus	Topic	Observer(s)	Method
Self as teacher			
Students			
Context			

not be operated by a colleague), or to get a colleague to observe you using some kind of checklist.

2. **Students**   Observing students engaged in a communicative task could be done by using an audio recorder: you probably wouldn't need help from anyone else.

3. **Context**   As far as context is concerned, you might be interested in looking at the appearance and layout of your classroom. You could do this in a chart with two columns: **at present** and **possibilities**, like this:

AREA	AT PRESENT	POSSIBILITIES
desks/chairs	circular arrangement in groups	open U-shaped arrangement of groups to allow easy transition to plenary mode
walls	five posters	poster section + area for displays of student work
teacher's desk	books, exercise books: small working space	relocate books/exercise books use open ring binder for field-notes

6.7 Methods of analysis

How are observed data to be analysed? There are basically two approaches. Let us call the first method *unstructured*. This is essentially an impressionistic approach whereby we note whatever seems of most importance and relevance, given our purpose for observing. It is in some ways the most straightforward but also the most subjective approach. It is important to remember that when we analyse something impressionistically, we do so in the light of our existing personal constructs: our ideas and beliefs related to what we are observing. If you ask a group of teachers to say what struck them as important while watching a lesson, they will usually come up with a lot of different ideas amongst them. There is also the degree of knowledge that we bring to the observation: an experienced teacher may view the classroom in a much more informed way than someone who has not been in a school since their school days. Similarly someone who is a specialist in the subject being taught may have different insights from someone who is not.

The great advantage of the unstructured approach is its flexibility. Given a certain focus of interest, student motivation, let us say, we can note anything that bears on this from the general appearance of the classroom to the teacher's feedback on student answers. So, even though the topic is an elusive one, by being flexible and observant we may manage to pick up some useful data.

How can one minimise the subjective element? It may be helpful to have more than one observer: sometimes on in-service courses it is possible to have feedback from several colleagues on one's teaching. If they are unanimous on one point, it probably says something for the reliability of the feedback. An impressionistic comment may also be considered along with other kinds of analysis of a more objective kind such as we shall be discussing shortly. Other investigative techniques may be used (e.g. questionnaires) which will yield a different kind of data which may or may not confirm observational findings. This is another example of the so called triangulation technique that we discussed in Chapter 3.

As far as possible, the observer should *observe* and not *assess* or *evaluate*. Avoid questions like: 'How good is this lesson in terms of motivation?' Concentrate on the evidence. Go to PERSONAL REVIEW 6.2.

6.8 Commentary (Personal Review 6.2)

The sort of questions you have come up with might look like this:

PERSONAL REVIEW 6.2: Unstructured Observation

Let us take the admittedly difficult issue of observing *motivation*. What sort of questions might you be looking for an answer to?

You might find it helpful to think in terms of:

- factors arising from the learner (personality, attitudes, etc.)
- factors arising from the teacher (as above)
- factors arising from the lesson
- factors arising from the context/situation

- What are the factors in the physical appearance of this classroom which promote/impair motivation?
- When during the lesson did the class seem most motivated? When least? What were the symptoms of interaction/non-motivation? What are the likely reasons for these states?

Such *fact-seeking* questions may develop understanding, as opposed to examination of issues of praise or blame, which probably will not.

It should be noted, of course, that the more detailed the list of questions prepared beforehand, the less 'unstructured' the observation is. So the difference between structured and unstructured observation is a matter of degree, not a clear-cut distinction.

6.9 Structured approaches: system-based

In structured approaches, the observer's analysis is guided by some kind of *observation schedule* which allows him or her to collect data, often of a more objective kind, in a systematic way. Structured approaches may be of two kinds: system-based or *ad hoc*.

In system-based observation the observational data are analysed in terms of an existing system of pre-specified categories. Such systems are usually *global* in nature (i.e. they are intended to give general coverage of the most salient aspects of the classroom process, as defined by the system being used). The systems consist of a *finite* array of categories.

The FIAC system (Flanders, 1970), for example, consists of only ten categories. Seven of these categories are used to categorise various aspects of 'teacher talk' and three are used to categorise 'pupil talk'. The last category is used when there is 'silence' or 'confusion' in the class (i.e. when there is no interaction to record, or when there are so many things going on that the observer is not sure what to record). The ten categories are:

Teacher talk
1. accepting feelings or attitudes expressed by the student;
2. praising or encouraging a student;
3. accepting or using students' ideas;
4. asking questions;
5. lecturing (explaining, informing);
6. giving directions or commands;
7. criticising students, justifying authority (e.g. when disciplining a student);

Pupil talk
8. pupil-talk response (e.g. answering a question);
9. pupil-talk initiation (e.g. volunteering information, asking a question of the teacher);
10. silence/confusion.

(Flanders, 1970: 34)

The classroom interaction is recorded using a pencil and paper technique. The observer (who has to have had some practice in using the technique) watches the class and categorises the interaction being observed at a certain fixed interval – usually once every three seconds. The categorisation is done on a tally sheet (for an example of a tally sheet, see Figure 6.1 in Section 6.12 below). At the end of the lesson, the tallies can be counted and it is then a simple matter of arithmetic to work out which of the categories have been most frequently used. This can yield data on, for example, the amount of 'teacher talk' as opposed to 'pupil talk', and whether the lesson is more student-centred (categories 1–4 and 8, 9) or teacher-dominated (categories 5–7).

What is the potential significance of such systems for the action researcher? Let us look at the advantages and disadvantages of using a technique like FIAC.

Advantages

One big advantage is that since the system is 'ready-made' you don't have to work out a different one for yourself. Another advantage is that a system like FIAC is well-known: it doesn't have to be trialled or validated. Also much research has been done using this approach which can be cross-referred to. It can be implemented in real time or using a recording, so it is quite flexible in that sense.

Disadvantages

But FIAC also has several disadvantages for the action researcher. One is that it cannot be used in real time by the teacher himself or herself. An observer is required, and one who is skilled in using the technique at that. It can, of course, be used by the teacher concerned if the target lesson has been previously taped.

Another important disadvantage is that the specified categories may not be of any relevance or interest to what you are researching. As it stands, for example, FIAC has only two categories for pupil talk, which might very well be the main focus of your investigation. Since all the categories refer to interaction, other issues that might be of interest (e.g. seating arrangements, chalkboard work) are excluded from observation.

Conclusion

If you are contemplating using observation for professional develop-ment, you might find it useful to familiarise yourself with some of the systems that are currently available, of which FIAC is only one example. You will find useful surveys in Malamah-Thomas (1987), Allwright (1988) and Wajnryb (1992).

Experience shows, however, that you are unlikely to find a system which will be exactly what you want. More likely you will want to either take an existing model and 'customise' it to your own needs, or to design a new system of your own. It is to this 'ad hoc' approach that we now turn.

PERSONAL REVIEW 6.2: Applying FIAC

Look back at the FIAC categories and think of your own teaching situation. Are there any general categories that seem important to you but which have not been listed by Flanders? Examples might be: use of the mother tongue/target language; use of group work/pair work. See if you can make up a new checklist which will be more relevant to your concerns.

6.10 Commentary

There have, in fact, been many adaptations of FIAC which have changed it to suit the particular needs of the trainer/researcher. Moskowitz

(1971), for example, has categories for whether the teacher uses jokes, and whether there is laughter or not, since one of the things in which she is interested is the affective dimension in foreign language class-rooms. In a communicative classroom you might want to have categories which cover learner-to-learner interaction. So, before using the Flanders system you would really have to look at it to decide whether there is coverage of all the areas of classroom activity that you are interested in.

6.11 Structured approaches: ad hoc

The term *ad hoc* is used to describe something that has been devised for a particular purpose, with no claims to generality. What we have called the system-based approaches start with a set of general categories which are applied to specific situations. The ad hoc approach is also a structured approach, but the categories derive from a particular problem or research topic. We shall be going into the implementation of this approach in some detail shortly, but at this point let us look briefly at how categories are established. Let us say we are observing a class to discover the involvement and application of the students in the work of the class. In terms of observable behaviour, two categories will immediately suggest themselves: *on-task behaviour* and *off-task behaviour*. For the purpose of our investigation, it might be important to know the forms that off-task behaviour may take. We could come up with the following list (taken from Hopkins 1993: 105):

Off-task behaviour
1. talking not related to task assigned
2. doodling
3. daydreaming
4. wandering around
5. working at other tasks
6. physically bothering other pupils
7. attempting to draw attention
8. pencil sharpener, fountain, washroom
9. other

Where do these categories come from? They could come from three sources. First, a list of off-task behaviours that we have received from our reading or similar source (just as this list has been taken from Hopkins' book). Secondly, from our own teaching/learning experience, perhaps augmented by brainstorming with other teachers/learners. Thirdly, the list might be the result of a period of unstructured observation, during which we have made a note of off-task behaviours as they have occurred. Or it could be a combination of these.

Which of these three sources we use will probably depend on the nature of the topic we are investigating. Not all areas are as accessible to experience as off-task behaviours, which we are all familiar with from our own student days. Others, such as categories of the linguistic behaviour of native speakers or of learners in various interactive situations may only emerge after long and careful observation, or else by utilising or adapting the categories of other investigators who have done work in this area.

It must be remembered that observations are not always a matter of recording naturally occurring behaviour, as it were. It is possible for investigators to intervene in the teaching/learning process in various ways in order to elicit various types of behaviour which can then be analysed and perhaps compared. You could, for example, give two different kinds of tasks to two groups, and compare the results. Or you could experiment with giving more thinking time to learners before they have to respond, and observe, perhaps even measure the results. The data from either of these investigations might give you reason to think again about your teaching style.

6.12 Approaches to observation: example studies

In this section, we shall look at some examples of approaches to observation in various areas. We shall take a few examples which mainly focus on the teacher and a few which mainly focus on the learner.

There are many aspects of teacher behaviour that we could look at. Areas that spring to mind are:

Aspects of teaching behaviour
- opening procedures (first five minutes or so of lesson)
- closing procedures (last five or so minutes)
- handling of critical incidents (e.g. discipline)
- use of chalkboard
- use of other teaching aids and resources
- patterns of movement from one group to another
- stance and posture
- use of voice (high and low pitch, volume, tone, audibility)
- eye contact
- psychological projection (e.g. of confidence, uncertainty, anger, good humour)

114

– management routines (for structuring class activities)
– interaction with students

Let us discuss the last area, interaction of students, in a bit more detail. We might be interested in the level of questions that we use. We can devise a simple tally sheet recording the use of whatever categories we wish to use in this respect. An example is given of questions related to a reading comprehension exercise.

Level of question	Tallies	Total
Literal (simple retrieval of information from the text)	ⵑⵑⵑⵑ ⵑⵑⵑⵑ ⵑⵑⵑⵑ ⵑⵑⵑⵑ ⅠⅠⅠⅠ	24
Inferential 'reading between the lines'	Ⅱ	2
Reorganisational combining information from different areas of the text (e.g. summary)	Ⅱ	2
Evaluative/reactive expressing a judgement or personal reaction	Ⅰ	1

Figure 6.1   Question tally sheet

This simple analysis shows a preponderance of 'low-level' literal questions, which may or may not be what you intended when planning the lesson. We could make this analysis more refined by distinguishing between (say) 'wh- questions' and 'yes/no questions'. Instead of using simple tallies we could use a code like W (for 'wh- questions') and Y (for 'yes/no'). How many of these questions are actually the same question redirected to another student? Now we have a new category: R for Redirect. Obviously we have to be careful how far we go down this road: we could end up making the coding procedure too complex to implement, at least in real time. (One of the advantages of recorded material is that it is amenable to complex analysis.)

Another focus of our research input might be concerned with how the questions are distributed among the class. Are some students 'favoured' (if that is the correct word) with the teacher's attention more than others? One way of recording this is by using another simple tally sheet, this time using the students' names in the vertical column thus:

Name	Tally	Total
Patricia	I	1
John	I I I I	4
James	I	1
Dorothy	I	1

Figure 6.2   Simple tally sheet

Again, it is possible to make the data collection richer by coding the questions instead of using simple tallies.

Another possibility is to use a *spatial* observation schedule, like this:

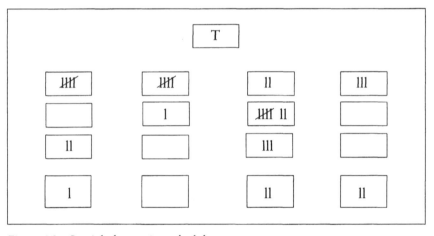

Figure 6.3   Spatial observation schedule

It would seem from this example that the students at the front are getting more than their fair share of attention!

6.13 Group-work observation

The examples we have just been exploring are focused on the teacher. Many teachers, however, will be at least equally interested in learner behaviour, and various ways of observing learner behaviour have been proposed.

For example, many teachers are interested in what actually goes on

i)   Recording frequency/distribution of participation

STUDENT TIME

	A	B	C	D	E
1					
2					
3					
4					
5					
6					
7					
8					
9					
10					

(30 second sweep) aligns with row 8.

ii)   Recording nature of participation

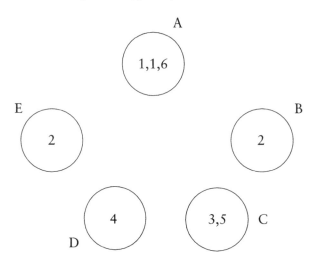

Figure 6.4   Group work: sample observation schedules

during group work. There are many different aspects you might wish to investigate, such as:

- What is the proportion of mother tongue and target language use? In a lesson, or a specified part of the lesson?
- What is the quality of the target language used? (This covers issues like: how accurate? how complex? how advanced?)
- What are the patterns of group interaction? Are there dominant group-members? Are there some who undermine the work of the group? Who are the active and passive members of the group? Are there different patterns of interaction for different tasks?
- More generally, what is the group process in performing a given task? Are there different group processes for different groups? For different tasks?

If your teaching style involves the use of a lot of group and/or pair work, the answers to such questions may be quite important. You may already have a pretty shrewd idea of what the answers to these questions are as they affect your own students, simply from informal observation as you have 'done the rounds' of the groups in your class. It may be the case, though, that your very presence may alter the group's 'normal' be-haviour: for example, there may be a tendency for a group to give you feedback on progress so far, or to ask questions (both of which are, of course, very appropriate activities). Also, it is usually not possible for a teacher to spend an extended period of time with any one group.

You may therefore decide that you want to find out more about the group processes that are going on in your classroom. The investigative technique you use will obviously depend on what aspect of the group process you are interested in.

How is the data to be recorded? One widely-used method is to tape record one of the groups. This has the disadvantage that the tape recording will probably have to be listened to in the teacher's own time, which could be quite time-consuming. Transcription of the tape would also clearly be extremely time-consuming, although it is occasionally desirable. (In some cases, of course, transcription may be a valid and 'meaningful' activity for learners. This is yet another example of how action research can be used to benefit learners.) If we are focusing on the use of the target language, tape recording is almost inevitable.

A second widely-used method is by real-time observation. The simplest method is by regular (say 30-second) 'sweeps' of a group to record who has participated in that time. Figure 6.4 i) could be used to record the frequency/distribution of participation in a group-work activity. This method tells us something about the quantity but little about the nature of the interaction. We may wish to analyse this in terms of various categories, such as:

1 = initiation
2 = response – simple agreement
3 = response – agreement and development
4 = response – simple disagreement
5 = response – disagreement with reasons
6 = structuring move (e.g. Why don't we discuss . . .?)

We could then record the nature of participation in the group work. Figure 6.4 ii) (not an actual example) shows that Student A has assumed a dominant role in the discussion (initiating and structuring) while C is the only member of the group fully engaged with A (in terms of developed responses).

As a result of this analysis, you might decide to allocate roles (such as chairperson, secretary) to different members of the group to see how far, and in what ways, this kind of structuring actually changes the nature of the group interaction. (This can be done more elaborately by using roleplay scenarios, where the members of that group have to assume given identities.)

We have already noted that this type of observation need not necessarily be done by the teacher himself or herself. Depending on the nature and maturity of the class, it might be possible for a member of the group itself to act as an observer and also, perhaps, report back to the group on his or her observations. This heightening of metacognitive awareness might actually be helpful to the group process.

PERSONAL REVIEW 6.3: Implementing Observation

1. Make a list of aspects of your own teaching behaviour or your students' behaviour that it might be useful for you to observe.

2. Pick one activity that you want to observe and decide how you are going to implement the observation. What do you hope to discover? What are the likely practical applications of what you hope to discover?

3. If you can, make a trial attempt at implementing your plan. How interesting/useful were the data you discovered? Is there any way in which the observation could have been improved?

6.14 Summary

In this chapter we have discussed methods of recording observed data, and different ways in which data can be analysed, from unstructured to highly-structured approaches. We have looked at some examples of how observation might be applied to teacher behaviour (with special references to questioning techniques) and student behaviour (with special reference to group work).

In the next chapter, we will look at how data can be obtained through asking questions of respondents through interviews and questionnaires.

6.15 Exemplar Article

The exemplar for this chapter is not, in fact, an article, but a short excerpt from a book:

G. Brown, A. Anderson, R. Shillcock and G. Yule (1984). *Teaching Talk: Strategies for Production and Assessment*. Cambridge: Cambridge University Press (pp. 70–72).

As the title indicates, this book is mainly concerned with ways of encouraging oral skills and also assessing them. The students in the research programme were native speakers, but the 'information gap' activity which is the focus of this excerpt will be familiar to most EFL/ESL teachers.

Read the article with the following questions in mind:

1. What are the special conventions used in the transcription here (i.e. how is the transcription different from 'normal punctuation')?
2. How easy or difficult did you find the transcription to read? What do you think was intended to be conveyed by the sign (+)? How useful/relevant did you find the transcription conventions used here?
3. What do the researchers tell us about their findings concerning 'co-operative tasks' or 'information-gap activities' in this excerpt?
4. Do you think these findings could have been discovered by a teacher without going through the procedure of audio taping and transcribing, as these authors have done?
5. The researchers have taken a common task and obviously audio taped a number of groups attempting the task, and then compared the interaction process. Would there be any other aspects of the group process that would be interesting to investigate in a similar way? How would you go about it? What practical problems can you foresee? Could they be overcome? How?

Co-operative tasks

So far we have been largely concerned with conditions where one speaker is the authoritative speaker, supposed to transfer information to another pupil who plays a fairly passive role. It is this type of task which we have most experience of, which we are able to grade with some confidence, and which we provide assessment procedures for.

There are clearly other types of task which make rather different demands on speakers, but which may have other drawbacks like being much harder to grade or to assess.

One such task, which is very popular with pupils, is where the information required to complete a task is distributed between two pupils and they have to co-operate to complete the task. Thus speaker A may have in front of him a map of an island containing a number of dangerous features with a safe route marked across it. Speaker B may have a map of the same island but one said to be 'made by an earlier explorer' which contains some of the features on A's map, but not all, and contains, in addition, three features which are not marked on A's map. A is asked to describe to B the safe route across the island so that B can draw it in on his map.

The reason a task like this is difficult to grade or to assess is because the behaviour of one member of the pair depends so much on the behaviour of the other member. Coping with incompatible information is difficult for any of us – we all need to construct a coherent representation. Speakers taking the A role, the authoritative role (i.e. knowing the route) can be more or less helpful in response to the announcement by another speaker that his information is different. Consider the behaviour of the speakers taking the A role in the following examples (14) and (15):

(14) A: draw a line from the start and do it round the beach + tree + + Palm Beach and do it round the swamp and round the waterfall
B: there is no swamp
A: well there is one on mine + well just draw a line round the waterfall
(15) A: go a bit further upwards and you'll come to a bridge
B: I haven't got a bridge
A: oh well + where it says 'Big River' + go along a bit and draw a bridge in

In the first of these extracts, the speaker makes no attempt to accommodate B's information – merely reiterates her own. In the second, the speaker takes on B's incompatible information and instructs him to draw in the bridge which he hasn't got. This suggests one way of grading co-operative behaviour, which is to value highly an attempt to help the other speaker out when he has incompatible information, and to value less highly a mere reiteration of the speaker's own information. We could then suggest valuing least highly of all behaviour when the speaker simply ignores B's problem as in (16):

(16) A: go past the pine trees + past the swamp + and past the waterfall
      B: where's the swamp?
      A: then past the mountain and a bridge

Where B responds in an appropriate manner, then we can usefully talk about A's behaviour. However B does not always respond in an appropriate manner:

(17) A: go over the Big River + over a bridge
      B: done it

In (17) B responds 'done it' in spite of the fact that she has no bridge on her map. Where B speakers take a passive role, A speakers have no opportunity to demonstrate whether or not they are capable of taking account of the other speaker's state of knowledge and framing a helpful reply.

It's perfectly possible to create a series of more or less difficult tasks using this format. The task will be simpler if (a) there are fewer rather than more incompatible features and (b) if the incompatibility lies in one speaker having a feature that the other lacks (e.g. B doesn't have the bridge over the river which A has) rather than two conflicting features in the same location (e.g. B has crocodiles where A has a swamp).

In spite of the difficulty of grading or assessing the task as it is actually performed, it still seems worthwhile including tasks of this sort in the teaching programme, precisely in order to give pupils practice in coping in a sympathetic and helpful way when the other speaker has incompatible information. Conversely, it also gives the pupil who takes the role of speaker B practice in taking on incompatible information and assimilating it to his view of the map. Consider the behaviour of B speakers in the following extracts:

(18) A: go to your left + just about come to the swamp
      B: where's the swamp + how far along?
(19) A: go over to quite a bit below the bottom of the swamp
      B: what swamp?
      A: swamp swamp
      B: how far is it away from Palm Beach?
(20) A: and across the bridge at Big River
      B: what bridge at Big River? + + + wait a minute + where's your bridge?

In each case the B speaker does not have the mentioned feature on his/her map. However, in each case they accommodate themselves to this new information and ask for the location of the feature. This is obviously going to be a more useful strategy than that employed by some pupils who simply state 'I've not got a swamp/bridge', leaving A to do all the work of telling them to draw it in.

This type of co-operative task does not, typically, give practice in long turns. What it does give practice in is transferring information in what the speaker may well have planned as a long turn, but what turns out to be a turn in which, in most cases, he keeps on getting interrupted because the listener needs to ask a question or check that he's understood. The ability to maintain a plan, and simultaneously cope with problems that the listener has, demands a considerable level of sophistication. Some of our population showed themselves to be sensitive and considerate speakers for at least some of the time. For others, the ability to perform under such circumstances obviously created considerable difficulty.

7 Questionnaires and interviews

7.1 Overview

In this chapter I am going to discuss two research techniques which both involve asking questions of other people, namely questionnaires and interviews. These techniques are usually classified as 'introspective', since they involve respondents reporting on themselves, their views, their beliefs, their interactions, and so on. They can also be used to elicit factual data (e.g. we can ask people what qualifications they have, which classes they teach). Also, if we have a big enough sample, responses can be statistically analysed. However, we have to remember that the only data we have is what the respondents choose to tell us.

I will be looking at some of the advantages and disadvantages of questionnaires and interviews as well as characteristics they have in common, and how they differ from one another. Finally, I will examine in turn their design and implementation.

7.2 Uses of questionnaires and interviews

We use questionnaires and interviews when we want to tap into the knowledge, opinions, ideas and experiences of our learners, fellow teachers, parents or whatever. We do this by asking questions. The answers are usually recorded in some way so that they become available for subsequent reflection and analysis. In questionnaires, the questions are usually set out in a very systematic way, and very often the questionnaire is answered by reading the questions, and then ticking responses, or writing in short answers. Interviews are by definition oral, more like conversations. Very often, though, in *surveys* (especially large-scale surveys) the questions asked orally are read aloud by the interviewer from a questionnaire. Interviews that are not of the survey type, on the other hand, can be quite free-wheeling and open-ended so the term 'interview' can cover quite a wide range of interaction from something like a spoken questionnaire at one end of the scale to something very like a conversation between professionals at the other.

7.3 Subject-matter of questionnaires and interviews

As I have just indicated, not only can questionnaires and interviews take a wide variety of forms, they can also be used to elicit many different kinds of data. For example, you can ask your colleagues or students questions on these topics:

Facts/personal perceptions
- How many hours a week do your students spend on homework?
- How long does it take them to do the tasks you set them compared with the tasks set by other teachers?
- If a student chose, let us say, English as a foreign language rather than another subject, what led him or her to make that choice?
- What are the main reference books (e.g. dictionaries, reference grammars) your colleagues use?
- How do colleagues teach or exploit a given chapter in the coursebook that is used in your institute? Do they all teach it in the same way or do they do it differently? Have they any favourite exercises or routines?

Experiences/anecdotes
- What was a colleague's most successful teaching experience? Worst experience? Funniest experience?
- What was a student's best/worst learning experience?
- What lessons has a colleague learnt about good classroom teaching practice after (x) years of experience?

Opinions/preferences
- What is your students' opinion/evaluation of their language course?
- What is your colleagues' opinion of the language teaching syllabus?
- What do people think are the qualities of a good language teacher/ learner? Who was your favourite teacher and why?

Ideas
- What ideas do your colleagues/students have for making the language course more stimulating/effective?
- What suggestions do colleagues have for successful 'Friday afternoon' activities when students are tired and motivation is low?
- What ideas do students have about activities they would like to do in the language class?

These questions are not necessarily in the form that you would actually use – we will be looking at the possible formats of questions later. They are intended to show that questionnaires and interviews are capable of generating a wide range of data, and your choice of format really depends on what you are interested in finding out.

It is normal for us as teachers to try to be aware of our students' feelings, and to try to tap into colleagues' expertise. The point at issue here is whether there is some aspect of our professional interest which is sufficiently important or troublesome to make us want to investigate it in a more structured way through action research, using questionnaires and interviews.

PERSONAL REVIEW 7.1: Topics for Questionnaires and Interviews

In the previous section you have been given some examples of questions which you might want to ask colleagues or your students. See if you can think of similar questions. You don't necessarily have to confine yourself to colleagues and/or students: you may want to extend your choice of informants to, for example, people with a management function, parents, or even ordinary people with no particular role in the language learning process. Try to characterise the response you want to elicit as either: *fact/personal perception/experience/anecdote/ opinion/preference/idea.* Use this layout.

Respondent (i.e. colleague/student, etc.) ....

Question ....

....

....

Category (i.e. fact/idea, etc.)...

See if you can generate *five* topics in the form of questionnaire/ interview questions. Don't worry about the format of the question at this stage: just decide on what you would like to know.

7.4 Problematic aspects of using questionnaires and interviews

Before we go on to consider how to implement questionnaires and interviews, it might be useful to consider some of the potential drawbacks or limitations of these techniques.

1. **Subjectivity**   When we ask someone a question, we have very often no way of ascertaining the truth of the reply. For example, if I ask a student through a written question how long it took him or her to do a particular piece of homework, and the reply is 'three hours', that is the answer I have to record. But does the student have a motivation for perhaps (consciously or unconsciously) exaggerating the amount of time spent on his or her homework? There is sometimes no way of checking on such feedback, even if we have the time to do so.

   Again, if I ask colleagues to evaluate a textbook, and they rate it 'very poor' this does not necessarily tell me anything about the true quality of the book. What it tells me is those teachers' *opinion* of the book, which is a different matter. This is not, of course, to devalue the importance of the teachers' opinion. If all the teachers using a textbook have a low opinion of it, then such a book is unlikely to contribute much to an effective teaching programme. In that case, we might want to know why they don't like it.

   The important issue here is to be sensible and realistic about evaluating data presented through questionnaires and interviews. Do our *respondents* have vested interests that will incline them to answer one way rather than another? What status can we give any opinions that are expressed? With regard to a particular issue, does the opinion of a newly-qualified teacher have the same status as someone who has twenty years experience? If the answer to the last question is 'no', should we disentangle the responses of less experienced and more experienced teachers? Depending on the information we are looking for, it may be worthwhile to do so.

   The fact that we are getting information from, say, a questionnaire does not make irrelevant the common-sense considerations that we normally employ when we get information, advice or opinion from others: considerations such as the quality of the source, possible hidden motivations, and so on. In such small-scale action research, of course, you will be getting responses from people you know well, which should make it easier to evaluate the resulting data, as we shall see shortly.

2. **Nature of the sample**   Sometimes we may ask ourselves how representative our respondents are of the larger groups of which they are a part. For example, how representative is our class of language learners of that age? Or of language learners as a whole? In such cases, we are thinking of our respondents as a *sample* of a larger group. *Sampling* can be quite a complex issue and I will be coming back to it later when I discuss the implementation of questionnaires and interviews.

   The fact is that for a lot of action research, sample size is not a major issue. For example, if we want to find out how popular a certain language exercise is with one of our classes, it is quite easy to get a 100% 'sample'. You simply ask the whole class! (In other words, you are not getting data from a *sample* as such, but from the entire *population* that you are investigating.) This does not necessarily tell you anything about other classes, or other learners in the school: but this need not concern you because perhaps it is only the reactions of your own class that matter to you.

Or again you may tape an interview with your colleague, Ms Smith. How representative are Ms Smith's views of these or other teachers in her department? This may not be a question that bothers you. You may say to yourself: 'Ms Smith is a teacher that I like and admire. She is, in my estimation, a very competent teacher. I am, therefore, interested in exploring her views and ideas, and I'm not at all interested in whether they are representative of what other people think or believe.'

This is fine as long as you are honest and open to yourself and others about the limitations of your sample. The important thing is not to generalise from your data unless you have a sound basis for doing so. For most action research you probably wouldn't want to, anyway.

3. **Intrusiveness** The third problem about interviews and questionnaires is that they can be quite intrusive techniques, in that they can eat into other people's time. Most of us do not enjoy filling in research questionnaires. It is true that occasionally in newspapers and magazines we see questionnaires with titles like *How ambitious are you?* or *Are you a good parent?*, and we fill them in. But there are two points about such questionnaires. First, we think that the results might be *relevant* to ourselves, to help us to know more about ourselves. Second, the feedback is *immediate*: we can usually check up on our score immediately, and we are given a rating on how ambitious we are, or whatever, and also perhaps we might be given some advice.

Research questionnaires are different usually. They may not be seen as benefiting ourselves, but only the researcher, and analysis of our responses is only made known to us much later, if at all. (Of course, if the researcher invites us to become collaborators in the project, then we may be more inclined to invest our time.)

Interviews may be even less welcome in that they can be threatening in all kinds of ways. If the respondents are busy people, how much of their time is going to be taken up with the interview? Are any awkward or personal questions going to be asked? And may the respondents have anxieties about how the results will be used?

The particular point being made here is that once you move away from your own immediate circle of people you know well, you should be very sensitive to such issues. Do you have to take up other people's time in this way, or can you investigate the issue you are interested in by some other means?

PERSONAL REVIEW 7.2: Alternatives to the Questionnaire/Interview

Look back at the five questions you generated for PERSONAL REVIEW 7.1. Take each one in turn and see whether you can think of another way in which you could either:

a) get similar information;   or
b) get information that would be complementary to (go along with) the information from your questions.

To give you a few examples, let us look again at some of the suggestions for questions which were given near the beginning of this chapter. Examples:

1. *How many hours a week do your students spend on homework?*
    Alternative/complementary strategy: you could get the students to do some homework tasks in class and measure how long it took them to complete the tasks. (Of course, this would not simulate 'home' conditions, but it might be informative, just the same.)

2. *How do colleagues handle a given unit in the textbook?*
    Alternative/complementary strategy: observation of a lesson when the unit was being taught.

3. *What was a student's worst learning experience?*
    Alternative/complementary strategy: give a student a list of bad teaching practices and ask him or her to select the five worst. (OK, this is cheating a bit, since it is an example of another questionnaire-type question, but it might give you useful complementary information.)

7.5 Comparing questionnaires and interviews as investigative techniques

Which is better to use, a questionnaire or an interview? The first answer to such a question is that this is not necessarily an either/or situation. We have repeatedly noted that the reliability of data can often be increased by checking it against data generated by some complementary technique. Indeed, PERSONAL REVIEW 7.2 which you have just done has probably given you some examples of that in relation to the questions you generated for PERSONAL REVIEW 7.1.

Questionnaires and interviews are thus often used in complementary fashion. If the questionnaires are filled in anonymously, then a certain number of respondents may be followed up at random for deeper investigation. If the questionnaires are not anonymous, then some of the respondents (perhaps those who give fuller or more intriguing responses) may be followed up for in-depth interviews, so that ideas may be explored more thoroughly.

7.6 Questionnaires

Questionnaires often take longer to prepare than interviews. This is partly because they tend on average to be more highly structured than interviews. Questionnaires usually also have to be very carefully written because of problems of ambiguity, since a lack of clarity in the questions cannot be immediately cleared up as they often can be in face-to-face interviews. On the other hand questionnaires can also *save* time. The greater the number of informants, the more economical of time it is to use a questionnaire. To interview 60 people for only ten minutes will take at least ten hours, and probably much more once travelling, etc. is taken into consideration. With such numbers, a questionnaire may be the only sensible choice.

The great advantage of the interview is its flexibility. If the respondent has problems with the questions, they can be explained. If the respondent says something intriguing, follow-up questions can be asked. If the structure of the interview is sufficiently loose, sometimes unexpected avenues of investigation can be explored.

In the sections which follow, other differences between the two techniques in terms of implementation will hopefully become clear.

PERSONAL REVIEW 7.3: Questionnaire or Interview?

Go back again to the five questions you generated for PERSONAL REVIEW 7.1. Which do you think would be more appropriate for investigating these areas, a questionnaire or an interview? Perhaps either would do equally well? Perhaps you would need both?

As an example, here are some possible responses based on the questions that have already been suggested.

1. *How many hours a week do your students spend on homework?*
    This looks as if it should be the subject of a question (or a series of questions) in a class questionnaire. There might be a case for follow-up interviews with students who spend very little, an average amount or a very large amount of time on homework. You might very well want to interview one or two students in each category.

2. *What was a colleague's most successful teaching experience?*
    This looks like a possible interview question: it would probably be tedious to write down a description of the whole incident; follow-up questions might be necessary for the informant or at least desirable.

7.7 Sampling

I have briefly touched upon this issue, and I would like to say a little bit more about it here, as it concerns the implementation of both questionnaires and interviews.

Researchers often refer to the total group being researched as a *population*. As has been previously noted, action research is often on such a small scale that the entire population (e.g. a learning group) can be investigated. So, if a teacher wants to find out about the attitudes of his or her class to something, or of the members of his or her department to the same thing, it may be quite feasible and convenient to give questionnaires to, or maybe even to interview, everyone in the target population.

You may wish to get data from a population that is too large for you to cover totally (e.g. you may wish to get the views not just of the teachers in your department but perhaps all the teachers in the school). You may decide that you want to ask only a sample of these to complete your questionnaire or to be interviewed. There are various ways you can do this:

– For example, you could interview colleagues that it is *convenient* for you to speak to. But this might mean that your sample might not be representative of the population as a whole: for example, most of them might be from your own department or be of the same age group as yourself. Do these issues matter? Only you can decide.
– Or you might decide to take a *random sample*. You could do this by, for example, choosing every tenth name on the staff list. Because it is random, this distribution may give unexpected results: it may be, for instance, that your sample may consist mostly of male students with only a few females: does this matter? Again, only you can decide. If you were investigating the kinds of books that students read for pleasure, you might want both sexes to be equally represented, just in case it turned out that the books selected by boys and girls were very different.
– You might decide that you want to be more in control of the sample by ensuring that different categories of people are represented (e.g. an equal number of men and women, so many people from each department, a certain number of promoted and unpromoted staff). This procedure is called *stratified sampling*.

If you want your sample to be statistically *significant*, you will be concerned with various technical issues which cannot be dealt with here. It may be useful to note that Cohen and Manion (1994: 89, 90) point out that, for statistical analysis, a minimum sample size of 30 is usually thought to be desirable: for further advice you are referred to their book (Chapter 4).

It is worth repeating that these issues need not worry you as long as you realise the limitations of your population or your sample, and don't attempt to generalise from your own case to others without very careful consideration.

7.8 Piloting

Another issue that affects both interviews and questionnaires, but particularly questionnaires, is that they should be *piloted* to see whether they work as planned. Even if you are going to distribute only a small number of questionnaires, it might be worth your while trying them out on one or two people beforehand. (If you were giving out a large number of questionnaires, you would want to pilot a correspondingly larger number.) Although conventional wisdom says that piloting should always be done, it has to be admitted that in practice this is sometimes very difficult. It may be that you simply want to get some feedback from a group that you haven't seen before and won't be seeing again. In such circumstances, piloting is difficult and probably wouldn't be attempted: you have to get it right first time!

In the piloting stage, you will want to ask questions such as:

1. Were the instructions clear and easy to follow?
2. Were the questions clear?
3. Were you able to answer all the questions?
4. Did you find any of the questions:
   – embarrassing?
   – irrelevant?
   – patronising?
   – irritating?
5. (Questionnaire) – How long did the questionnaire take to complete? (Note: in an interview you, as the interviewer, would similarly want to check the length of the interview.)

Don't forget to ask your respondents for any other comments and suggestions that help to make your questionnaire or interview more effective.

7.9 Questionnaire preparation

Purpose

The first thing to be very clear about is your *purpose*. Why are you setting up the questionnaire? What do you hope to find out? Try to imagine the range of responses. Will they tell you what you need to know?

Handling the data

Again, it is important to imagine the completed responses. Will they be in a form that is simple and convenient to analyse? This might mean organising the questionnaire form so that it is easy for you to record the results.

Practical details

How many copies of the questionnaire will you need? Will you need spares? How are you going to ensure maximum return of the completed questionnaires?

Anonymity

Are the questionnaires going to be anonymous? If they are, people may be more honest and informative in their responses. If they are not anonymous, you may be able to have follow-up interviews on selected questionnaires. You may also be able to send reminders to those who have not responded.

7.10 Questionnaire design

Clarity

It should be clear to the informants why they are filling in the questionnaire: what it is intended to achieve. It should be clear whether or not the questionnaire is supposed to be anonymous.

The instructions should be very clear and explicit. Have answers to be ticked, crossed, circled or written out? Where? It may be a good idea to provide one or two examples.

Simplicity

Is the questionnaire laid out in a straightforward manner? Does the layout help respondents to find their way through it?

Closed and open questions

In a questionnaire the respondent may be asked to choose from a limited range of possible answers. Questions of this type are sometimes called *closed* questions. Here is an example of a closed question:

Example 1

(Please tick (✓) the appropriate box.)

How many years have you been studying English?

0–3 ☐   4–6 ☐   7–10 ☐   more than 10 ☐

In contrast, we have *open* questions, where the response is open-ended.

Example 2

Why did you decide to learn English rather than some other foreign language? (If you have several reasons, pick the most important.)

_____

_____

_____

The advantage of closed questions is that they usually make the questionnaire easier and quicker to fill in. They also make for quicker and more reliable scoring of the responses.

The disadvantages of closed questions is that they usually take longer to devise than open questions. Instructions on how to answer them have to be very clear. It also means that the questionnaire designer has to anticipate all or most of the possible answers, so there may be little unexpected information in the responses.

One corresponding advantage of open questions is that they are comparatively easy to design, but you may have some headaches in trying to score and/or analyse the responses. Open questions are good for exploratory research where you have difficulty in anticipating the range of responses. They are also more likely to yield more unexpected (and therefore, perhaps, more interesting) data.

It is also possible to combine closed and open elements within the same question, or to have a question of one type with a follow-up question of another type. Here are examples of each of these:

Example 3

What is your main reason for studying English? (Please tick ONE of (i) – (iii), or write in an answer to (iv).)

(i)   For business   ☐

(ii) For further study   ☐
      (e.g. university course)

(iii) For social reasons   ☐

(iv) Other (please specify)..
      ....

Example 4

1.   Did you enjoy your EFL evening class?   YES/NO
     (Please circle appropriate answer.)

2.   (a) If your answer to (1) was YES, what did you enjoy

          most about it?

          ....

          ....

     (b) If your answer to (1) was NO, why did you not enjoy

          it?

          ....

          ....

As you will already have noted, there is a wide range of different ways in which closed questions can be planned. The simplest one is probably the YES/NO format in Example 4. We can also have a range of choices (Example 3), or a scale (Example 1). If you are using a scale, make sure the categories don't overlap (i.e. in Example 1, don't use categories like 0–4, 4–6, 6–10, where respondents who have been learning English for four years or six years will be confused about which box to tick).

Instead of using figures, you can sometimes use *verbal categories*:

Example 5

How helpful did you find the textbook we used this term?
(Please tick.)

Very interesting .... OK .... Not interesting ....

You can also use a scale for this of, say, 1–5, or 1–7. (See Question 1 of the Example Questionnaire in PERSONAL REVIEW 7.4 which comes later in this chapter.)

If you are using verbal categories, please make sure that they are meaningful:

Example 6 (negative example)

How much homework do you do in a typical week? (Please tick.)

A lot .... Average .... Not much .... None ....

You can see that the only really informative category here is 'none'. How much is 'a lot'? What is 'a lot' for a lazy student may be 'not much' for a hard-working one!

How would an individual student know what was 'average'? And so on.

A better example might be:

How many hours homework do you do in a week? (Please tick.)

0–1 ☐   2–3 ☐   4–5 ☐   more than 5 ☐

7.11 Relevance

Probably the most frequent mistake made in designing questionnaires is asking unnecessary and/or irrelevant questions: for example, wanting to know whether the respondent is male or female, or his or her age, when this information has nothing whatever to do with the purpose of the questionnaire.

7.12 User-friendliness

A lot of what we have been saying can be summarised by making the point that, since no-one enjoys answering questionnaires, they should be made as 'user-friendly' as possible. This means they should not be too long, they should not be intrusive (e.g. by asking questions that may embarrass the respondents), and they should not be confusing or perplexing. It also means being sensitive to the respondents in other ways. As teachers, we may very often want to get feedback from our students. If they are beginner learners, or very young, questions should be kept short and simple, and may have to be framed in the mother tongue to make sure that you are getting valid data. Alternatively, you may decide to use graphics such as 'happy/unhappy faces'.

PERSONAL REVIEW 7.4: Question Formats

Although most of us have filled in questionnaires at some time, it would probably be helpful at this point to look at an actual example of a questionnaire that someone has used. I have chosen the questionnaire used by George Murdoch in his investigation into 'Language development provision in teacher training curricula' (*ELT Journal*, 48/3, 1994: 253–265). Although it is quite a long questionnaire, it has the advantage of displaying a range of possible formats for questions (and of course it also asks some interesting and very pertinent questions!).

Have a look through the questionnaire, and then think about this question:

Murdoch uses *five* different formats for his questions. They are:
− a numerical scale, 1–5
− ranking
− a verbal scale
− yes/no response
− open-ended response

Can you find examples of each format?
(Try to answer the question before reading on.)

Appendix 1

Survey questionnaire of the views of student teachers in Sri Lankan teacher training institutions on curriculum provision for language development.

1 To what extent would the following activities in methodology classes on teaching reading aid the growth of your language skills? Rate each one using the five point scale (1 = most effective, 5 = least effective).

a. Listening to a lecture about teaching reading skills.	1 2 3 4 5
b. Ranking different materials according to their interest value for pupils.	1 2 3 4 5
c. Creating teaching materials/activities for classroom teaching.	1 2 3 4 5
d. Brainstorming pre-reading stimuli for a course book reading text.	1 2 3 4 5
e. Comparing different lesson plans for teaching the same material from the textbook.	1 2 3 4 5
f. Summarizing orally and then in writing the main points the lecturer has made about the key reading strategies.	1 2 3 4 5
g. Categorizing texts in terms of different functional/rhetorical categories, e.g. narrative, argumentative, etc.	1 2 3 4 5
h. Student presentations on a topic or set reading.	1 2 3 4 5
i. Discussions after viewing a film or observing a class being taught.	1 2 3 4 5
j. Copying down a lecturer's note.	1 2 3 4 5

2 Rank these groupings for activities in methodology sessions according to their value for language development (1 = most valuable). Write the appropriate number in the box provided.

☐ working individually

☐ working in pairs

☐ working in groups

☐ whole class with teacher directing

In questions 3–9 tick the column with the heading that best summarizes your reaction to each statement.

Q	Strongly agree	Agree	Not sure	Disagree	Strongly disagree
3 Teaching skills and techniques should be developed by methods that maximize opportunities for students to develop/practise their language skills.					
4 Student teachers cannot improve their English enough simply via studying methodology and preparing for teaching practice.					

continued

Learner strategies and learner interviews

Q	Strongly agree	Agree	Not sure	Disagree	Strongly disagree
5 The way in which language is taught in teacher training institutions has a very strong influence on the procedures student teachers adopt for teaching English in schools.					
6 The teaching of spoken English during formal training should be based largely on the interactions which take place in the school context.					
7 If student teachers are taught classroom language, this will have a very beneficial effect on their later classroom performance.					
8 A teacher's confidence is most dependent on his/her own degree of language proficiency.					
9 I would like to find out about how best to learn English and study effectively during my language development course.					

10 Rank the four skills according to their degree of importance for an English teacher in Sri Lanka (1 = most important)

☐ Speaking

☐ Reading

☐ Listening

☐ Writing

11 Which of the following activities do you find useful for improving your English? Circle the appropriate answer.

singing	Yes	No
role plays	Yes	No
drama activities	Yes	No
pronunciation practice	Yes	No
problem-solving activities	Yes	No
dictation	Yes	No
learning and practising grammar	Yes	No
writing about personal experience	Yes	No
debates/discussions	Yes	No
reading widely	Yes	No
activities to practise particular reading/writing skills	Yes	No
simulations	Yes	No

12 Are there any other language learning activities you feel are valuable but are not mentioned in 11?

---

13 Which of the following subjects would best provide sources of stimulating input for language development activities? Tick ($\sqrt{}$) the appropriate boxes (you can choose as many as you want).

☐ modern literary texts

☐ classroom situations, experiences, and issues

☐ other subjects in the training course curriculum

☐ current affairs

☐ students' own writings

☐ other societies and cultures

14 What other topics/subjects, not mentioned in 10, could be dealt with on a teacher education language course?

---

15 What percentage of your time would you like to spend simply developing your language skills on your training programme? Tick the appropriate box.

☐ less than 5%

☐ 05–10%

☐ 10–20%

☐ 20–30%

☐ 30–40%

☐ 40–50%

☐ more than 50%

16 Consider the value of these components of a training programme for English teachers. Rank them in order of personal importance from 1 to 10 (1 = most important).

☐ educational psychology

☐ principles of education

☐ language improvement

☐ teaching practice

☐ ELT methodology and techniques

☐ testing

☐ linguistics/sentence structure

☐ phonology

☐ study of literary set texts

☐ classroom observation/microteaching

THANK YOU

Learner strategies and learner interviews

7.13 Commentary

Some examples are: numerical (Q1), ranking (Q2, Q15), verbal (Qs 3–9), yes/no (Q11), open-ended (Qs 12, 14).

In Q15, notice that Murdoch's categories overlap (e.g. 5–10% overlaps with 10–20%). In this case, the overlap has no significance, since Murdoch is not looking for real-life data (as he would if he were asking a question like: 'How many hours a week do you teach?' or 'How many students are in your class?'). Here, he is interested only in rough hypothetical percentages, so the responses are still valid.

PERSONAL REVIEW 7.5: Analysing Questionnaire Data

Now look at the data from Murdoch's questionnaire. What do they show? How have they been organised? Does the way in which they have been organised help understanding? What conclusions do you derive from studying these data? (e.g. generally speaking what sort of activities do teachers find beneficial for improving their language skills?)

Appendix 2
Survey results

1 To what extent would the following activities in methodology classes on teaching reading aid the growth of your language skills?

Results (in rank order, 1 = most effective):
  1 Creating teaching materials/activities for classroom teaching.
  2 Discussions after viewing a film or observing a class being taught.
  3 Brainstorming pre-reading stimuli for a coursebook reading text.
  4 Student presentations on a topic or set reading.
  5 Ranking different materials according to their interest value for pupils.
  6 Summarizing orally, and then in writing, the main points the lecturer has made about the key reading strategies.
  7 Categorizing texts in terms of different functional/rhetorical categories, e.g. narrative, argumentative, etc.
  8 Comparing different lesson plans for teaching the same material from the textbook.
  9 Listening to a lecture about teaching reading skills.
  10 Copying down a lecturer's notes.

2 Rank these groupings for activities in methodology sessions according to their value for language development.

Results (in rank order: 1 = valuable):
  1 working in groups
  2 working in pairs
  3 whole class with teacher directing
  4 working individually.

3–9 Results are given in percentiles.

Tick the column with the heading that best summarizes your reaction to each statement:

Q	Strongly agree	Agree	Not sure	Disagree	Strongly disagree
3 Teaching skills and techniques should be developed by methods that maximize opportunities for students to develop/practise their language skills.	52	43	1	1	2
4 Student teachers cannot improve their English enough simply via studying methodology and preparing for teaching practice.	21	41	9	23	5
5 The way in which language is taught in teacher training institutions has a very strong influence on the procedures student teachers adopt for teaching English in schools.	23	36	18	15	2

continued

Q	Strongly agree	Agree	Not sure	Disagree	Strongly disagree
6 The teaching of spoken English during formal training should be based largely on the interactions which take place in the school context.	20	35	21	12	5
7 If student teachers are taught classroom language, this will have a very beneficial effect on their later classroom performance.	39	46	7	4	1
8 A teacher's confidence is most dependent on his/her own degree of language proficiency.	49	40	5	3	2
9 I would like to find out about how best to learn English and study effectively during my language development course.	34	50	9	4	1

10 Rank the four skills according to their degree of importance for an English teacher in Sri Lanka.

Results (in rank order; 1 = most important):
1 Speaking
2 Listening
3 Writing
4 Reading

11 Which of the following activities do you find useful for improving your English?

Results (percentage of students that selected each activity):
Role plays 95%; Debates/discussions 95%; Learning and practising grammar 94%; Activities to practise particular reading/writing skills 91%; Pronunciation practice 89%; Drama activities 84%; Reading widely 84%; Dictation 73%; Simulations 72%; Singing 65%.

12 Are there any other language learning activities you feel are valuable but are not mentioned in 11?

Results (most mentioned activities):
language games; creative writing tasks; solving problems; quizzes.

13 Which of the following subjects would best provide sources of stimulating input for language development activities?

Results (in rank order):
1 modern literary texts; 2 classroom situations, experiences, and issues; 3 current affairs; 4 students' own writings; 5 other subjects in the training course curriculum; 6 other societies and cultures.

14 What other topics/subjects, not mentioned in 13, could be dealt with on a teacher education language course?

Results (subjects most mentioned):
aesthetic subjects; social studies; religion; personal experience.

15 What percentage of your time would you like to spend simply developing your language skills on your training programme?

Results (number of students selecting each option):
more than 50%: 115; 40–50%: 45; 30–40%: 30; 20–30%: 8; 10–20%: 2; 5–10%: 2; less than 5%: 1.

16 Consider the value of these components of a training programme for English teachers. Rank them in order of personal importance from 1 to 10 (1 = most important).

Results (overall ranking):
1 language improvement
2 ELT methodology and techniques
3 educational psychology
4 linguistics/sentence structure
5 teaching practice
6 principles of education
7 phonology
8 study of literary set texts
9 classroom observation/microteaching
10 testing

It is worth noting at this point that Murdoch has provided in these appendices both the format of his questionnaire and the data resulting from it. This is usually considered good practice, as it allows the reader:

- to check the actual questions asked;
- to directly examine the data;
- to come to his or her own conclusions (in addition to reading the author's conclusions).

We will come back to this issue in the last chapter when we discuss how you go about sharing the findings of your research.

One final question on this article: why do you think it was more appropriate for Murdoch to use a questionnaire for this type of data collection than an interview format?

7.14 Interviews

Like questionnaires, interviews come in many different forms, but perhaps it is most helpful to think of interviews as falling into three broad categories, namely *structured, unstructured* and *semi-structured*. I will briefly discuss each of these in turn.

7.15 Structured interviews

By structured interviews I mean interviews that have a very tight structure, and in which the questions will probably be read from a carefully prepared *interview schedule*, similar to a questionnaire but used orally. Structured interviews have therefore most of the advantages (and disadvantages) of questionnaires. The main disadvantages are, first, that it obviously takes much longer to implement questionnaires orally than in writing, and, secondly, there is less possibility of anonymity (unless the interviewer and interviewee (respondent) are complete strangers to one another, as sometimes happens in surveys). The main advantage is that misunderstandings, or a lack of understanding, can be immediately sorted out during the exchange.

7.16 Unstructured interviews

The word 'unstructured' is perhaps not completely accurate, in that, by definition, an interview must have *some* kind of structure otherwise it would simply be a conversation. One necessary element of structure even in an 'unstructured' interview is that the interviewer must have a research purpose in mind when initiating the interview. Another necessary element of structure is that the interviewee must know that he or she is taking part in an interview, and should preferably also know what the purpose of the interview is. To engage people unknowingly in interviews which they think are private conversations would, of course, be quite unethical. Apart from this, an unstructured interview can be quite free-wheeling, without losing sight of the research purpose. This open-ended approach may engender a relaxed atmosphere where personal data can be revealed which might otherwise be withheld in a more formal setting.

7.17 Semi-structured interviews

As its name indicates, the semi-structured interview is a kind of compromise between the two extremes. There will almost certainly be a prepared interview schedule, but most of the questions will probably be open questions. The schedule may also contain *prompts* (i.e. comments, examples or follow-up questions intended to encourage the interviewee to give fuller, more detailed responses). Semi-structured interviews therefore combine a certain degree of control with a certain amount of freedom to develop the interview. This is why it is probably the most popular format for interviews. Attend carefully the next time you watch an in-depth interview of, say, a politician on TV: you will probably discover that it has a semi-structured format. You will be aware that the interviewer has his or her own agenda; and you may well see him or her checking a prepared list of questions.

7.18 The time factor

Time is an important aspect of interviewing, for several different reasons. If you have piloted your interview (as I recommended earlier), you should have a rough idea how long it will take. The proposed duration of the interview should be made known to the interviewees, when you are inviting them to take part. Having agreed on that time, you must stick to it, and not over-run.

Remember also that the more people you decide to interview, the more work you are going to have to do in preparation, making arrangements, possibly travelling to the interview venue, and the analysing and perhaps also transcribing of data. Powney and Watts (1987: 118) suggest that for each hour of interviewing, a further three should be allowed for preparation and summary – and this does not include transcription. They analyse the total time taken in an actual

research project relating to 90-minute interviews (p.126) : each interview in fact took up 15 hours of the researcher's time, including travel
time and transcription.

Earlier, you were asked why George Murdoch used a questionnaire
rather than interviews for his research: the answer is clear when you
look at the number of students involved in his questionnaire – 208!

For someone contemplating doing action research through using
interviewing, the moral is obviously to be very realistic about how
much interviewing you are going to do, who are the key people to be
interviewed, and how you are going to handle all the other things that
go with the interview process. You may wish to consider: fewer interviews; shorter interviews (how much do you really need to know?);
group interviews instead of individual interviews; simpler forms of
analysis (e.g. no transcription); simpler administration (e.g. very little
travel), and so on.

If you have access to the Internet, this of course raises interesting
possibilities of who you can interview and when. In the present context
it also affords the possibility of being able to download interviews and
having hard copy without going through the time-consuming drudgery
of transcription.

7.19   Recording interview data

There are three ways in which interview data can be recorded. The
easiest, but in many ways least satisfactory, is by *simple recall* (i.e.
depending on your memory). Obviously, this is not a very reliable
method as most of our forgetting occurs shortly after the event. If you
have to use this approach, your recollection should be written down or
audio recorded as soon as possible after the interview is over. Much
more reliable is *note taking* during the interview. In structured interviews, the note taking may take the form of filling in a questionnaire. In
less structured interviews, note taking may be more difficult, as there is
an obvious conflict between being an attentive and reactive listener on
the one hand and taking extensive notes on the other.

The third method is by *taping* the interview either through audio or
video, and this usually is the richest method, in terms of the amount of
data available for analysis. It is also not without its problems, of course.
The recording machines must be carefully checked to make sure they
are functioning. If you are using batteries, make sure that they are fully
charged. Some potential interviewees may either object to being taped,
or may be very ill-at-ease. The tapes will have to be listened to or
watched again, and also may have to be transcribed, either in whole or
in part.

7.20   Individual and group interviews

Most interviews are one-to-one, but it is also possible to have an 'interview' with a group, which could take the form of a kind of structured discussion. It might be that the discussion could proceed with very little intervention for the interviewer. For example, the topic we mentioned earlier of 'Good ideas for Friday afternoon' might be best handled by a group interview using a brainstorming approach.

7.21   Prior notification of questions

Interviewees may be more relaxed if they know what questions they are going to be asked. This may also help them to provide fuller, more informative, answers. It is also important to check in advance whether the interviewee is happy about being recorded, if this is what you wish to do. If the interview is a sensitive one, the interviewee may wish to check your transcript, to agree that what you have written down is what he or she actually said.

7.22   Conduct of the interview

Interviews should begin and finish on time. The atmosphere should be friendly and relaxed. If you are using a recording machine, check that it is working properly, and that the sound level is OK. You can start off with easy 'lead-in' questions that the interviewee will have no problem in answering: this can help break the ice, and build up the interviewee's self-confidence and confidence in you.

7.23   Interviews: variety of focus

I am using the term interview *focus* here in the same sense that it is used by Powney and Watts (1987: 28), that is, any stimulus (e.g. a video tape, text, task) which is used to elicit responses from the interviewee. In this sense, the interview schedule is itself one kind of focus. Some other examples, using different kinds of focus:

1. **Teacher interviewing student**   The teacher plays back a video recording of his or her lesson, stops it from time to time, and asks the student for his or her reactions at that point.
2. **Teacher interviewing teacher**   The interviewer asks the interviewee

to read a short controversial article from a professional journal, and asks him or her to react to it.
3. **Teacher interviewing student** Teacher gives the student a task to do. Teacher asks questions before, during and after the task.

7.24 Example interview schedule

You will see here an example of a short interview schedule. Note the 'basic data' recorded at the top of the schedule.

Interview Schedule

Interviewee:. . . . . Intended duration:. . . . . . . mins

Date:. . . . . Interview began:. . . . .

Location:. . . . . Interview finished:. . . . .

Actual duration:. . . . . mins

Topic: Student Motivation (EFL)
1. How long have you been studying English?
2. Why did you choose to study English?
   (*Prompts*: Business/further studies/social/hobby . . .)
3. How would you describe your motivation (i.e. desire to study English) at this time: HIGH/AVERAGE/LOW?
4. Would you say that your motivation has changed at all during your period of study?
   (*Prompts*: Constant/up and down? More/less now than at beginning?)
5. What would you say are the things that have affected your motivation over your period of study?
   (*Prompts*: Teachers/textbooks/fellow students/something in you? How did these affect you?)
6. Can you suggest anything that could happen or could be done at this time to improve your motivation?
   (*Prompts*: Career development/more leisure? Better syllabus/teacher/textbook?)

PERSONAL REVIEW 7.6: Devising a Semi-Structured
Interview

Choose any topic that you are interested in. (You might want to
go back again to PERSONAL REVIEW 7.1 to pick up some of
your initial ideas.) Devise a semi-structured interview on that
topic. You can use the format given for the example Interview
Schedule above, or you can devise your own. If you have the
opportunity, actually use the interview with someone relevant to
the topic who's willing to be interviewed. If possible, record the
interview, and play it back to yourself later to evaluate how it
went. Think of the criteria that you are going to use for your
evaluation (e.g. Did I get the information I wanted? Was it
interesting? Did communication break down at any point?) After
listening to the tape, decide whether there is anything you
would now do differently.

7.25 Summary

In this chapter, we have discussed two techniques, interviewing and
questionnaires, both of which involve gathering data by asking people
questions. We often use questionnaires when we are going for *breadth*,
(i.e. wanting to get responses from a comparatively large number of
people). We often use interviews, on the other hand, when we want to
investigate people's views, attitudes, experiences etc., *in depth*.

It is sometimes the case, however, that the best way forward is to
combine these two techniques, so that the strengths of both procedures
can be exploited (e.g. by using questionnaires to elicit basic factual data,
and interviews to follow up on attitudes and experiences).

Since we have just spent some time looking at a questionnaire, we are
going to round off this chapter by looking at an article which relies on
the interview technique.

7.26 Exemplar article

The examplar article illustrates the use of interviews to find out about
learner strategies.

The article is:

Eloise Pearson (1988). Learner strategies and learner interviews. *ELT Journal* 42/3, July 1988, 173–178.

Read the article with the following questions in mind:

1. The writer did not set out in the first place to focus narrowly on learner strategies, but to find out about other things. What were they?
2. How many people were interviewed? Where were they interviewed?
3. There were two *follow-up interviews*. Where were they held? What was the purpose of these interviews, do you think?
4. Notice how in her conclusions Pearson relates her findings to 'the literature' (pp. 157–159). Pick out three or four of the findings from other writers and researchers referred to by Pearson, and consider whether or not these findings correspond with what Pearson discovered from her interviews.
5. How convinced are you by the findings of Pearson's research?
6. Pearson tells us that her interviews were 'basically unstructured' (p. 153). Supposing she had decided to use a semi-structured approach: what are the questions she might have asked?
7. Do you know anyone who strikes you as being a very good language learner? If so, why not interview them to find out the secret of their success!

Learner strategies and learner interviews

Eloise Pearson

This article describes a series of interviews between the author and a number of Japanese speakers of English as a second language. The interviewees were men on long-term job assignments in South East Asia. All but two of the interviews took place on site. The initial aims of the interviews were to determine the uses to which the interviewees put English; to identify the conditions under which they used English; and to characterize in general terms their life styles while living and working outside Japan. However, the results were also found to be interesting in relation to the interviewees' second-language learning strategies in general, and in relation to certain implications of those strategies for classroom content and methodology.

In her work on the good language learner, Rubin defines 'learning' as 'the process by which storage and retrieval of information is achieved' (1981:118). Elsewhere, learning strategies have been referred to as 'operations or steps used by a learner that will assist in the acquisition, storage, or retrieval of new information' (Chamot and O'Malley 1986:9). The purpose of this article is to discuss the relevance of these views in relation to a small selection of learners.

Five interviews were conducted on site in South East Asia with a total of twelve employees of a major Japanese company and some of its subsidiaries. The interviews were basically unstructured. The first two interviews were with Mr J. and Mr S., two businessmen in different offices in Singapore who had both lived and worked in Singapore for three years. The third interview involved a group of three engineers supervising the construction of a large steel-structure building in Singapore. The fourth interview was with a group of five supervising engineers on a large construction site on the west coast of Malaysia, and the last interview was with two supervising engineers on a large construction project near Kuala Lumpur. With the exception of Mr J. and Mr S., all of the men had been abroad only six months or less. The businessmen were interviewed in their offices, and the engineers were interviewed on their respective job sites. In all cases, the visits included tours of the working areas.

Interview one

Mr J. never used English in his office, as all his associates were Japanese or Japanese speakers. In his free time, he usually associated with them or other members of the Japanese-speaking community. He spoke Japanese at home with his family. His uses of English were limited to business conversations with local clients and to very rare golf games with them. His other uses of English were restricted to conversations with restaurant employees, parking attendants, ticket clerks, and so on. All his information about business and current affairs was obtained through Japanese. He did not have local friends, nor did he associate with the local people or culture. He had not studied English since university. Nevertheless he claimed that, to his surprise, his level of English had not improved in the three years he had been in Singapore. He mentioned that his job was stressful due to his lack of English, and he was looking forward to returning to Japan.

Interview two

By contrast, the second businessmen, Mr S., worked in an office with all Singaporeans. He spoke only English in all his working contacts. Both he and his Japanese wife had Singaporean friends and associated mostly with them, speaking English with them. Mr and Mrs S. both made exclusive use of English-language sources of information and entertainment and were trying to learn and improve their English through their own efforts. Mr S. reported that his English had improved 'somewhat' in his three years. He enjoyed living and working abroad, and said he had no language-related problems with his work.

Interview three

The third interview, with three supervisor-engineers on a large construction site in Singapore, revealed that they associated only with themselves and with some Japanese-speaking members of a local trading company that was in charge of their part of the project. Despite some proficiency in English, they reported that they had never attempted to communicate with any of the workers on the job site or in the community in the three months they had been in Singapore. At the end of the working day they went to their rooms, where they ate only Japanese food prepared by a cook provided by the trading company. They mentioned that they only communicated with her through the trading company, although they thought she probably knew some English. During their time off they stayed in their rooms reading Japanese papers and books and sleeping. They reported they had no need or desire to have any dealings with anyone else, as the trading company did everything for them. They mentioned that their life was boring, that they were lonely and depressed, and that they wanted to go home as soon as possible. They had all been abroad before on projects and had lived and worked in a similar manner. They said they found working abroad to be troublesome because of their lack of language, but that they had no time to study. They mentioned that their English had not improved since graduation from university.

Interview four

The fourth interview, with five engineers on a coastal project in west Malaysia, revealed a quite different response to their situation. The oldest among them, Mr T., mentioned that he had been in Indonesia on two previous long-term projects and spoke fluent Indonesian, his second language. His English, however, was very limited. He reported that the first thing he always did upon arrival at an overseas project site was to buy a small motor bike which allowed him to get into the nearby community every night for dinner and entertainment (usually drinking). He said he had picked up the Indonesian language that way, and by taking every opportunity to talk and make friends with local people both on and off the job site. Although his company provided an almost completely Japanese 'home from home' life style, Mr T., preferred to experience Malaysian life style as much as possible.

The four younger engineers had mostly followed his lead and were all 'picking up Malaysian', their second language, through their associations with native speakers. They were better speakers of English than Mr T., but they preferred to try Malaysian whenever possible. On most evenings they went into town for dinner and greatly enjoyed Malaysian food and life style. After six months, none of them reported any symptoms of 'culture shock'.[1] All of them seemed well adjusted and claimed to be 'really enjoying' their time abroad, even though the work was hard. They said that their English had not improved at all, but that they could handle most of their communication needs in Malaysian. They reported that they experienced no language-related problems with their jobs.

Interview five

The fifth interview was conducted with two engineers on a large construction site near Kuala Lumpur. Both men appeared to be introverts. English was their only second language, and their command of it was very poor indeed. In fact, the interview was conducted in Japanese as their command of English was not sufficient to communicate, and they obviously did not want to struggle with it. They reported nothing but problems with their work and daily life because of language difficulties, and although their housing, meals, and daily necessities were all provided for, as with the other interviewees, there was no one around who could speak Japanese. They felt totally isolated. They said that they never went anywhere or did anything besides work, were afraid all the time, had never eaten Malaysian food in the four months they had been there, and had not tried to make any friends or communicate with anyone. They both said they were trying to endure their terrible loneliness and difficulties at work and were anxiously looking forward to their return home. They explained that they felt overwhelmed by everything and were very depressed and unhappy. Overseas work and any dealings with non-Japanese speakers were very stressful for them.

Two follow-up interviews

Later, in Tokyo, I undertook two follow-up interviews, one with Mr J., the first businessman who had been in Singapore for three and a half years, and the other with Mr T., the oldest of the engineers on the coastal site in Malaysia who had previously reported his success in acquiring Indonesian as a second language. Again, the interviews were basically unstructured, although they were focused more directly on discovering what, if any, second-language learner strategies they had employed while abroad.

When asked what he did to try to improve his English, Mr J. said that he had not tried very hard. He said that he had not spoken English unless it was unavoidable. He reported constant frustration because he did not understand everything. He did not try to guess, or work out meanings. He tried to cover up when he did not understand. He did not really try to figure out any general rules or to use any new words or expressions unless he was entirely sure they would be correct. He mentioned that he was always afraid of making a mistake, even though he felt he was not often misunderstood because of linguistic errors. In addition he always felt frustrated because he could not express himself on anything other than business topics, and so he avoided such topics or non-professional situations. He said he rarely planned or practised what he wanted to say in English. He had not seriously considered actively trying on his own to learn English because, he claimed, he had not had the time. He explained that for about a year he and his family had hated Singapore, but that things had improved after that. He reported that he often used gestures and had 'picked up' local expressions for beginning and ending a conversation, and other common situations.

Mr T., from the coastal Malaysian site, was quite different. He explained that he had never encountered Indonesian before going to Indonesia the first time, and that in the beginning, when he was eating and drinking with native speakers he would point to different objects to elicit vocabulary, and he would repeat each word several times to memorize it. He would listen to conversation and then try to put together sentences with new words and expressions and would always receive immediate feedback, sometimes in the form of laughter. It was all fun and like a challenging game to him. He mentioned attempting to find general rules and then trying them out. Above all he was always listening and trying to work out meaning, often by guessing, which was immediately followed by checking for verification or clarification. He often gestured, used paraphrasing, simplification, and synonyms, but he always tried to find out the correct or better way to say what he wanted to say. He claimed never to have experienced anything like culture shock, and he thought this might be due to his desire to learn the language and to his enjoyment of his own increasing fluency. He never planned his learning, and his only monitoring was in recognizing his own production errors, which he then tried to correct. He explained that in Tokyo he tried to keep up his Indonesian by practising with Indonesian-speaking office colleagues and by reading Indonesian newspapers. The interview concluded by his saying that all four of the other younger engineers who were with him on the site had 'mastered' Malaysian in the ten months they were there, and that they had not experienced any of the symptoms of 'culture shock' as I have described it (see footnote 1).

It is clear from the interviews that the three engineers in Singapore and the two engineers near Kuala Lumpur did not employ successful second-language learning strategies and that their command of their second language, English, had not been improved by their experiences abroad. It is probably equally clear that they were suffering from some aspects of 'culture shock' and that there were perhaps personality factors that pre-vented their using good learning strategies. They were noticeably unhappy abroad, and because of their linguistic handicaps, they had also had problems with their work.

On the other hand, it is quite evident that the autonomous learners, Mr S., the second businessman in Singapore, and the entire group of engineers in coastal Malaysia, were making extensive use of many of the strategies referred to in the literature (for example, Wenden (1985), Stern (1983), Brown (1980) and Rubin (1982)). The second-language ability of these individuals had reportedly improved, and they had adjusted to their new environments well.

However, Mr J. in Singapore employed few learning strategies and reported little progress in his second-language ability. He had suffered from culture shock and again there may have been personality factors inhibiting his use of learning strategies. He was not very happy abroad and he found work difficult.

Some conclusions

Although these interviews yield only a small amount of data—and subjec-tively reported data at that—they do confirm the findings of researchers (for example, Wenden 1985, Chamot and O'Malley 1986) that successful language learners do apply specific strategies to the task of learning.

But these interviews also suggest other important factors in the language-learning process which are less explicitly dealt with in the research with which I am familiar. The interviews suggest that there are complex but describable relationships between personality factors and approaches to language learning; that the phenomenon generally known here as 'culture shock' may inhibit language learning; and that successful language learning in these contexts is clearly associated with a life style which is from the personal point of view comfortable and which is from the professional point of view effective. Research findings which touch on these issues point to the importance of global strategies, in which learners create practice opportunities with native speakers (Wenden 1985); social learning strategies, with their emphasis on the striving for independence, and affective strategies, with their emphasis on coping with the emotional stress of being in a second-language situation (Stern 1983). Brown in his work distinguishes between learning strategies on the one hand, and personality factors and socio-cultural variables on the other. But he cautions that researchers need to determine if personality factors 'are something that one can "learn" in the adult years especially cross-culturally' (1980:109).

In her advice to second-language learners, Rubin (1982) includes both cognitive factors and personality factors as being equally relevant and important to successful second-language acquisition (for example, personality factors: make opportunities to use the language, don't be afraid to make mistakes, tolerate ambiguity, and so on).

Two factors implicit in the literature are that learners must be consciously prepared to invest a great deal of their own time and energy in second-language learning, and that learners must desire learner autonomy for their own learning. In fact, Larsen and Smalley (1972:27) explicitly advise the learner: 'There is no way to learn a second language without devoting time to it, not just a good block of time each day, but rather a significant segment out of the learner's life'. However, it is practically impossible to expect learners in the throws of adjusting to life in another culture to be able to invest as much time and energy as might be required for successful language learning. Indeed, the effects of the time spent in a foreign culture may not benefit second-language learning at all—in fact it may create additional inhibiting factors by creating negative attitudes towards other cultures and encouraging ethnocentric and prejudiced thinking.

Sonia Eagle (1986) strongly recommends that second-language learners who are going abroad should clearly understand concepts like ethnocentrism, cultural relativism, culture shock, prejudice, stereotyping, and so on. She suggests that teachers should include such information as part of their classroom training. Thus, if the poor learners (Mr J., the three engineers in Singapore, and the two engineers near Kuala Lumpur) had received training in learning strategies and had been advised of personality factors and certain socio-cultural concepts that inhibit or enhance learning potential, they might have been able to make more effective use of their time abroad, and they might have been happier both personally and professionally.

The second factor which is implicit in the literature is that learners must want to become responsible for their own learning—in other words, to become autonomous. Both Rubin (1982) and Wenden (1985:7) discuss two attitudinal obstacles to learner autonomy: previous second-language learning experience which leads learners to expect that learning is dependent on a teacher, textbook, and a formal course; and a belief on the part of learners that they cannot learn on their own. Certainly, these interviews suggested to me that the learners who were autonomous and who were actively participating in their own learning experience were the most successful learners.

As Wenden puts it: 'Learners must learn how to do for themselves what teachers typically do for them in the classroom. Our endeavours to help them improve their language skills must be complemented by an equally systematic approach to helping them develop and refine their learning skills. Learning training should be integrated with language training' (1985:7). Conducting the interviews described in this article has helped me to appreciate the need for such integration. ☐

Received April 1987

Note

1 I am using 'culture shock' to describe what Brown calls 'feelings in the learner of estrangement, anger, hostility, indecision, frustration, unhappiness, sadness, loneliness, homesickness, and even physical illness. The person undergoing culture shock views his [*sic*] new world out of resentment, and alternates between being angry at others for not understanding him and being filled with self-pity' (1980:131).

References

Brown, D. H. 1980. *Principles of Language Learning and Teaching*. Englewood Cliffs, NJ: Prentice-Hall.

Chamot, A. U. and J. M. O'Malley. 1986. 'Language learning strategies for children.' *The Language Teacher* 10/1:9–12.

Eagle, Sonia J. 1986. JALT Seminar on Anthropology for Language Teachers (Kyoto).

Larsen, D. N. and W. A. Smalley. 1972. *Becoming Bilingual: A Guide to Language Learning*. William Larey Library.

Rubin, Joan. 1981. 'A study of cognitive processes in second language learning.' *Applied Linguistics* 2/2:117–31.

Rubin, Joan. 1982. *How To Be A More Successful Language Learner*. Boston: Heinle & Heinle.

Stern, H. H. 1983. *Fundamental Concepts of Language Teaching*. Oxford: Oxford University Press.

Wenden, Anita L. 1985. 'Learner strategies.' *TESOL Quarterly* 19/5:1–7.

The author

Eloise Pearson teaches at Sophia University, Tokyo.

8 The case study approach

8.1 Overview

In this chapter I will discuss something which is not so much a specific technique (like questionnaires or diary studies), but more of a general approach to research, namely the case study approach. This approach will be explained in contrast with traditional empirical research approaches. We will be looking at some limitations of the case study approach, and suggesting why, nevertheless, it might be a useful approach for action researchers to consider. There will be a brief discussion of examples of case studies, and the chapter will conclude by looking at two related case studies in more depth.

8.2 Traditional empirical research

The case study approach is perhaps best understood by contrasting it with the traditional forms of empirical investigation. Traditional *empirical research* is typically concerned with establishing general scientific laws which apply to the whole class (population) of people or phenomena being investigated. This is usually done by establishing two *matching groups* which are representative of the total population. (*Matching* means that the groups are as identical as possible in any way that is important for the investigation.) One group is called the *control group* and the other the *experimental group*. The two groups are tested using identical tests in order to establish their relative performance level. Then some *treatment* (e.g. a lesson, a syllabus, new materials, etc.) that is given to the experimental group is not given to the control group. The groups are then tested again to establish relative improvement. If the 'treatment' has been effective, the experimental group should perform significantly better. If the groups have been properly selected, then we can predict that the successful treatment will have a certain statistical likelihood or probability of working well for the population *as a whole*.

8.3   The case study approach

Case studies work on quite a different principle. Case studies concentrate on what is *unique* (i.e. with individual units: an individual student; an individual event; a particular group; a particular class; a particular school, etc.). The results will *not* therefore be statistically generalisable to the whole population of learners, classes, institutions, or whatever, of which this particular example is a member. You as a researcher might decide, of course, that this particular student, let us say, that you have investigated is in fact a quite typical member of the group or population to which he or she belongs, but this will be your subjective judgement.

We can make this more concrete with an example. At the end of the previous chapter (Chapter 7), there is an article by Eloise Pearson on learner strategies. One of her interviewees is a Japanese learner of English ('Mr J') who has made very slow progress in English because he hardly ever interacts with English speakers. It would clearly be very dangerous to generalise from this that all Japanese operating in a non-Japanese speaking environment behave in this way. Indeed, the very next interviewee ('Mr S') demonstrates completely contrasting behaviour.

It is, of course, true that a case study could be used to *disprove* a generalisation. If a generalisation predicts that all the members of a population will behave in a certain way, then only one exception would be enough to disprove the generalisation. It has to be said, though, that generalisations of this kind play a much less important role in social sciences like education than they do in the natural sciences (i.e. physics, chemistry, etc.). In the social sciences, generalisations are more often made in terms of *probability* rather than in terms of universal laws, so they are not likely to be disproved by one or two exceptions.

If the case studies do not give statistically generalisable findings, why should they be used?

8.4   Reasons for adopting the case study approach

Action researchers are usually interested in their own unique situations: *their* students; *their* lessons; *their* classes, and so on. The *specific focus* of the case study therefore becomes a positive advantage for action researchers, since it may meet their professional needs better than more traditional empirical research studies relating to large target populations.

The specific and limited nature of the case study approach may make it *more accessible* to the practising professional. I have used the term 'more accessible' rather than 'easier'. It is probably meaningless to categorise one research approach as 'easier' than another. With research,

PERSONAL REVIEW 8.1: Brainstorming Ideas for Case Studies

For this 'Personal review' section, you will have to use a 'mind-mapping' approach.

Take a blank sheet of A4 paper and lay it sideways ('landscape' layout), thus:

Now draw a rough circle or oval in the middle and put in the heading 'Ideas for case studies'. Then have lines coming out from the circle/oval listing categories of case studies that you might be interested in: for example, individual students, specific groups or classes, my school/college, etc., colleagues, myself, learners, critical incidents (i.e. significant events in class or wherever [see chapter 4]), and any other individual categories that you can think of that you might want to investigate. An example of how this 'Personal review' section might be developed is as follows:

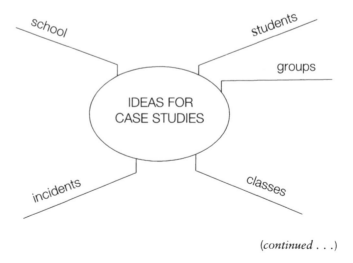

(continued . . .)

Out of each 'spoke' or 'branch', you could put actual names/ examples of individual students, etc. that you might want to investigate and why you could. For example, the students 'branch' might look like this:

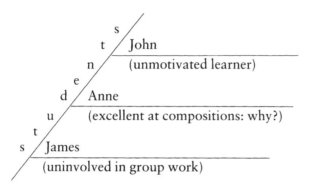

Of course, the case studies might well be related: you might be thinking of investigating three students, one who appears to have low motivation, one who is average, and one with apparently exceptionally high motivation.

as with most things in life, the amount of benefit gained is usually more or less proportional to the amount of effort you put into it. In this sense, case studies can be just as demanding as any other form of research. By its nature, also, case study research often generates more *human interest* than generalised statistical findings. For practitioners of a caring profession like teaching, this fact makes case study research more accessible, and indeed more valuable, than some approaches.

Although, case studies are not generalisable, they *can* be used as *evidence* to support a theory. For example, you could have a theory that a teacher with, say, a class of beginners will use the mother tongue in certain specified situations (e.g. to explain the meaning of different words). By carefully studying and analysing the discourse of one particular class you can show how this works out in practice. Or you could find out what your own practice is by taping your own interaction. This evidence can then be used to support a theory about the use of the mother tongue in beginners' classes. (For an extended discussion of the use of case studies to support theoretical propositions, see Yin, 1994.)

There are also other particular research objectives that can be achieved through case studies which I will discuss later (see below: 'Aims of case studies').

Now try PERSONAL REVIEW 8.1.

8.5 Aims of case studies

I have suggested that action researchers might want to use the case study approach because it may lead to studies that are more focused or specific, more accessible (especially to inexperienced researchers) and possibly also more interesting in human terms. So what kind of purpose might we have in mind in performing case study research? Here are some possible aims for case study investigations:

1. **Solving problems**   You might have a *particular problem* that you want to know more about with a view to perhaps finding a solution. For example:
   – Why does Student A do badly in tests though his or her work is otherwise good?
   – When I, as a teacher, give Student B feedback on his or her compositions, why does Student B appear to ignore it?
   – Groups X and Y are supposed to be about the same level of ability: why does Group X do its group tasks so much more effectively?
2. **Applying theories to practice**   You might want to see if a theory advanced by some writer *applies* in your particular case. If it is argued that students should survey passages before they read them, how does that work with your class? A teacher-training article recommends that you should give feedback on essays, etc. to your students by dictating the feedback onto tapes instead of writing it down: how would that work for you and your students? So theories, hypotheses, sample suggestions can be tried out and the results monitored.
3. **Generating hypotheses**   Case studies can also be used in the opposite way: as a way of *generating hypotheses*. What *is* the most effective way for students of a certain level to go about reading a text? By trying things out with a particular student or a particular class, you may arrive at reading strategies that work for one student or one class and may not work for others. You can report the case study and perhaps persuade colleagues to use the same technique: obviously, the more often it works with different students and different classes, the more confident you will be in recommending it to other colleagues, at, say, an in-service workshop.
4. **Providing illustrations**   Case studies can make interesting *illustrations* if you are describing your work or your ideas to other colleagues (e.g. in an in-service presentation, staff development session or in an article in a teachers' journal). We have already noted that case studies can add human interest to accounts of research, and sometimes can flesh out what might otherwise be overly abstract.

In the 'Personal review' section which follows I will give same examples of investigations which seem to me to come under the category of 'case studies'.

PERSONAL REVIEW 8.2: Reacting to Example Case Studies

In the following section there are brief summaries of six articles which appeared in *ELT Journal* during the period 1989–1993. The articles were not described by their authors themselves as case studies but, in spite of this, I would suggest that they fall within the category of case studies as I would define it, since they are involved with the investigation of 'bounded' classes or groups (i.e. groups with a clear membership so that it is easy for the researcher to specify who is a member of the target population and who is not). The membership of each group is defined in the section labelled 'population'. It is this specified population and the analysis of data generated from it which characterises these articles as case studies, as opposed to, say, suggestions derived from teaching principles, teaching hints and tips, advice or recommendations.

Read each of the summaries with the following questions in mind:

1. What kind of data might have been generated in each study? For example, in Case study 3 (Jordan: Pyramid discussions) possible data might have included:
    - the results of the choices (i.e. the 'requirements' chosen at each stage of the discussions)
    - tapes/transcripts of the interaction generated by the exercise both for the pairs and the groups of four
    - completed evaluation questionnaires from interviews with students
    - observation of pairs/groups, with/without observation schedules
    - tutor's impressions

2. Is there any information about the population not given in the summary which you would like to know? For example, taking the Jordan article again, you might like to know:
    - What were the 'seven different countries'? Were any (or perhaps all) of the students from developing countries?
    - How long had the students known one another?
    - Were any of the students particularly shy? (And did this affect their performance?)

The answers to such questions might substantially affect the way that you interpret the findings, and decide on the extent of their relevance to your own situation.

8.6 Some example case studies

---

1. Joachim Appel. 'Humanistic approaches in the secondary school: how far can we go?' *ELT Journal*, Vol. 43/4, October 1989, pp 261–267.
   [Literature]

   Population Class of 17–19 year old students in top secondary school stream in Southern Germany.

   Description The author's Gymnasium (academic-type Secondary school) students are used to studying literature in a very academic way. As a change the teacher did not go straight to the text, but tried discussing the themes of the text (e.g. running away from home) for about half-an-hour, in a way that related to the students' knowledge and experience. The less academic students liked the approach, the more academic students didn't.

---

2. Alan Fortune. 'Self-study grammar practice: learners' views and preferences'. *ELT Journal*, Vol. 46/2, April 1992, pp. 160–171.
   [Grammar]

   Population 50 intermediate/advanced EFL learners studying part-time at Ealing College, London.

   Description The writer argues that there are two basic types of grammar practice. Type 1 is deductive (i.e. the rule is given first and then the learner practises the rule). Type 2 is inductive (i.e. the student 'discovers' the rule by doing certain tasks). Over a three-week period, the students worked their way through fourteen exercises, seven of each type. By the end, the number of students preferring Type 2 practice jumped from 24% to 42%, although the majority (58%) still preferred Type 1. Even for those preferring Type 2, a clear statement of the 'rule' at some point, is still valued.

---

3. R. R. Jordan. 'Pyramid discussions'. *ELT Journal,* Vol. 44/1, January 1990, pp. 46–54.
[Oral English]

Population   The group involved consisted of twelve postgraduate economics students at post-intermediate level coming from seven different countries.

Description   The technique used was 'pyramid discussion'. Each student was given a list of twenty requirements for a country to improve its economic development. Each student had to choose the three requirements that they thought were most essential. Next grouped in pairs, they had to agree on three requirements with a partner (which inevitably meant that some previously chosen requirements had to be dropped). The exercise was repeated with groups of four, and concluded with a whole-class discussion and agreement on the final selected three requirements. The exercise generated a large amount of spoken language, but more so in pair work than group work.

4. B. Kumaravadivelu. 'Language-learning tasks: teacher intention and learner interpretation'. *ELT Journal.* Vol. 45/2, April 1991, pp. 98–107.
[Teaching Techniques]

Population   The study focused mainly on two intermediate ESL classes, taught by two different teachers.

Description   The aim of the study was to look for potential sources of mismatch between what teachers intended and what learners actually understood. The researcher discovered ten potential sources of mismatch (e.g. taped classroom interaction shows that 'simple' instructions can be misunderstood by learners).

5. D. R. Ransdell. 'Creative writing is Greek to me: the continuing education of a language teacher'. *ELT Journal,* Vol. 47/1, January 1993, pp. 40–46.
[Language Learning]

Population   One student learning elementary Greek (the student is the writer herself, otherwise a teacher of EFL).

Description   Attending a beginner's class in Greek taught the writer 'more than I had learned in several years of attending conferences and sifting through journal articles'. Specifically, she learns the motivating value of creative writing, which she successfully transfers to her own EFL teaching.

---

6. Susan Vincent. 'Motivating the advanced learner in developing writing skills: a project'. *ELT Journal.* Vol. 44/4, October 1990, pp. 272–278.
[Writing]

Population   5th year students of EFL on a five-year degree course leading to the award of MA, Institute of Applied Linguistics, Warsaw, Poland.

Description   Students on a writing skills course were unmotivated. Teacher arranged a brainstorming session to identify English-speaking institutions outside the University. Shell International Petroleum office in Warsaw was one of those identified. Students composed letters to the Shell office, visited it and subsequently wrote articles for the Shell magazine. The teacher noted significantly increased motivation.

8.7   The methodology of case study

It will probably have occurred to you when doing PERSONAL REVIEW 8.2 that the case study approach is capable of being realised through a wide range of techniques. Most, perhaps all, of the techniques that we have been looking at can be used in case studies: observation (Chapter 6), questionnaire and interview (Chapter 7), verbal report (Chapter 5), and so on. It is worth remembering that case studies can be made of individuals just as well as groups, and in such cases diary studies (Chapter 4) and think-aloud data (Chapter 5) could very well be appropriate.

PERSONAL REVIEW 8.3: Your (Parallel) Case Study

Is there any one of the case studies you have just looked at that deals with topics that you would like to investigate for yourself as a parallel case study? In other words, would you be interested in taking the ideas put forward by Jordan or Vincent, or whoever, and applying them to your own context? (If the answer is 'no', then pick a topic that you *would* like to investigate as a case study. You should find the ideas you generated during the brainstorming exercise that you did for PERSONAL REVIEW 8.1 useful here.)

Then answer these questions:

1. What would be the 'population' (target group) for your study?

2. If you are adapting a case study, would you alter the structure of it in any way? (For example, if you chose 'Pyramid Discussions' [Jordan article], you might decide that you would have a different number of topics [i.e. not 20] and that they would deal with a different topic [i.e. not developing countries].)

3. What sort of data would you generate and how would you generate it?

4. How would you analyse the data?

5. If the case study involves experimenting with new methods or new materials, how would you go about satisfying yourself whether or not the materials, etc. were 'successful'?

The decision as to which technique to use will partly depend on the precise nature of the case study. For example, one of the things which distinguishes Kamaradivelu's study from most of the other examples is that most of the others were concerned with making methodological or materials-related proposals. Kamaradivelu's research, on the other hand, is *heuristic* or *exploratory*: he is looking at classroom data to see whether there are any mismatches between teacher intention and learner interpretation, and, if so, how these might be categorised. As we have seen, he has found that this is in fact the case, and prepares ten categories for describing these teacher/learner mismatches. Kamaradivelu therefore makes extensive use of classroom observation and transcripts of classroom interaction. Since the other researchers are anxious to show that their suggested methods/materials are 'successful', they have to generate data which will support this evaluation.

The Ransdell article is also different from the others in that the 'case' in question is the writer herself. It is, in fact, as you may already have noted, a self-report. Since a case study is usually of someone or some group other than the researcher(s), perhaps we should call this a *personal case study* to distinguish it from the more usual type.

If you intend to write up a case study for a journal or a conference presentation, there is a very important issue which relates to the *target population* of the case study. The description of the case study population has to be *sufficiently detailed* to give a clear picture of all the relevant aspects of the case study population to interested readers. For example, if the case study relates to an individual learner, it will probably be necessary to know various personal details concerning the learner. These might include age, sex, status (e.g. student, manager), mother tongue, number of years learning the target language, and so on. Since we are only talking about one learner (or one class or one college), the reader has to know enough about this unique case to decide whether the data generated by it might also relate to his or her own situation.

8.8 Summary

In this chapter we have been considering the case study approach, and we have seen that it is an approach which fits very comfortably into the action research framework. This is because it tends to be tightly focused and personalised and therefore is a highly appropriate tool for teachers wishing to promote their own professional development within their own context.

In the next chapter, we shall look at and discuss techniques of trialling and evaluation, with particular reference to materials.

8.9 Exemplar article

The exemplar article is

Sara Cotterall (1995): Developing a course strategy for learner autonomy. *ELT Journal* 49/3, July 1995, 219–227.

It will be obvious from the title this article is concerned with the issue of *learner autonomy* (i.e. the mental outlook of some learners by which they take responsibility for their own learning).

Read through the article carefully, then think about these questions:

1. In Section 8.5, we discussed four of the possible purposes that people might have in mind when doing case study action research, namely: *solving problems*, *applying theories to practice*, *generating hypotheses* and *providing illustrations*. Which of these purposes do you think Sara Cotterall's article is intended to serve? (Remember, it could be more than one.)

2. What do you know about the *context* in which Cotterall's programme works? How similar or different is it to your own teaching context, or any context that you are familiar with?

3. What are the main components in the Victoria University programme, and how do they work?

4. What have the programme organisers learned from implementing this programme?

5. Do you think that a programme like the one described here would be (a) desirable and (b) feasible in your own teaching context? Could you use it as described or would you have to modify it in some way?

6. What has reading this article revealed to you about the strengths and weaknesses of the case study approach? (Note: in answering this question, you may be interested to know that in the same issue of *ELT Journal*, (49/3, July 1995, 190–196), there is a companion article by Jeremy F. Jones about a self-access programme in a very different context, namely Phnom Penh University in Cambodia. He describes the way in which a somewhat similar programme is run along very different lines because of the context and the culture, e.g. there is much greater emphasis on group work rather than individual work.)

Developing a course strategy for learner autonomy

Sara Cotterall

Autonomy in language learning is a desirable goal for philosophical, pedago-gical, and practical reasons. However, although many language programmes claim to be learner-centred and supportive of learner initiative, much classroom practice appears to subvert this goal. This paper discusses ways in which mechanisms for promoting learner autonomy have been incorporated into one English language programme. It also discusses the crucial role played by teacher/learner dialogue about learning in the classroom, and considers the implications for materials, task design, and time management.

Why is autonomy desirable?

According to Boud (1988: 23):

> The main characteristic of autonomy as an approach to learning is that students take some significant responsibility for their own learning over and above responding to instruction.

Learners who are autonomous might take responsibility by setting their own goals, planning practice opportunities, or assessing their progress. But why should we wish our learners to behave in this way?

Autonomy is considered desirable for philosophical, pedagogical, and practical reasons. The philosophical rationale behind autonomy is the belief that learners have the right to make choices with regard to their learning. Furthermore, many writers (see Knowles 1975) have pointed out the importance of preparing learners for a rapidly changing future, in which independence in learning will be vital for effective functioning in society. Helping learners become more indepen-dent in their learning is one way of maximizing their life choices. Littlejohn (1985) suggests that one outcome of learners acting more autonomously may be an increase in enthusiasm for learning.

Promoting learner autonomy can also be justified on pedagogical grounds, since

> adults demonstrably learn more, and more effectively, when they are con-sulted about dimensions such as the pace, sequence, mode of instruction and even the content of what they are studying. (Candy 1988: 75)

Learners who are involved in making choices and decisions about aspects of the programme are also likely to feel more secure in their learning (Joiner, cited in McCafferty 1981).

The practical argument for promoting learner autonomy is quite simply that a teacher may not always be available to assist. Learners need to be able to learn on their own because they do not always have access to the kind or amount of individual instruction they need in order to become proficient in the language. Finally, learners become more efficient in their language learning if they do not have to spend time waiting for the teacher to provide them with resources or solve their problems.

How is autonomy fostered?

Many programmes, and most ESL teachers, claim to believe in autonomy, yet many of the same teachers regularly subvert that goal by excluding learners from decisions about planning, pacing, and evaluating classroom tasks. Consequently learners do not always perceive the link between classroom tasks and the language skills they wish to develop. In our programme, we have come to believe that autonomy is principally fostered by means of *dialogue* about learning. The programme components which are described in the next section all contribute to that dialogue.

This paper discusses a strategy for promoting autonomy within the overall language programme and not just that of the classroom, since autonomy as a goal cannot be realized until it is translated into the structure of the programme:

> An innovation needs to be incorporated into the structure and functioning of its host institution within a short time if it is to survive: it needs to be institutionalized. If it is not institutionalized but merely tolerated as a minor aberration, it is unlikely to be taken seriously by learners or faculty, and may well fail completely. (Hammond and Collins 1991: 208)

This observation highlights the need to embody the goal of learner autonomy in the timetable, the materials, the tasks, and the talk which surround learners. Our experience suggests that autonomy is not something which can be 'clipped on' to existing learning programmes, but that it has implications for the entire curriculum.

An autonomy-based course

The EAP course has been run at the English Language Institute of the Victoria University of Wellington for more than thirty years. It is a twelve-week intensive course for international students intending to enrol in tertiary institutions in New Zealand. It runs during the summer months and finishes just before the start of the academic year. The course comprises ten classes, including three which are subject-specific, and has approximately twenty teaching staff. Certain programme components are common to all and were originally designed with the explicit objective of encouraging learners to take more responsibility for their language learning. These components are:

1 Learner/teacher dialogue
2 Learning a Language study theme
3 Classroom tasks and materials
4 Student record booklet
5 Self-access centre

The components presented separately here together make up an overall strategy for fostering autonomy which has grown in strength and coherence over the past five years. The programme components focus on learners' understanding of how language learning proceeds, the language used to discuss that process and records for charting it, the support provided for learners, and learners' access to resources and feedback. These concerns are realized through the five components discussed below.

Learner/teacher dialogue

The first component of our strategy for promoting autonomy is the dialogue between the learners and their class teacher. Every learner is interviewed by the class teacher at the beginning, mid-point, and end of the course. Each interview has a different focus: the first is principally aimed at establishing a personal relationship between teacher and learner, and setting and clarifying objectives; the second aims to assess and discuss the learner's progress, and to offer advice; in the final interview, teachers advise learners on their future study of English.

Learning a Language study theme

The second component of the strategy is the unit of work on learning a language which, since 1987, has occupied the first week of study on the course. This unit presents some key concepts in language learning, and encourages learners to explore issues such as the amount and type of language input they are getting, and the use they make of it in arranging adequate practice opportunities. The unit also provides an introduction to a basic metalanguage for language learning. This makes it easier to discuss learners' difficulties with them. Some important distinctions made in this first week of study (for example, the distinction between fluency and accuracy work) are recurring concepts in dialogue throughout the course.

Classroom tasks and materials

The third component of the strategy involves the design of tasks. The tasks we design aim to replicate those which learners confront in 'real-world' situations, and to incorporate language support. The fact that most course members are destined for university study inspired the introduction of a Guest Lecture series, which exposes learners to the kind of academic listening task they will face in their future studies. Preparatory help is given before the lecture, learners' difficulties are talked through afterwards, and a variety of follow-up classroom activities is provided.

Virtually all materials used in our language programme are developed by members of the Institute's staff. Through our materials, we seek to encourage learners to take the initiative in their language learning. This is achieved principally by making overt the relationship between classroom language learning activities and learners' developing language competence. Learners are encouraged to use the dialogue with the teacher to explore the purpose and relevance of tasks to their needs.

Student record booklet

The fourth component adds an element of monitoring to the learning process. Each learner on the course receives his or her personal copy of the student record booklet at the start of the course. This booklet is divided into two sections: the first section contains a series of self-assessment scales and a place to record personal objectives. Self-assessment on the scales is completed on three separate occasions during the twelve-week course. The second section is primarily concerned with monitoring learning activity. It contains a number of graphs and charts on which learners can record their activities and progress during the course. The booklet encourages learners to develop their ability to judge their language performance, and helps them to monitor their developing language competence. The booklet also provides a starting point for discussion of learners' experience of the course, and can serve to prompt out-of-class practice.

Self-access centre

The final component of our strategy for fostering autonomy is the provision of independent study facilities. In 1987 a small temporary self-access centre was established for learners enrolled on the course. The centre provides a selection of self-study reading and vocabulary and grammar practice materials, as well as a collection of self-access listening materials. The centre is open four hours a day for independent study but is staffed for only one hour. The staff member's functions include orienting students to the materials, advising them on the election of activities and materials, and issuing reading materials. Learners are encouraged to discuss ways of using the centre with their class teacher (to ensure coherence in the dialogue), and are directed to the documentation there for further information. The centre provides for learners who have identified needs which they wish to address in their own time, at their own pace, in the way they feel most comfortable.

Reflections and modifications

The experience of constantly evaluating our language programme has sharpened our perception of which features have contributed most to fostering autonomy among learners. This has led to certain modifications in the overall strategy.

Learner/teacher dialogue

Dialogue between learners and the class teacher on our programme is now seen as central to the fostering of autonomy. At first the learner/teacher dialogue consisted principally of formal interviews. However, most teachers had difficulty keeping to the scheduled twenty minutes per person, and many found that learners appeared disappointed with the outcome of the interviews, since they had been hoping for instant solutions to their language problems. It became clear that the purpose of the interviews was not always well established in learners' minds. Gradually, however, learners started to relate concepts presented in the Learning a Language study theme to their own language learning, and requested more frequent, less formal opportunities to talk about their learning with the teacher. Our programme has been adapted accordingly, and class teachers now aim to speak to each learner for fifteen minutes every week (sometimes within the context of a writing workshop). We believe that a great deal of language learning activity proceeds without learners fully comprehending its purpose or relevance. It is therefore important to provide frequent opportunities for learners to ask the teacher questions and receive feedback on progress. Such activities seem ideally suited to the encouragement of learner autonomy. While this discussion demands time, the quality of feedback for teacher and learner, and the level of dialogue about all aspects of the course, justify the innovation.

One of the aims of learner/teacher dialogue is for learners to better understand their language learning experience. This dialogue arises naturally out of classroom tasks, and may involve clarifying the purpose of an activity or discussing ways of evaluating performance. Teachers and learners are able to refer back to concepts about language learning introduced in the first week of the course. By making this process public, learners who are less skilful at addressing their weaknesses can learn from others who are more expert.

The dialogue can also communicate powerful messages about the learners' responsibilities. This might happen, for example, when a teacher asks learners which learning activities they have practised out of class. This kind of inquiry signals that individual practice in one's own time should accompany classroom language activity, and that progress and achievement depend on independent (autonomous) activity.

Learners who have no previous experience of talking about their learning require a special kind of support. Teachers must be sensitive to their needs and confidence so as to transfer responsibility to learners only gradually. This requires considerable skill on the part of the teacher, and imposes a substantial burden when dealing with large numbers of learners. Teacher education courses need to incorporate experience with one-to-one counselling skills.

Learning a Language study theme

The Learning a Language study theme has helped encourage learners to assume more initiative in their learning. This comes about principally because the study theme extends learners' understanding of what they can and should do to help themselves. Learners come to the course with a wide range of previous learning experiences and 'myths' (Harri-Augstein and Thomas 1991) about language learning. This study theme challenges learners' preconceptions and relates them to information about factors contributing to success in language learning. This component of the autonomy-fostering strategy is also important because it gives learners a vocabulary with which to talk about their language learning, and introduces them to concepts which help them set realistic objectives, and find appropriate solutions to problems they face.

This unit also allows us to spell out the rationale behind our teaching language through content. Failing to do this can result in learners complaining that they joined the course in order to learn English, and not to learn about, for example, the greenhouse effect! Teachers who adopt pedagogic approaches without explaining their reasons for doing so are denying their learners access to valuable information. A course which aims to promote learner autonomy must incorporate frank discussion of objectives, methodology, roles, and expectations. We have found our Learning a Language study theme provides a natural way of opening up this discussion.

Classroom tasks and materials

The importance of learners' understanding the purpose of classroom tasks has become a major concern in our strategy for autonomy. Learner autonomy implies an appreciation of the link between classroom practice and learning needs. However we believe that learners do not always perceive this link. Accordingly, language tasks on the summer course now incorporate a consciousness-raising element, aimed at making learners think about the application to their future needs of skills practised in the task. Teachers frequently ask questions such as: 'How easy or difficult did you find that task? Why was it difficult? What would have made it easier? Why did we do it? How might it help you in the future? What do you need to do to improve your performance?' Learners are also encouraged to see the 'out-of-class' dimension of tasks which take place within the classroom. In this way they are constantly reminded of the need to practise in their own time.

Staff have recently started work on a materials publication project. The intention is to design materials which make explicit to learners the aspect of language knowledge or skill being developed. We hope that this will foster autonomy by clarifying for learners the way they might use such practice activities. Each task incorporates the prompt for a 'learning conversation' (Harri-Augstein and Thomas 1991) with the learner. Learners will be encouraged to provide feedback on the usefulness of these prompts in the materials.

Our work on classroom tasks also emphasizes the importance of providing high quality feedback on performance to learners. In order to assume greater control of their learning, learners need ways of assessing the quality of their language performance. Without feedback on their performance, learners can think they have mastered something when they have not, can fossilize in errors, become discouraged, or resent the effort they have put in. Sometimes feedback can be built into the task itself (Crabbe 1991); where it is not, teachers need time to respond adequately to learners' efforts. The student record booklet provides learners with a means of recording such feedback. This feedback may be formal or informal, solicited or spontaneous, but it is our conviction that such discussion plays a central role in promoting autonomous learning.

Student record booklet

Our experience with the student record booklet presents a dilemma which faces all those who wish to encourage their learners to become more autonomous. Originally we sought, through the booklet, to encourage learners to monitor and record significant moments in their experience of the course. This aim is in harmony with the goals of autonomous learning, in that it encourages learners to take an active role in formulating their learning objectives and assessing how and to what extent these are met. In practice, however, many learners never really made the booklet their own. While there are several possible explanations for this, it can also be argued that if learners do not readily see a role for the booklet in their own learning, then the approach is in some way deficient.

While we now acknowledge that the pre-determined nature of the booklet represents a teacher's rather than a learner's point of view, we maintain that record keeping and monitoring of language performance are important aspects of autonomy. We are currently seeking a compromise position. The issue remains one of how to allow for greater negotiation of the booklet's use and function without losing the practical advantage of having available at the beginning of the course a ready-made log for student records.

Self-access centre

The final component of our strategy for promoting autonomy has perhaps seen the greatest modification in approach. Initially, resources went into acquiring a large bank of materials and developing a user-friendly system of organizing and displaying them. This was to enable learners to practise independently. Recently, however, the centre has come to be seen more as a laboratory where learners test out solutions to specific language problems. These efforts provide the content for learners' discussions with the teacher. Our approach, therefore, has shifted away from encouraging general language practice activities in the self-access centre towards promoting individualized problem-solving. Furthermore, the self-access centre is seen as only one resource among others for solving language-related problems.

In line with this shift in perspective, the self-access centre team has recently been responsible for two initiatives. Firstly, the reference section has been considerably expanded to include a collection of dictionaries, encyclopaedias, grammars, and other reference books. In addition, staff have published a number of self-access centre guides aimed at providing information on possibilities for further study and language practice in the community. At the same time, efforts have gone into making documentation on materials in the centre as clear and straightforward as possible. All these resources offer good starting-points for learners seeking information on a variety of topics.

Secondly, the centre's listening resources have been greatly expanded. A considerable number of staff hours were committed to making many existing listening resources truly 'self-accessible'. The transformation of many of these materials has been complemented by the production of a clearly organized catalogue of self-access listening resources, and the production of users' guides to accompany all tapes. The investment of staff hours, always a critical issue in development terms, was justified by our conviction that listening skill development is ideally suited to independent practice.

During the past five years, our view of the role of staff working in the self-access centre has been modified by experience. Initially they were encouraged to assume an active role in advising learners in the centre. However, experience showed that only staff who were seriously committed to the idea of encouraging learner autonomy were able to successfully assist learners in the centre. The role of staff nowadays is limited to the issuing of reading materials. This has come about because we believe that discussion of the best way to use the centre belongs to the dialogue between learner and class teacher. However, this does not prevent learners from seeking advice elsewhere.

In spite of the great popularity of self-access centres in language teaching, our experience has alerted us to two possible abuses of such learning facilities. Firstly, there is a tendency for some learners to occupy their time in the centre with 'busy work' which may not result in learning, or to consistently choose materials which do not challenge them. Clearly, providing a large number of attractive self-study resources does not automatically turn dependent learners into autonomous ones. Rather, it highlights the need for learners to be encouraged to monitor and evaluate their learning, ideally through discussion with the class teacher.

Secondly, some learners treat materials in the self-access centre as a 'quick fix' solution to their language problems. Learners who complete practice activities without considering their appropriateness run the risk of seeing little return for their investment of time. Learners need to be encouraged to adopt a systematic approach to their problem-solving and independent study. This would involve frequent consultation with the class teacher over resources used, the approach adopted, and monitoring and evaluating activities. If this approach is to be successful, teachers need to be allocated time to pursue this important dialogue with their learners.

Conclusion

Our experimentation with this course-wide strategy for fostering autonomy has been productive and encouraging. It has led us to draw the following conclusions:

1 Autonomy in language learning is desirable.
2 Dialogue is more important to autonomy than structures.
3 The relationship between the learner and the class teacher is central to the fostering of autonomy.
4 Autonomy has implications for the entire curriculum.

In this paper, the importance of learners talking about their learning has been emphasized. Several implications derive from this central theme. Firstly, a vocabulary of language learning shared by all participants is required. Secondly, time must be made available within programmes for teachers and learners to engage in dialogue about the learning process. Finally, teacher education programmes need to incorporate practice in the skills required for management of the learning dialogue.

Note

This article was presented as a paper at the Third National Conference of Community Languages and English for Speakers of Other Languages, Auckland, New Zealand, September 1992.

References

Boud, D. (ed.). 1988. *Developing Student Autonomy in Learning* (2nd edn.). New York: Kogan Page.
Candy, P. 1988. 'On the attainment of subject-matter autonomy' in D. Boud (ed.).
Crabbe, D. A. 1991. 'Bringing evaluation and methodology closer together' in S. Anivan (ed.). *Issues in Language Programme Evaluation in the 1990s*. Singapore: SEAMEO Regional English Language Centre.
Hammond, M. and **R. Collins.** 1991. *Self-Directed Learning: Critical Practice.* London: Kogan Page.
Harri-Augstein, S. and **L. Thomas**. 1991. *Learning Conversations: The Self-Organised Learning Way to Personal and Organisational Growth.* London: Routledge.
Knowles, M. 1975. *Self-Directed Learning: A Guide for Learners and Teachers.* New York: Association Press.
Littlejohn, A. 1985. 'Learner choice in language study'. *ELT Journal* 39/4: 253-61.
McCafferty, J. B. 1981. *Self-Access Problems and Proposals.* London: The British Council.

The author

Sara Cotterall has an MA in Applied Linguistics, and taught English in Europe and China prior to her appointment as a lecturer at the English Language Institute, Victoria University of Wellington, New Zealand. She is co-director of the Institute's English Proficiency Programme, and is also involved in teacher education and the teaching of undergraduate writing. Her research interests include autonomous learning and strategy instruction.

9 Evaluation and trialling: teaching materials

9.1 Overview

This chapter is concerned with two important aspects of teachers' work: evaluation and trialling. Since these both cover very wide areas of potential action research activity, they will be discussed with particular reference to issues and activities that are relevant to most teachers: materials evaluation and the trialling of new materials. The chapter concludes with the study of a survey article on ELT textbooks.

9.2 What we mean by 'evaluation'

The word *evaluation* is obviously derived from *value*, and in its most basic sense means putting a value or estimation of worth upon something or someone (i.e. deciding how bad or good he/she/it is). So we evaluate other colleagues when we say they are 'good' teachers, we evaluate ourselves (and/or perhaps our learners) when we say we have taught a 'terrible' lesson, we evaluate a syllabus when we say it is 'impossible to get through', and we evaluate a coursebook when we say it is 'really useful and helpful'.

Evaluation is clearly at the heart of the action research philosophy, since it is usually a self-evaluation of our work (especially a negative evaluation) which gives us the motivation to attempt to improve it through action research.

Statements of the kind quoted at the beginning of this section are commonly heard whenever teachers informally converse or exchange views. However, such statements are usually impressionistic judgements and far less often the result of systematic action research investigation. I have suggested that action research involves the systematic collection and analysis of data. Therefore, a research approach to evaluation will naturally involve a more systematic approach than intuition or impressionistic judgement. (This, by the way, is not a negative evaluation of the intuition or judgement of experienced teachers. If you asked some experienced teachers about the suitability of a textbook they had used in a given situation, and they all agreed that it was 'very useful', then you would probably be right to feel confident in using it in that situation.)

In this chapter we will be looking at more systematic ways of going about evaluation with particular reference to a specific area.

PERSONAL REVIEW 9.1: Areas for Evaluation

You will find listed below a selection of language teaching areas that could be evaluated. Look through the list to get an idea of the range of possibilities. Tick any of the areas that you have informally or formally evaluated. For example, if you have ever thought or expressed an evaluation of yourself as a teacher, or of another colleague (which nearly all of us must have done at one time!), then you would put a tick opposite these categories. In the second column, tick if the evaluation has been in a more formal way: for example, most of us will have formally evaluated our students through tests, performance in public examinations, and so on.

Finally, pick one of the areas that you have evaluated informally, but not formally (i.e. with a tick in the first column only). Try to think of ways in which you could go about evaluating that area in a more systematic way. Self-evaluation as a teacher, for example, could be done by writing down five positive and five negative comments on yourself as a teacher. One of the comments (either positive or negative) could be chosen and a plan of action drawn up to exploit/overcome that strength/weakness. Or you may have a better idea . . .

Language teaching areas	Informal evaluation	Formal evaluation
myself as a teacher (self-evaluation) other teachers students (learners) lessons teacher's materials (e.g. textbooks) resources (e.g. self-access courses) teacher's methods courses syllabuses/curricula		

---

institutions (e.g. the school we teach in) organisations (e.g. teachers' associations) educational projects research projects management (classroom/depart- mental/school, etc. training (trainers/methods/materials/ institutions, etc.) supervision/Inspection (supervisor or inspector/methods/ observation checklists, etc.) teacher support provision other (specify)		

9.3 Range of evaluation areas

Clearly, the range of possibilities for evaluation is vast. Further, it is by and large true that different areas require the use of different evaluation techniques, although there are some principles of evaluation that have a very wide relevance. It would obviously be impossible to cover all these areas in one chapter here, so I will not attempt to do so. Instead I am going to select one area, which hopefully will be of relevance to most classroom teachers, and make suggestions about some ways in which it might be approached. As for the other areas, I will give you some references in which the topic of evaluation is dealt with more extensively.

9.4 Teaching materials

I have decided to focus on teaching materials, as this is an aspect of evaluation that nearly all teachers do at some time, even if it is only on an informal basis. Within the area of teaching materials, I am going to concentrate on coursebooks, although most of the issues that will be raised apply equally well to other kinds of teaching materials. I am not at this point considering teaching materials designed by teachers themselves, although I will be coming back to this issue later, when the issue of *trialling materials* will be discussed. In this section, I am assuming that the materials being used are materials currently in use, published either by a commercial publisher or by an official publisher, such as a Curriculum Unit within the Ministry of Education.

9.5 **Purpose of evaluation**

The purpose of the evaluation is very important, because it very much determines how you will go about the evaluation. Thinking of published materials, there are two possibilities:

1. You have a range of possible books to use, and you want to compare those that are available on the market, in order to choose the most suitable one for you;
2. You have little or no choice: you are supplied with teaching materials that you have to use, although perhaps you may be able to modify or supplement them in various limited ways.

In many, probably most, teaching situations, the second scenario is the more common one. Therefore that is the scenario that I will concentrate on in this chapter. To redress the balance a little, however, the exemplar article at the end will relate to the first 'consumer survey' type of evaluation. In any case, many of the issues we shall be looking at have equal relevance to both possibilities.

PERSONAL REVIEW 9.2: Pre-Evaluation – Developing Criteria

Before you can evaluate something, you have to have some idea of the qualities which could make it either 'good' or 'bad'. For example, if you evaluate your Head of Department as being a very effective manager, then you must have some ideas or assumptions about what it is to be an effective manager (and, by contrast, what it is to be an ineffective one), and indeed about what 'effectiveness' implies.

Since we are going to be looking at coursebook evaluation, write down at least six qualities that you think a good coursebook should have.

1 ....

2 ....

3 ....

4 ....

5 ....

6 ....

9.6 Commentary

One benefit of doing a task like PERSONAL REVIEW 9.2 is that it should be possible to turn the qualities into *criteria* for evaluating materials. In the section which follows below you will find a description of possible criteria for evaluating teaching materials. The possible criteria are:

1. cost
2. rationale
3. context
4. level
5. relevance to needs
6. facility and practicality
7. layout and organisation
8. coverage
9. range of tasks/activities
10. learner support materials
11. interest/motivation
12. teacher support material.

Are *your* six 'qualities' represented somewhere on this list?

In Section 9.7 following, I intend to go through each of these criteria and comment on them. I have incorporated 'Personal review' sections into most of the criteria: this will allow you to apply that 'Personal review' section to a particular coursebook, if you have one that you wish to evaluate.

I suggest that you read through the whole of Section 9.7 skipping the 'Personal review' sections, in order to give yourself an overview of the issues. Then you can come back and do the 'Personal review' sections.

9.7 Teaching materials: Possible criterion areas

1. **Cost** Expense is an obvious criterion for evaluating materials. The materials may be good, but are they also value for money?
2. **Rationale** This refers to the reasoning behind the book (e.g. its justification for its type, style and organisation among other things). What is the purpose of the book, and on what methodological assumptions is it based? Here you may have to be careful to distinguish between the *stated rationale* and the *actual* rationale. Sometimes the writers of a textbook will justify the book in terms of principles which are actually not realised to any significant extent in the actual text. For example, the author of a coursebook

185

may describe its methodology as 'communicative', but you may decide on examination of the actual activities, that it does not merit this description at all (e.g. because it does not include authentic materials or because it does not provide opportunities for genuine communication).

PERSONAL REVIEW 9.3: Investigating the Rationale

Choose a textbook or coursebook that you frequently use. (You can use the book you have chosen as a kind of 'case study' for the various criterion areas which follow.) See if you can find a stated rationale for the book as a whole. The rationale may be explicitly stated in the foreword of the book, or in the teacher's book (if there is one); or it may have to be pieced together from various comments made, say, in the publisher's 'blurb' on the cover or from the kinds of exercises given, etc. For example, you could take a typical unit and examine it in detail in terms of the criteria that have been listed here. Or you could look carefully at the instructions and how the activities are organised to see whether you can work out the explicit or implied roles of the teacher and the learners. How far does the stated rationale fit in with your perception of the book's rationale? Do they match exactly? Or do they only overlap? Or are they actually quite contradictory? And how do the book's stated and real rationale relate to your own ideas of an acceptable rationale for a book of this kind?

---

3. **Context** For what context is the book intended? Does it have an 'intended' audience, or is it specific to a particular country or region? Is it intended to be used in a school or university, or is it intended for private, personal use?
4. **Level** What is the stated target level of learner? What subcriteria are used to establish that level (e.g. public examinations or years of study)? And would you say that, in the particular context that you are concerned with, the materials are actually appropriate to that level?
5. **Relevance to needs** This criterion overlaps with the previous one. What are the needs of the learner in this area of study and is the coursebook relevant to them?
6. **Practicality** Practicality reveals itself most easily in use. How practical and easy to use is the book? Are the exercises easy to set

up, for example? Are the teaching units a convenient length for the teaching periods? What is your experience in using the book in your own context? Did it ever let you down?

7. **Layout and organisation** This is another overlapping category, as good layout and organisation can make a textbook significantly more 'user-friendly'.

   Layout incorporates features such as:
   - clear signposting (use of list of contents, headings, sub-headings);
   - clear and systematic use of conventions (e.g. [OO] for audio tape);
   - attractive and appropriate use of typeface (e.g. **bold**, etc.);
   - helpful and attractive use of illustrations (photographs, diagrams, drawings, etc.)

   Organisation
   - What are the different main sections of the book and how do they relate to one another?
   - Are the language topics dealt with in an appropriate order?
   - What is the system of organisation for the elements of the course? (For example, is the course divided into units and each unit divided into certain sections? What do you think is the rationale for the organisation?) See PERSONAL REVIEW 9.4.

8. **Coverage** Are all important aspects of the course covered, or have some been omitted? (If you are working to a syllabus, you will want to check the coursebook against the syllabus.) Are topics included that could have been omitted?

9. **Range of tasks/activities** Is there a wide range of activities for the learners to be engaged in? Or is there some sense of repetitiveness? Is there perhaps some element of choice? You may find it useful to list the types of activities, so that you can decide whether there are any gaps or inconsistencies.

10. **Learner support materials** Are there extra back-up materials in the form of cassettes, workbooks, authentic materials, posters, etc. to support and motivate learners? Are there extension materials for more gifted students and/or remedial materials for the less able? Are there answer keys provided to support autonomous learning?

11. **Interest/motivation** There is obviously considerable overlap between this and other criterion areas. For example, it is obvious that materials which are at the wrong level and badly organised will tend to demotivate learners. However, it seems such an important consideration that it merits a category of its own. Is the overall effect of the material on most learners motivating or the reverse? What are the factors which you think contribute to the effect of motivation/demotivation? See PERSONAL REVIEW 9.5.

PERSONAL REVIEW 9.4: Level/Relevance/Facility and Practicality/Layout and Organisation

Once more, look at the textbook you have chosen and evaluate it according to the above criteria. What are your findings? You may find it useful to use a rating-scales layout, like this:

Name of book/materials: . . . .

Target level:. . . . .

Criterion	Rating Good Poor ⟵——————⟶ (Circle as appropriate)	Comments
appropriateness to level	1 2 3 4 5	
relevance to students' needs	1 2 3 4 5	
facility/practicality in use	1 2 3 4 5	
layout	1 2 3 4 5	
organisation	1 2 3 4 5	

A problem in this area is that many learners, especially less sophisticated ones, will find it difficult to separate out their feelings towards the materials from their feelings towards the subject as such. Perhaps a questionnaire would be useful. It could elicit:

- feelings towards the subject (e.g. by a 1–5 rating scale)
- feelings towards the materials (similarly)
- listing of three things they liked and didn't like about the coursebook, perhaps with some kind of rating (stars?) to show how strong their feelings were about each of the likes/dislikes.

PERSONAL REVIEW 9.5: Coverage/Range of Tasks and Activities/Learner Support/Motivation

Continue your evaluation of the book you have chosen by evaluating it against these criteria. For MOTIVATION you can either use your own judgement, or you may decide you want to enrol the help of your students. As well as the questionnaire referred to in the previous paragraph, they could also interview one another and make reports to the class on their findings.

---

12. **Teacher support material** A very important consideration in terms of evaluating teaching material is: What help is given to the teacher? Of course, some of the things that help the student also help the teacher (e.g. clear layout and sensible organisation). Teacher support may be part of the text (e.g. in the form of teacher's notes at the beginning) or it may take the form of a separate teacher's handbook. Many of the criteria (e.g. rationale) that have already been applied to the textbook could also be applied to the teacher's book. But there are others which might well appear only in the teacher's book: one thinks of suggestions on methodology, aims and objectives, rationale, reference data (e.g. the new vocabulary items, grammar items introduced in each unit), supplementary activities, suggestions for further reading and suggested answers to exercises, and so on.

PERSONAL REVIEW 9.6: Teacher's Support Material

What criteria would you use to evaluate teachers' support material? Are all the criteria just mentioned relevant to you? Have you any other suggestions? If the coursebook you have chosen has a teacher's book, then you could evaluate it using your selected criteria.

9.8 Evaluation: the outcome

Evaluation is not usually something that is done for its own sake. As with other aspects of action research, it is performed in order to improve performance in some way. In the case of teaching materials, evaluation either helps us to make the right choice of materials or helps us identify areas where the materials we currently use can be improved in some way.

In this chapter, we have paid special attention to the evaluation of materials currently being used rather than with the choice of new materials. Usually, teachers only go to this trouble if they are currently aware of some sense of dissatisfaction with the materials they are currently using, either on the part of the students or on their own part.

Let us imagine that in evaluating some materials you currently use, you have identified some aspect of these materials that you think can be improved. What next?

9.9 Adapting materials

You will probably decide that you want to adapt the materials in some way. This can be done in two ways:

1. Retain the materials basically as they are, but teach them in a different way (i.e. either different from the way you normally teach them, or from the way recommended in the Teacher's Book).
2. Change the materials in some way, for example by devising new materials either instead of or in addition to some part of the existing materials. (This still comes under 'adapting materials', because I am assuming you are not rewriting the entire course!)

Although these are rather different strategies, I will not attempt to make any distinction between them in what follows.

9.10 Trialling

How will you know if your adaptation will work better than what you had previously? The best way of answering this question is by trying out the materials (trialling). This is something which as teachers we tend to do a lot of: try out things and see if they work. But if we intend to do this as a form of action research, we have to be a bit more systematic. How can we organise this procedure in a more systematic way to give ourselves data that might be more informative?

PERSONAL REVIEW 9.7: Improving/Changing Materials

For a coursebook that you are currently using or have used in the past, choose one or more aspects of it that you think could be improved, or simply done in a different way. Plan in detail how you would go about improving the materials.

9.11   Pre-trial specifications

Before starting to try out the new or revised materials, it is best to write down the answers to these questions:

1. Specify clearly your learning/teaching goals with the new materials. What are you trying to achieve?
2. How will you know whether or not you have succeeded? How will you evaluate your trial materials?

Try to make criteria which will generate objective evidence. Take this, 'criterion' for a group-work task, for example: *The students will interact better.*

How would you evaluate whether this criterion has been achieved? One way would be to make a subjective judgement. By simple observation, you might decide that in comparison with other lists the quality of student interaction was, say, *much better, better, about the same, worse than before* (with other tasks.)

A more objective criterion would be: *Every member of the group will make at least one contribution to the discussion.*

This is more objective, but it doesn't tell us anything about the quality of the contribution. Also it assumes that members of a group can only interact by saying something. You might decide to make a 'sweep' of the group every minute to judge the level of interest on say a 3-point scale using the following code:

V = apparently very involved or interested (2 points)
I = apparently involved or interested (1 point)
U = apparently uninvolved or uninterested (0 points).

For a ten-minute task, our recording instrument might took like this:

	1	2	3	4	5	6	7	8	9	10	Total
Student A											
Student B											
Student C											
Student D											
Student E											

Grand total

The 'Grand total' will provide an overall index of the level of interest during the task. If there were several groups working at the same time, you could delegate the observation schedule to student observers (see Chapter 6): this would make your data more comprehensive, but clearly less reliable.

PERSONAL REVIEW 9.8: Designing Criteria for Evaluation of Revised Materials

With reference to the materials that you adapted in the last 'Personal review' section, work out a set of criteria for evaluating the success of your revised materials. You could use the kind of layout I suggested for PERSONAL REVIEW 9.4, incorporating a rating scale, with a space for comments.

9.12 Process and product

When evaluating the trialling of new materials, you can evaluate the *process* or you can evaluate the *product*, or you can evaluate both. For example, if you are experimenting with new methods of teaching writing, you could evaluate the product (the eventual compositions) or the process (how the students go about writing the compositions), or both. Usually, when you introduce innovations in materials, you are interested in the product or outcome of the new materials. Nevertheless, evaluation of the process can also reveal how the improvement (if any) has actually come about. Sometimes, of course, the process *is* the product, as in the case of the example we have just been looking at, of materials designed to promote discussion. We discussed in Chapters 4 and 5 (using diaries, verbal reports, etc.) how learners could be involved in the gathering of data on process. Questionnaires and interviews (Chapter 6) could also be used.

PERSONAL REVIEW 9.9: Process/Product Evaluation

Still thinking of the new materials you have devised, would it be helpful to make a distinction between the evaluation of the process and the evaluation of the product? Look at the criteria you worked out for PERSONAL REVIEW 9.8. Do they refer to *process* or *product* or both? If you haven't already done so for PERSONAL REVIEW 9.8, think of ways in which you could evaluate both of these aspects.

9.13 Summary

I suggested at the beginning of the chapter that there is a sense in which evaluation lies at the heart of the action research process. Indeed it also lies at the heart of professional development. The question is, having identified a source of professional concern, how do we go about meeting that concern? Since in this book, I have been proposing an action research strategy, the emphasis in this chapter has once more been on systematic data collection and analysis.

In this chapter, I have discussed the process of evaluation with special reference to teaching materials. I have also looked at the trialling process and how it too can be evaluated. I have emphasised the importance of establishing valid criteria, and indicated the potential use of checklists.

9.14 Exemplar article

As the exemplar article for this chapter, I have chosen:

Bill Reed and Sharon Nolan. Survey review: Two series of Business English materials. *ELT Journal* 48/1, January 1994, 80–89.

Although this article is concerned with ESP-type materials, it provides some useful ideas for any type of materials evaluation report.

Read through the survey carefully, and think about these questions:

1. Think about the way the review is organised. Do the authors

compare each series step by step according to certain criteria, or do they deal comprehensively first with one series and then with the other? What are the advantages or disadvantages of the way in which they have chosen to organise their review?

2. What are the criteria that the authors use to evaluate these two series?

3. Imagine that you were actually able to use these materials with students. Can you think of any ways in which you could involve your learners in the process of evaluation? (Think of the range of research techniques we have been looking at: journals, reports, think-aloud, observation, interviews, questionnaires, case studies . . .)

4. Think back to your evaluation of the textbook you chose earlier. Now that you have read the article by Reed and Nolan, are there any other criteria that you now think you could use for your own textbook evaluation?

Survey-review: *two series of Business English materials*

Bill Reed and Sharon Nolan

Business Management English
Nick Brieger and Jeremy Comfort
Prentice Hall   1992

Language Reference for Business English
ISBN   0 13 093428 3   Book

Marketing
ISBN   0 13 093469 0   Book
          0 12 093584 0   Cassette
          0 13 105750 2   Self-Study Pack

Personnel
ISBN   0 13 093451 8   Book
          0 13 093576 x   Cassette
          0 13 105678 5   Self-Study Pack

Finance
ISBN   0 13 093444 5   Book
          0 13 093592 1   Cassette
          0 13 105743 X   Self-Study Pack

Production and Operations
ISBN   0 13 093477 1   Book
          0 13 093600 6   Cassette
          0 13 105776 6   Self-Study Pack

Longman Business English Skills
Series editors: Mark Ellis, Nina O'Driscoll and Adrian Pilbeam

Longman   1987–1992

Making Contact
Nina O'Driscoll and Fiona Scott-Barrett
ISBN   0582 066447 3   Book
          0582 064465 5   Cassette

Exchanging Information
Christine Johnson and Nina O'Driscoll
ISBN   0582 06445 7   Book
       0582 06444 9   Cassette

Presenting Facts and Figures
David Kerridge
ISBN   0582 09307 4   Book
       0582 20957 9   Cassette

Meetings and Discussions
Nina O'Driscoll and Adrian Pilbeam
ISBN   0582 09305 8   Book
       0582 85262 5   Cassette

Socializing
Mark Ellis and Nina O'Driscoll
ISBN   0582 09308 2   Book
       0582 85260 9   Cassette

Telephoning
Kay Bruce
ISBN   0582 09306 6   Book
       0582 85266 8   Cassette

Giving Presentations
Mark Ellis and Nina O'Driscoll
ISBN   0582 06441 4   Book
       0582 06440 6   Cassette

Negotiating
Philip O'Connor, Adrian Pilbeam, and Fiona Scott-Barrett
ISBN   0582 06443 0   Book
       0582 06442 2   Cassette

Introduction

The development route for most Business English publications has been through mainstream EFL thinking, and this has caused confusion in some quarters. 'What is Business English?' and 'Are we teaching Business or English?' are common cries in language schools, conferences, and teacher training workshops. Many language schools have perceived a potential market in the Business English sector, leading them to expect their EFL-trained teachers to cope with the particular demands of business and professional people. At the same time, publications, such as *Business Assignments* (Casler and Palmer, 1989) which have departed significantly from mainstream EFL by incorporating quantities of management training

196   *Bill Reed and Sharon Nolan*

material, may only partially meet learners' needs and arouse distrust among those required to teach them. EFL-trained teachers fear for their own credibility, while those who come to Business English teaching from a management background are not always able to cope with the particular constraints of language training for management. Whereas the RSA-trained teacher can make a good stab at teaching general English from virtually any bit of material, published or improvised, the teacher of English to business people may be confronted with masses of alien information, and obliged to deal with it in front of more mature, more experienced, worldly-wise learners. Only recently have appropriate trainer training courses appeared.[1]

Business English publications, therefore, have to fulfil an awkward dual role, which is to inform and support the learner, while, at the same time, and in entirely different ways, informing and supporting the teacher. Even with the provision of teachers' books, publications can fail in this difficult task. Below the intermediate level, the job is done reasonably successfully by courses such as *Business Objectives* (Hollett, 1991). But what can be done for those learners who (whatever their level in English), expect intellectual and communicative challenges on a par with those they experience in their own language?

This review considers two series which provide different types of answer to this question.

The Prentice Hall *Business Management English* (BME) series appeared in 1992. The first volumes of *Longman Business English Skills* (LBES) appeared in 1987, and the series has recently been extended and re-launched in colour. Both series are written by well-established teams who have specialized for a number of years in Business English, in the UK and abroad. The main markets for these books are probably the UK, Germany, France, Italy, Spain, and Japan, with a growing potential in Eastern Europe, where it is quite possible that a certain amount of management training is mediated by EFL teachers and books—a disturbing thought, which highlights the need for books to be based on good management practice, as well as on sound teaching and learning practice.

Business Management English

The Business Management English series consists of five books. The first, *Language References*, covers structures, functions, and notes to help in communication situations (presentations, meetings, telephoning, reports, letters, and social occasions); each of the others is devoted to a management discipline: *Finance, Personnel, Marketing,* and *Production and Operations.* Exercises in these four 'discipline' books are cross-referenced to the language reference volume, and there is a key at the back of each book.

The stated aims are to provide language development exercises and communication skills practice to specialists and non-specialists at post-intermediate levels, in the context of key management disciplines, which are dealt with in some depth. These aims are ambitious, and target very specific business areas.

The approach is through business and management reading texts, and listening passages on audio cassette. The reading texts are mostly taken from the publisher's own management textbooks—Prentice Hall being a specialist in this field. While these texts do not provide a management course in themselves, they are clearly related to management training themes, and will be instantly recognisable to MBA and Business Studies students as topics and theories for discussion. Thus, the stimulus in each unit is a matter of management concern, introduced via a short explanation which is useful to both teacher and learner, and by a warm-up activity which raises some basic issues. For example, Part One of Unit 5 in *Marketing* is on pricing. The warm-up questions are: 'Does a lower price always mean higher sales?' and 'For what types of product do higher prices sometimes mean higher sales?', leading in to a short but relatively sophisticated and concentrated text, illustrated with graphs, on the relationship between price and demand. The text and the diagrams form the basis for a series of exercises—comprehension/interpretation; language focus (in this case on cause and effect, appropriate enough for the price/demand topic); word study; and a transfer exercise where new graphs are to be used for interpretation, decision-making, and presentation. This overall pattern is repeated in Part Two, with a listening exercise in place of reading, and language focus on 'asking for clarification'. The language exercises are cross-referenced to the relevant units of the language reference book—Unit 77 on 'Cause and effect', and Unit 73 on 'Checking and confirming information'.

All the units in the discipline books work in the same way: raise and discuss the theme; read or listen; interpret the meaning; work on the language; practise in a slightly different context. There is a great deal of input in each unit, and the skills of speaking, listening, reading, and writing are all covered. Tasks are imaginative: the heading 'Comprehension/interpretation', for example, shows that opinion and discussion are encouraged. Learners have to read between the lines of the texts and use a more exploratory approach than in most EFL books.

Although these books look quite dense at first sight, they are clearly organized. Each of the discipline books has seven or eight units. Each unit is in two sections, A and B, which in turn have two parts, 1 and 2. A header on each page (e.g. '3.A.2') and a footer giving the main theme and sub-theme (e.g. 'Operations capacity: deciding capacity') make it easy to keep track of where you are. It would be helpful if the headers to the key at the back of each book were blocked in grey instead of black, to distinguish them from the main part of the book.

Units always begin on a right-hand page—we are pleased to see that the publishers have been prepared to include blank pages where necessary. Tapescripts are included in the key.

Given the denseness of the books, we would have liked to see more sophisticated graphics in place of the rather spindly charts and diagrams. Symbols could have been used in the margins to indicate, say, reading or listening exercises; but perhaps the publishers have deliberately cultivated a 'management textbook' look rather than an 'EFL' look.

The language reference volume naturally has its own layout reflecting its twin aims of providing reference material both for language knowledge and communication skills.

The Grammar Structure section (61 per cent of the book) is a sort of scaled-down *English Grammar in Use* (Murphy, 1985) with business examples, and none the worse for that. There are no exercises, as these are to be found in the other four books. Each unit contains sample sentences; brief rules under the heading 'Form'; applications under the heading 'Uses'; and further notes and references to related units.

The Function section (17 per cent of the book) is organized in the same way, with seventeen appropriately chosen headings, such as 'Describing trends', 'Comparing and contrasting ideas', 'Obligation and requirements', and 'Scale of likelihood'. Some of these units use simple diagrams, such as those used by the same authors in *Business Contacts* to explain concepts. We feel there would be potential for extending this section, to include common management tasks such as project planning, or explaining mathematical calculations, which have their own implications for likely language functions.

The Communication section (22 per cent of the book) gives tips and useful language exponents on presentations, meetings, telephoning, report-writing, letter-writing, and social language. Unlike the Structure and Function sections, this section does not give rise to specific exercises in the discipline books, which reinforces the self-study bias of the series. The trainer using this material will need to create links between the communication notes and the warm-up and transfer exercises in the books to ensure the skills are put into practice.

This volume is exactly what it claims to be: a reference book. You can refer back from exercises in the discipline books but you can't easily find an exercise to practise a particular structure or function. For example, while testing the material, we found a need to practise the conditional in the context of company finance. (The springboard was 'If my company wasn't making a profit it wouldn't be so attractive to potential buyers.') It took a detailed search through *Finance* to find an appropriate exercise—we eventually used pages 49 (Language focus: Conditions), and 51 (Language focus: Conditional I and II). The use of subject-matter, rather than language, as a starting-point is characteristic of the series, and while we have no argument with this in principle (language being a means to an end, not an end in itself), it would be useful to have an extra cross-reference here.

The language content of the series is both varied and sophisticated. All examples are clearly business-oriented, and the language reference volume has a practical approach throughout. No apology is made for the complexity of some of the texts: the implied assumption is that interest in the subject-matter will carry the learner through. There is no difference in level between the beginning and the end of the books; and there is no artificial attempt to present language systematically or progressively. The series has a clear commitment to subject-matter first, and language work as a consequence.

Word study rightly plays an important role. Words with suffixes and prefixes, phrasal verbs, and similar words (e.g. *rise, raise, arise*; *lie, lay*) are examined in some detail. Some terminology is very specific and conceptual (e.g. *net operational cash flow*; *man–machine time chart*).

Each discipline book contains a 500-word glossary of terms at the back, based, according to the authors, on 'frequency of usage within this subject area'. The entries are not confined to words used in the book. Many entries have an example as well as a brief definition. As a spot-check, we compiled the following random list of terms to look up:

Value analysis—appears in *Production and Operations*: 'a methodical examination of each product in order to minimize cost without reducing its functional value'.
Total quality management—doesn't appear in any glossary, though 'total quality control' appears in *Production and Operations*.
Cash cow—doesn't appear in *Marketing* or in any of the other books.
Internal rate of return—doesn't appear in *Finance*, even though the topic is dealt with in Unit 4.
Bull market—appears in *Finance*: 'period when share prices are rising'.
Organigram—appears in *Personnel*, with the same definition (correctly) as 'organization chart'.
Up-market—appears in *Marketing* along with eight other collocations using the word 'market'.

There is relatively little overlap in the glossaries. 'Turnover' appears in

Personnel ('staff turnover') and in *Finance* ('gross sales of a company'); but 'stock turnover' is not included in *Production and Operations*, although four other collocations with 'stock' are listed. 'Account' does not appear in *Production and Operations*, but appears in *Marketing* as 'account executive', in *Finance* along with 'accountancy' and 'accountant', and in *Personnel* as 'accountable'.

Thus, while they cannot vie with other Business English dictionaries such as Longman's *Concise Dictionary of Business English*, with upwards of 10,000 main entries, the four books together provide a glossary of getting on for 2,000 entries: a valuable resource for teacher and learner alike.

A cassette accompanies each of the discipline books and contains listening passages for the second part of each unit. The transcripts are to be found in the key. These listening passages are scripted meetings, conversations, and telephone dialogues, and while they are fairly realistic, they are more 'EFL-like' in character than the reading texts. The exercises focus on understanding the information and also, usefully, on evaluating the quality of the exchange. For example, a telephone conversation in *Marketing*, 6.B.2, gives rise to the comprehension/interpretation questions 'How do you think the supplier handled these telephone calls?' and 'How do you think the customer handled these calls?' The answer in the key, appropriately enough says, 'Up to you!' This is another way in which the series bridges the gap between language training and Business Studies, and is an implied reference to the communication section of the language reference book. As with the reading texts, the exercises then focus on language items, word study, and a transfer activity.

A large part of the books is given over to a very wide variety of exercises: comprehension, interpretations, gap-filling, evaluating, summarizing, word study, report-writing, and many more. Not all of these are dynamic in themselves; but the emphasis of the series is on the exchange of opinions on the management content, leading to individual work on the language exercises.

We find this series quite flexible. It is possible to delve in to any unit for an appropriate text on a particular subject, and then refer back to *Language Reference* for relevant language and communication items. You can follow different paths through the books: you can focus only on the reading or the listening texts if you wish, as each part of each unit stands alone. The series can be used as a reference for someone on an immersion course, or as a complete course for a Business Studies student.

Through its use of Business Studies and MBA-type texts, *Business Management English* has a weight found in few other Business English course materials. Largely theory-based, it avoids discussion of particular products and services: all the topics raised in the discipline books can be applied to the individual business and management interests of the learners, and this gives the series greater flexibility than, say, the case study approach of Business Assignments. It should not date too quickly.

For the business content, the authors have chosen to concentrate mainly on 'hard' issues—that is, those which are definable and quantifiable. The focus on specific disciplines means there is little opportunity to raise wider management issues such as strategic planning, or the implementation of change within organizations, or the overall social and economic conditions under which businesses operate—'softer' issues which are more difficult to define, and therefore naturally provoke discussion and speculation. In deciding this format for the series, and in limiting themselves to Prentice Hall texts, the authors have had to omit such thought-provoking authors as Drucker, Handy, Peters, Adair, or Heller—writers whose work is increasingly on the reading lists of MBA and Business Studies students, and who raise general management issues which have to be confronted in all disciplines.

We would advise potential users not to be put off by the initial impression of dryness and complexity. While many of the issues raised are indeed complex, about 80 per cent of the content (at a rough estimate) is mainstream language teaching material which should not be alien to the experienced trainer, the Business Studies trainee, or the management course participant. With a little practice you can find your way around easily. The series is entirely suitable for Business Studies students and professional people on extensive courses, and can easily be 'dipped into' on short intensive courses.

These books contain a wealth of information on the running of businesses. However, even well-founded theories are open to interpretation. Language trainers should see in this series many opportunities to facilitate the presentation of arguments and the exchange of views, putting into practice the communication skills outlined in the language reference volume.

Longman Business English Skills

Longman Business English Skills is a three-level series comprising eight slim volumes, each with an accompanying cassette: Pre-intermediate (*Making Contact* and *Exchanging Information*); Intermediate (*Telephoning, Socializing, Presenting Facts and Figures*, and *Meetings and Discussions*), and Upper-intermediate/Advanced (*Giving Presentations* and *Negotiating*). The division into levels is not rigid—for example, parts of *Giving Presentations* could certainly be tackled at a lower level. However, the cassettes for the highest-level books are faster-paced, and have longer listening passages.

Giving Presentations and *Negotiating* are also distinguished by the inclusion of useful tips which go slightly beyond language training into the communication training sphere. The first books in the series appeared in 1987 and the latest in 1992, when the whole series was relaunched in colour.

The publishers state that 'This series is for business and professional people who need to use English successfully at work. Through a series of carefully guided activities [it] helps you develop appropriacy, fluency and confidence.'

The audio cassettes are central to the work in all the units, giving practice in listening to language used in a variety of business situations. Each unit presents language appropriate to a specific situation (e.g. in *Making Contact* Unit 11, entitled 'Introducing others', we have 'explaining position' (i.e. job), 'introducing', 'explaining job function', 'greeting'). There is practice in using this language in controlled situations, and in using formal and informal styles. Each situation has different objectives, but overall the pattern is: listen; present language; practice; produce. It is possible to use the material in classroom teaching, but the main bias is towards self-study.

While the books are all very similar in approach, they are organized slightly differently. Answers are provided either at the back of the book, or after a group of units, or (in the case of *Negotiating*) after each unit. The use of colour, cartoons, wide margins with symbols or notes, and boxes with extra information help to make the books attractive and inviting. Headers on each page give unit or section titles, which are often language functions.

Every unit is constructed in a logical, 'building-block' style for self-study, with task-based language exercises, and plenty of listening tasks which use a variety of international accents. This tightly-controlled approach means the series can be a useful support to newly qualified teachers, but the lack of an interactive dynamic makes it rather dry and repetitive for classroom work.

Exercises follow a consistent pattern in each book. In *Socializing*, for example, the pattern is 'Background' (a few lines introducing the listening passage); 'Comprehension check' (using the cassette); 'Focus on language' (gap-filling with prompts in the margin pointing out discourse functions); 'Language summary' (function-based tasks, e.g. 'Thanking people for hospitality' in Unit 5); and 'Practice' (responding to discourse function prompts, e.g. 'thank your host (you don't know this person very well)' to elicit 'It was very kind of you to invite me'). Pronunciation exercises are prominent only in *Telephoning*.

The two higher-level books are a little less dry. To counteract the lack of real exchange, *Negotiating* incorporates 'self-record' prompts with a microphone symbol, to encourage learners to speak on cassette instead of simply writing in the book. This idea could usefully be incorporated throughout the series. *Giving Presentations* includes a certain amount of guidance on presentation skills in the form of checklists (e.g. on 'Involving the audience' in Unit 1 or 'Using visuals' in Unit 4). *Negotiating* contains a 'Cross-cultural summary' in each unit, which is an attempt to raise awareness of these issues in negotiating across national boundaries. We have reservations about some of the generalizations involved here—for example, is it really true that in American culture, 'meaning is mainly conveyed through words ... (and) relatively little is left to be understood from the context'? (p.27) In explaining their approach to the question of negotiation, the authors refer to the Harvard Negotiation Project, and state that their emphasis is on 'pursuing your own interests while maintaining good human relations with people whose interests conflict with yours.' This means that learners who seek to emulate the Arthur Scargill stabbing-finger style, or the Margaret Thatcher handbagging style, will not find appropriate language exponents here. 'No way!', or 'You're off your trolley!', or 'You must be joking!' are rendered as 'I'm afraid we couldn't accept that' and 'I'd say that was the least favourable option for us.' Negotiation can be competitive as well as co-operative, but this is not reflected in the book.

Units in the books can be used in any order, and are complete in themselves. However, flexibility within each unit is very limited, as each task builds progressively on the last.

The series is designed to look attractive to business people, with high-quality back-lit cover photographs replacing the harsher, rather dated pictures of earlier editions. Page layout is lively. Unit themes are appropriate, and cover a range of communication skills quite thoroughly. The content of the series has not dated appreciably and does not look likely to do so.

The step-by-step approach is very supportive of both learner and teacher. However, the experienced teacher who does not need such a tight framework could find this too restrictive. At the same time, less linguistically inclined learners using the books for self-study may have difficulty in dealing with some of the discourse analysis prompts. Nevertheless, learners who work through the books will get a sense of having studied English, and will have listened and read a lot. They can see what they are going to learn, follow a predictable pattern, and feel comfortable within a safe framework. They come out armed with a bank of functional language.

What the series does not do, given its self-study bias, is challenge the learner to be inventive or creative with the language, or give real experience of coping in the target situation, possibly under pressure. There is little which engages the intellect of the learner beyond functional description and analysis of the language. Even in the higher-level *Negotiating*, there are no role plays to put the language learned into practice. For appropriate support in creating and facilitating real exchanges in the classroom context, the trainer will need to look elsewhere.

Conclusion

The *BME* series and the *LBES* series set out to achieve very different aims, and do so in very different ways. In some senses, they are complementary: what is played down in one series is played up in the other. For example, *LBES* has virtually no 'business information' content, whereas *BME* has a great deal. On the other hand, *BME* simply lists appropriate language exponents for, say, telephoning, in a five-page section of the *Language Reference* volume, whereas *LBES* covers them step-by-step. In other ways, their respective philosophies are quite opposed: *BM* works downwards from whole texts, whereas *LBES* works upwards from component phrases. Paradoxically, *LBES*, which concentrates on interaction, contains very little truly interactive material, because it is designed for self-study; whereas *BME*, although it focuses largely on description, provides opportunities for presentations and discussions in the classroom. In Table 1 we summarize the relative strengths of the two series as we see them.

Whereas both series should clearly be on the shelves of any Business English training centre, the choice of which to use in any particular situation will depend on the nature of the participants and the aims of the course or session.

Table 1: relative strengths

Aim	BME	LBES
Use with Business Studies students	√	√
Use with business and professional people	√	√
Core material in Business Studies English course	√	√
Core material in short intensive course	×	×
Back-up material in short intensive course	√	√
Self-study	√	√
Provide business background knowledge	√	×
Comprehensive language reference	√	×
Study interactive language functions in detail	×	√
Present and discuss business management questions	√	×
Dynamic frameworks for extended interaction	×	×
Listening passages	√	√
Reading texts	√	√
Analyse discourse in detail	×	√
Intrinsic interest of subject matter	√	×
Support to teachers: discourse analysis	√	√
Support to teachers: business background	√	×

Bill Reed and Sharon Nolan

Note

1 For a list of Business English teacher training courses, see the ARELS/IATEFL publication *English for Business: Survey of teacher training*, available from ARELS, 2 Pontypool Place, Valentine Place, London SE1 8QF.

References

Adam, J. H. 1985. *Concise Dictionary of Business English*. Harlow: Longman.

Brieger, N., J. Comfort, S. Hughes and **C. West.** 1987. *Business Contacts*. Hemel Hempstead: Prentice Hall.

Casler, K. and **D. Palmer.** 1989. *Business Assignments*. Oxford: Oxford University Press.

Hollett, V. 1991. *Business Objectives*. Oxford: Oxford University Press

Murphy, R. 1985. *English Grammar in Use*. Cambridge: Cambridge University Press.

The reviewers

Bill Reed and **Sharon Nolan** hold qualifications in modern languages, education, TEFL, and business management, and have trained in interpersonal skills with the Human Potential Resource Group of the University of Surrey. They are the authors of *Business English Teacher's Resource Book* (Longman, 1992) and *English for Business: Survey of Teacher Training* (ARELS/IATEFL, 1993). As partners in Abbey Communication Training, they provide intensive English language and communication skills courses, trainer training courses, and consultancy services for business and industry.

10 No teacher is an island: some approaches to sharing ideas

10.1 Overview

This chapter will explore some ways in which involvement in action research can help us break out of the isolation of the teacher's role and tap into the expertise of the wider language teaching community. Two aspects of this process will be discussed:

1. making use of the ideas, insights and findings of colleagues, other teachers, writers and researchers;
2. sharing your own ideas, insights and findings with others.

Although it is convenient in some ways to separate these two aspects, they are very often also complementary and simultaneous activities.

10.2 'No teacher is an island'

There is a sense in which the heading of this section is actually not true. Paradoxically, although teachers by definition spend their lives in the company of others (sometimes a very large company, if we think of the size of certain classes!), it is in many ways a lonely profession. Apart from team teaching, which only affects a few teachers and then usually for brief periods, most teachers face their classes alone. Our lapses and failings very often do not come to the attention of our peers (mercifully!), but on the other hand our successes are also usually unnoticed and therefore ignored by those colleagues whose good opinion we would value.

Apart from personal and morale considerations, this professional isolation is ultimately a barrier to professional development. I would suggest that action research can be a helpful means to break down the professional isolation just referred to.

Notice that I said 'can be' not 'will be'. It is possible, of course, for action research to be a totally private activity. As a practising teacher, I can decide to investigate some aspect of my own teaching, collect the relevant data and analyse it, come to certain conclusions, and keep

207

whatever findings I have arrived at completely to myself. Indeed a lot of the reflection we do on our own practice is of this purely private nature.

However, if all our professional development were of this kind, we would surely be unnecessarily handicapping ourselves, as well as depriving ourselves of a lot of stimulus and interest. Being aware of other colleagues' ideas can give us a fresh slant on problems and ideas for our own action research, to say nothing of the saving of time when solutions are presented to us ready-made. Similarly, sharing our own ideas with others can be beneficial in many obvious ways. Sometimes, the mere necessity of having to articulate our ideas to an audience can help us to develop them in ways that might not otherwise have happened. The feedback from colleagues can be motivating and rewarding, as well as providing the basis for further reflection. These points may seem so self-evident that they hardly need stating, but the fact remains that the amount of 'sharing of ideas' that takes place among language teachers is probably far less than it could and should be. This may be for a number of reasons, among them, pressure of work, lack of motivation or reward for professional development, natural diffidence, professional insecurity, and so on. In other words some of the inhibiting factors are organisational and some are personal: but, whatever their origin, their continued existence must be a source of regret. The greatest share of responsibility for improving this situation must rest with management and with training institutions, but in at least some teaching contexts there also exists the opportunity for individual initiative. The rest of this chapter makes some suggestions as to how that individual initiative might be exercised. Let us start by thinking about collaborative action research.

10.3   Collaborative action research

Again we run into a paradox, for one of the most effective ways of exercising our individual initiative in the context of action research is through collaboration! Collaboration can be with:

– our students
– colleagues in the same department/school/institution
– colleagues outside our own school/institution
– colleagues with a different area of expertise (e.g. teacher and trainer; teacher and full-time researcher; teacher and manager, etc.)
– colleagues in other disciplines (e.g. foreign language teacher/mother tongue teacher)
– colleagues in other countries

Let us now look at some of these possibilities:

1. **Collaboration with students**   We have frequently noted (e.g. Sections 3.17, 5.10) that there are ways in which getting our students involved in the action research may benefit both themselves and us. With regard to composition, for example, researching their own writing processes and comparing the results could be, for students at a certain level, a very helpful exercise. It may also benefit us as teachers by giving us insights into how our students write.
2. **Collaboration with colleagues in the same department/school/ institution**   The main advantage here is ease of contact. Proximity means that it is more convenient when planning activities and analysing data. It may also make certain kinds of data collection easier (e.g. observing one another's classes).
3. **Collaboration with colleagues outside our school/institution**   Teachers who collaborate in action research with colleagues in other institutions often remark how stimulating it is to get insights from fellow-professionals operating in different contexts.
4. **Collaboration with colleagues with a different area of expertise**   This kind of collaboration can lead to useful division of labour. For example, collaboration between a teacher and a trainer can lead to the pooling of different kinds of data, or the trainer may have access to better reference facilities. The danger here is that the teacher can end up in the role of the 'junior partner', rather than at least an equal partner.
5. **Collaboration with colleagues in other countries**   This is becoming much more possible with facilities such as e-mail and the Internet. Again, interesting comparative and contrastive data could be found (e.g. some action research done in another country to see if the results are similar). Also foreign language and mother tongue comparisons of, for example, reading and writing processes can be set up.

10.4   Advantages and disadvantages of collaborative action research

There are three advantages of collaborative action research. They may be characterised as:

1. **Depth and coverage**   The more people are involved in an action research project, the more data can be gathered, either in depth (e.g. a single case study) or in coverage (e.g. several complementary case studies; a bigger population), or in both.
2. **Validity and reliability**   Involving others makes it easier to investi-

gate an issue from different angles, perhaps using different research techniques (i.e. using *triangulation*, as we discussed in Section 3.3). Triangulation should make our findings more reliable, and subjecting them to different people's scrutiny within the action research team should help to make the findings more valid.

3. **Motivation** Perhaps the most important aspect, though, is that, if the 'vibes' are right (i.e. if the group dynamic is positive), working as a member of a team is much more motivating than working on our own. We are much more likely to follow through on the action research tasks we set ourselves if others are there to spur us on.

There are, of course, potential disadvantages in collaborative action research. You have probably heard stories of friendly colleagues who have never spoken to one another again after going on a holiday together! The same thing is possible in an activity like action research which can make unusual demands of a professional relationship. This is something you have to consider when deciding on whether to seek collaborators within, say, your own department or further afield. I have already mentioned the potential problem of status when professionals with different kinds of expertise come together.

Perhaps the solution is to spend time discussing the ground rules:

– What are we trying to do?
– Why are we doing this? (Do we share the same motivation, or do we have different motivations?)
– How are we going to do it? (Who does what and when?)
– How much time are we each prepared to spend on this?
– How often do we meet, where and when?
– What is the end product going to be? (A talk or article, or simply a shared experience?)

Now try PERSONAL REVIEW 10.1.

10.5 Commentary (Personal Review 10.1)

If you have been able to respond to this 'Personal review' section, you may have felt that the next suggested step would be to find a collaborator and begin negotiations! In fact, we all know that collaboration rarely comes about in such a logical, calculating way. It is much more likely to arise from discovering a shared concern or enthusiasm in the course of a conversation, or while participating, say, in an in-service workshop.

The intention of the 'Personal review' section is simply to alert you to some of the ground-rules that might be usefully established before you get launched on a collaborative action research project. Even close

---

PERSONAL REVIEW 10.1: Collaborative Research

1. Note down one or more action research topics that you are considering.

2. For each topic, note down a list of potential collaborators or types of collaborators (e.g. 'someone who knows about management').

3. Write down what form you see the collaboration taking in terms of:
    – your contribution
    – collaborator's/collaborators' contribution(s)
    – how much time you are prepared to spend on the topic
    – how much time you expect collaborator(s) to spend on the topic
    – how you expect the collaboration to be structured (e.g. arrangements for meetings)

If you are working in a group, discuss with one or more members how you could collaborate with each other on your projects. This is just an exercise, so you don't have to follow through (but you never know . . .).

---

colleagues working together can have totally different expectations and level of commitment – and grief lies in that direction. It is much better to have a frank and full discussion of what is involved before anyone commits too much of their own time and resources.

Next we will look at some other ways of sharing ideas, which you can use whether or not you are involved in a collaborative arrangement.

10.6   Sources of ideas

The most congenial way of getting ideas about teaching methods and materials is probably in *informal conversation with colleagues*. First-hand recommendations from colleagues are very often highly relevant because they spring from our immediate environment and teaching context. Further, being personally acquainted with the person originating the idea, we will probably have a shrewd notion as to whether it might suit us, or whether it may be actually a function of our colleague's perhaps quite different personality.

Thanks to the miracle of modern electronic technology, it is possible for those who have the appropriate hardware and software to have something approximating to this kind of informal professional discussion on a national or international scale using the Internet. This can be done through electronic mail ('e-mail') or by accessing electronic discussion lists. One such list (known as 'TESL-L') had in 1997 a membership of over 19,000 members in 90 countries, thus creating, in Ricardo Calil's words, 'a virtual community of professionals where contact and interaction are facilitated, and a vast amount of information and knowledge are brought together to be shared' (see Calil (a) and (b), 1995; Carrier, 1997).

Another popular way of getting ideas is from *talks* or *workshops*. Again, this has the advantage of allowing some degree of personal acquaintance. Just by listening to the speaker, we can form some kind of impression of their teaching style and whether what works for them might also work for us. In a workshop setting we might even have a chance to try out teaching materials, or put ideas into action. There is often an opportunity to ask questions or discuss problems.

One of the best ways of getting involved in talks and workshops is through membership of a teachers' EFL organisation. Large international organisations such as IATEFL or TESOL International, and their affiliates, spring to mind, but there are obviously others. Within the larger organisations there also tend to be special interest groups (SIGs) devoted to, say, Computer Assisted Learning or Teacher Development.

Another source of ideas can come from teachers' programmes on *radio or television,* especially if we can record them for repeated playback.

The most readily accessible supply of new ideas is probably to be found in written sources such as *books, magazines,* and *journals.* A magazine like *Modern English Teacher (MET)* may be a rich source of ideas for practising teachers who might not think of themselves as 'researchers', but who are nevertheless very much open to new techniques and approaches. An example article has been reproduced at the end of this chapter (second article, by Douglas Buckeridge).

Clearly it would not be too difficult to generate data from the kind of activity that Douglas Buckeridge describes. We could, for example, turn some of the interviewers into 'reporters' for the local 'ELT Radio Station', duly equipped with small portable audio cassette recorders. The quantity and quality of the recorded interaction could be analysed using techniques that we have discussed earlier in this book (see Chapter 6). Student reactions to the technique could be assessed using questionnaires and interviews. The written follow-up activity ('Step three' – short paragraphs concerning what the students have in common) could also provide data. You may have thought of other ways.

PERSONAL REVIEW 10.2: Practical Ideas from
Magazines

1. Read the article from *MET* by Douglas Buckeridge at the
    end of the chapter, and think about these issues:
    a) What was the main 'message' that the writer was trying
       to get across?
    b) Was the message clear, or was the article in any way
       confusing or ambiguous?

2. How (a) useful and (b) relevant in your situation would you
    reckon the suggestions presented in this article to be?
    Why?

3. If the answers to the previous question were positive to at
    least some degree, would you use the ideas exactly as they
    are described here, or would you modify them in some
    way? If so, in what ways?

4. Now you can try on your 'teacher as action researcher' hat!
    Certain claims are made in this article, either explicitly or in
    an implied way, for the benefits and effectiveness of the
    technique described. How would you go about collecting
    data on the effectiveness/appropriacy, etc. of this
    technique in your own situation?

Finally, this article may also have given you further ideas. For
example, what about devising contexts for teaching and learning
comparatives instead of superlatives? What about getting students to
generate their own sets of questions (see 'Step one')? What about
creating lists ('The five things I value most'; 'The four household chores
I like least'; and so on)? Notice that Douglas Buckeridge was motivated
to write this article by something he read by Gertrude Moskowitz
(1978), and also other writings by Klippel (1984) and Ur (1989). You
could be stimulated by his article to write something that will interest
other teachers, who may in their turn want to share their ideas in print:
and so a very productive kind of chain reaction is set up which benefits
everyone involved.

10.7   Literature search

So far, we have been looking at ways of getting hold of ideas in a rather
informal, unstructured way, or being fortunate enough to come across a

suggestion that motivates or intrigues you. It is also possible to tap into other people's ideas in a much more directed and purposeful fashion. To do this you have to have a *focus* or specific area of interest. The article we have just been looking at contains a number of overlapping areas of possible focus, for example:

- grammar
- grammar practice
- grammar practice activities
- motivation
- affective dimension
- opinion gap
- conversation/discussion activities

Let us say that you decided that you wanted to know more about 'grammar practice activities'. What are the other possibilities for ways of practising grammar? Maybe you would like to expand your repertoire in this area. What is the next step? Well, of course, you could think up your own activities: but perhaps you don't have too many ideas.

One way forward would be to start searching out other ideas in a systematic way by trying to find out what has been written on this topic.

You have now embarked on what is sometimes called a *literature search*. This term has little to do with *literature* in its usual sense, as in *language and literature*, but actually means a search for the books, articles and other writings which may have a bearing on the research area that you are interested in. There are various ways in which you can go about this, partly dependent upon the resources you have at your disposal. The basic requirement is that you should have access, directly or indirectly, to a reasonably well-stocked library.

Very often the starting point for a literature search is a *bibliography* or list of references attached to an article that has caught your interest. If you were interested in doing action research in the area covered by the article by Buckeridge, for example, the references to Klippel (1984), Moskowitz (1978), and Ur (1992) might be well worth following up. If you succeeded in getting hold of any or all of these books, they might lead you on to other references in *their* bibliographies. So, bibliographies can have a 'ripple' or 'chain' effect, one set of references leading you on to another.

Knowing the title is not much good to you unless your library stocks the book. In my experience, most librarians take pride in their ability to help 'serious' readers find what they are looking for. In any case, there should be an *author catalogue* and/or *title catalogue* which helps you to track down the book you are after. The catalogue will have a *shelf-mark* which will tell you where the title you are looking for is located. Sometimes there is also a *subject catalogue* where all the books relating to the same or similar topics are grouped together. (In the Dewey Decimal System, for example, all the books about Language are grouped under 400–499.) Many libraries now have *computer-accessed catalogues*, which make life even easier: all you have to do is type in the author's name, and the availability of the books by that author held in the library is shown on the monitor screen. Similarly, it is usually possible to type in subject headings (such as those we listed for the *MET* article), and any relevant titles will be displayed. If your library does not have the book you are after, it may be able to get it from another library on *inter-library loan*.

Very often, the best source of ideas is from magazines and journals. They cover a wider range of topics, are sometimes more specialised, and very often more up-to-date. You may already subscribe to one or more journals, and, if you do, it is worthwhile holding on to back copies for future reference: even language teaching association newsletters can come in handy for references, as well as useful contacts. Remember that the value of an article is not just in the article itself, but in the further references that very often go with it.

10.8   Other sources

If you are involved in some action research which you intend to write up in a journal (or perhaps for a higher degree) then you may want a wider range of references, or you may want to be fairly confident that there are no major references that you have overlooked. Before you get started on this, you should have decided:

– the specific topic areas you are interested in;
– how far back you want to go for your sources: five years? seven years? Obviously the wider the scope of your enquiry, the more work will be involved, and the more time it will take;
– what kind of sources you are interested in: books? articles? theses/ dissertations? CD-ROM?

Once you are clear about the kind of information you are looking for, you will find that there are basically two kinds of support that you can get:

– lists of sources which give you only the bibliographical information that you need to locate any source you are interested in;
– lists of sources which, in addition to the above, also provide an abstract or summary of the main points in each source.

Such a list of sources could be seen as a kind of 'database'. Obviously, databases which provide abstracts can save you a lot of time (e.g. in

PERSONAL REVIEW 10.3: Source Material – Books and Journals

The purpose of this 'Personal review' section is to encourage you to make an inventory of the sources that are available to you in terms of books, journals, magazines, newsletters, and so on.

1. What library facilities are available to you? If you live in a large town, there may be public libraries, and also university libraries, which may be open to you under certain conditions.

2. What access, if any, do these libraries give you to other libraries (e.g. through inter-library loan)?

3. Within any library you have access to, do you know what catalogues there are, and how they work?

4. Does the library have a readers' adviser, or an assistant who is willing to help?

5. Do you know what system the library uses for organising its collection of books? (These are sometimes called *shelf-mark* systems. One common shelf-mark system is the Dewey Decimal System. It is called a *decimal* system, because it divides all human knowledge in ten areas; each of these is subdivided into ten areas; and so on.)

6. Do you know the main shelf marks associated with language teaching? (For example, in the Dewey Decimal System a lot of ELT Methodology texts will be found under section 428.) Don't forget, however, that there may be books that are very relevant to your interests in other areas. For example, if you are interested, let us say, in the management of an ELT department, you may find some useful ideas from books located in the business studies section. Similarly, if you are interested in motivating students to learn language, you are almost certain to find helpful texts in the psychology section.

7. What magazines and journals does the library hold in the area of language teaching? Which of them are likely to be of use to you? (For example, they may be too 'academic' or too 'popular' for your purposes.) Do they contain regularly updated indexes of topics that have appeared in the journal?

8.   As I indicated in (6) above, not all human wisdom resides in the discipline of ELT! Make a list of journals, etc. in related areas that may be worth your while looking at from time to time (e.g. business studies, psychology, or whatever).

9.   Have you come across any *survey articles* in an area you are interested in? These are articles which are intended to give comprehensive and authoritative overviews about the current 'state of the art' in a particular area. The potential usefulness of such articles, if they relate to an area you are interested in, is obvious.

10. Is there any professional journal that you subscribe to, or would consider subscribing to? You are more likely to contribute to a journal that you are 'at home' with because you read it regularly.

sorting out the sources that are really relevant and/or useful from those that are not). Even in the case of relevant/useful sources, the abstract may provide you with enough information for you not to have to read the original source. (This can be especially useful in the case of dissertations or theses, which are often quite difficult to get hold of.)

If you identify sources which you want to read in full, then you have to check for their availability or, failing that, order them through inter-library loan if that service is available to you.

There are four main ways of accessing databases:

– by means of print medium
– electronically, by means of CD-ROM
– electronically, on-line (i.e. by direct contact with the source database [perhaps via the Internet])
– by means of microfiche

In the future, it will probably be the case that all major databases (and, indeed, all major reference works) will be available on CD-ROM, partly because that takes up much less storage space than in print medium, but also because it is usually much faster to locate information on electronic databases. It is usually possible to find what you are looking for if you know *either* the author's name, *or* the title (or even a keyword from the title), *or* the subject-matter (topic).

For books, many libraries will be able to give you access to national and/or subject bibliographies, such as the *BNB: British National Bibliography* (available either in print medium or CD-ROM), Whitaker's *Books in Print* (UK books, on microfiche) and R. R. Bowker's *Books in Print* (US books, also on microfiche).

The *Education Index* (New York: H. W. Wilson) formerly listed only journals, but from September 1995 it has also listed books. It provides very useful short abstracts. A similar publication is the *Current Index to Journals in Education* (Phoenix, Arizona: Oryx).

Another useful source, available on CD-ROM, is the *ERIC* database (Washington, DC: US Dept. of Education, Educational Resources Information Centre). As well as listing articles etc., *ERIC* also lists its own documents on various educational topics. It also provides short abstracts of all the references it lists. Although a US publication, *ERIC* lists many international sources. There is additionally another database, also available on CD-ROM, called *International ERIC,* which lists sources from the Australian, British and Canadian Education Indexes. It does not, however, provide abstracts. For an example of information provided by each of these databases, both with reference to the same source, see Figure 10. 1.

If you wish your search to cover theses and dissertations as well, a very useful international source that is available in a variety of media is *Dissertation Abstracts International* (print medium), *Dissertation Abstracts On Disc* (CD-ROM) and *Dissertation Abstracts On-line.* This database provides usually very full abstracts, which can sometimes provide you with all the information you need. There are also national databases: for example, for the UK there is the *ASLIB Index to Theses* (available in print medium and CD-ROM).

For many teachers who are involved in research, or who simply want to keep up with 'what's new', a very convenient type of database will be one which gives reasonably full abstracts of new publications in their own subject-area. For language teachers, a good example of this type of database is *Language Teaching: The International Abstracting Journal for Language Teachers and Applied Linguists* (Cambridge: Cambridge University Press). A sample page of this database is reproduced in Figure 10.2. (PERSONAL REVIEW 10.4, which follows on after Figure 10.2, relates to 'Using Databases'.)

i)   5 of 5 Complete Record
     00173949   British Education Index (BEI)
     Creative writing in foreign language teaching
     Morgan Carol
     Journal Name: Language Learning Journal; No.10: Sep 94
       Publication Year(s):   1994
       Physical Description: p4447
       British Library Document Supply Centre Shelfmark: 5155.710200
     Language: English
       Country of Publication: England
     Notes: Secondary Education
       Descriptors: Modern Language Studies; Creative Writing; Poetry

ii)   5 of 5 Complete Record
      EJ506765   FL524808
      Creative Writing in Foreign Language Teaching.
      Morgan, Carol
      Language Learning Journal, n10 p4447 Sep   1994
      ISSN: 0957–1736
      Language: English
      Document Type: NON-CLASSROOM MATERIAL (055);
      JOURNAL ARTICLE (080)
        Journal Announcement: CIJNOV95
        Discusses the use of creative writing in second language
classrooms, focusing on techniques that can help students construct
their own poetry and poem-like creations in the target language.
Maintains that student poetry can help enliven the classroom
experience and allow students to express their own ideas.
(39 references) (MDM)
        Descriptors: *Classroom Techniques; *Creative Writing;
Elementary Secondary Education; English (Second Language);
FLES; Language Usage; *Poetry; *Second Language Instruction;
Student Attitudes

Figure 10.1   Records from (i) International Eric *and (ii)* Eric *Databases*

Teaching particular languages

English

95–445   Abuhamdia, Zakaria A. Coordination in ESL writing: is its use culture-specific? *Multilingua* (Amsterdam), **14**, 1 (1995), 25–37.

It has repeatedly been claimed in the literature on ESL writing and rhetoric that excessive coordination as a means of structural linkage typifies Arab ESL writing. The interpretation generally given attributes this norm-deviant feature in writing to the learners' native language, viz. Arabic. While this feature appears to be dominant in Arabic, the negative transfer explanation does not take into consideration facts about the overuse of coordination by other groups of learners of written English, including native speakers of English at a certain stage of acquiring the appropriate norms of discourse. This paper examines the role of other intervening variables and concludes that the use of coordination is more universal than the culture-specific position argues.

96–446   Balcom, Patricia and Kozar, Seana. An ESP speaking course for international graduate students. *TESL Canada Journal* (Montreal), **12**, 1 (1994), 58–68.

A critical issue in English for Academic Purposes (EAP), is whether a 'wide-angle' or more discipline-specific approach should be taken. If a course attempts to address students' needs in their area of study, even an EAP-trained teacher cannot be conversant with the concepts, issues, vocabulary, and discourse in a variety of scientific fields, especially with students at the graduate level. This article describes an academic speaking programme in which international graduate students are grouped according to their academic discipline (e.g. hydrology, chemistry, pharmacy) and participate in activities that simulate situations where they need to use English in their academic programmes. In such a situation, the peer group members are the content experts, providing discipline-specific guidance and discussion, whereas the ESL teacher is the language expert, helping the students in the areas of organisation, grammar, pronunciation and presentation skills.

95–447   Bax, Stephen (Canterbury Christ Church Coll.). Language across the curriculum in an ESL context: how teachers deal with difficult texts. *Language, Culture and Curriculum* (Clevedon, Avon), **7**, 3 (1994), 231–50.

This article addresses the use of English to teach 'content' subjects across the curriculum, and the ways in which English language teachers operate in such circumstances. In particular, it examines how South African teachers, working in situations where English is a second language, approach the teaching of a 'content' lesson based on a Geography text. Although their strategies are useful in some areas, the range and variety of their approaches could be extended, perhaps through training. This has implications for the many other contexts around the world where English is being used or introduced as a medium of instruction, and for English teachers and teacher trainers in those countries.

95–448   Ernst, Gisela (Washington State U.). 'Talking circle': conversation and negotiation in the ESL classroom. *TESOL Quarterly* (Washington, DC), **28**, 2 (1994), 293–322.

Language classrooms are often said to provide little opportunity for student-generated talk and meaningful use of language. However, this research shows that one classroom event, the talking circle, can provide a rich opportunity for students to extend their receptive and productive repertoires in the L2. Moreover, this type of instructional activity creates opportunities for learners to engage in meaningful communication, on the one hand, and to practice recently acquired social and linguistic knowledge, on the other. Both are appropriate activities for the L2 classroom. Results of a microethnographic analysis of one talking circle in an elementary ESL classroom are examined in relation to specific academic, social, and communicative requirements that constrain or enhance language use and language learning. Discussion of these results illustrates the value of ethnographic research in increasing our understanding of talk and interaction in L2 classrooms.

Figure 10.2   Sample page from Language Teaching.

PERSONAL REVIEW 10.4: Using Databases

1.   Compare the two entries in Figure 10.1. They are both about the same article. Which one do you find more informative/useful?

2.   Find out what databases are available to you. Pick a topic that you are interested in, and compare the information provided by the different databases.

3.   The purpose of the next task is to increase your awareness of the advantages and limitations of abstracts. Look at the four sources listed in the extract from *Language Teaching* reproduced in Figure 10.2. Pick the one which interests you most and read the abstract. Does the abstract tell you everything you want to know about this article?
     If not, what information is lacking, in your view? Do the same for any of the other articles that interest you. Which of the original articles are available to you, either locally or through inter-library loan?

4.   How enlightening/frustrating did you find this task?

10.9   Decision time . . .

In the previous four sections we have been looking at ways in which you can get ideas from written sources. At this point you have to decide how you see yourself sharing your own ideas (and perhaps your views on other people's ideas) with colleagues.

You may either:

a) be thinking of some kind of a fairly formal presentation (e.g. at a conference, or for an academic qualification);   or
b) have decided that, if you share your thoughts with any one at all, it will be in an informal setting.

If you are going to do the former, then you may find the (fairly technical) advice given in Sections 10.10–10.15 which follow of some use.

If you are not contemplating this kind of formal presentation, then you should go on to Section 10.16, which gives a few hints on presentations in general.

10.10   Logging sources

If you are going to be involved in any kind of long-term action, which involves scanning and reading many resources, it will save you much time and not a little frustration if you are organised from the beginning in the way that you log, or keep a systematic record of, these sources that you have spent your valuable time tracking down and studying. Unless you are very organised, it will almost inevitably happen that you will want to refer again to something that you read some time ago, and you will not be able to remember where you read it. This has happened at some time to most people involved in research, and it can be most exasperating. How can you avoid this happening to you?

10.11   Source cards: Books

As we have already said, the secret is to be organised. The technique used by many researchers is the use of *source cards*. (If you have access to a wordprocessor, you might find it more convenient to make up your own database of sources on the wordprocessor. Don't forget to save your records! Whichever method you use, you will be logging the same kind of information.) On the source cards (or wordprocessor database) you must record all the bibliographical information relating to the book or article, which simply means all the information required so that you, or someone else, will be able to locate the book or article again. Source cards can be any convenient size. Most people use cards that measure about 5 inches by 3 inches (128 mm x 76 mm).

For a *book* the required information is:

- the author's name or the editor's name (or the authors'/editors' names, if there is more than one)
- the title of the book
- the year when it was published
- the city where it was published
- the name of the publisher

There are no rules about how you put this information on source cards, because these cards are for your own private use. It would probably be useful, though, to set out the information in the way that you are going to present it for your own bibliography or list of references. (We will be coming back to this issue later.)

The information you need will be found on the *title page* and the *imprint* page of the book. (The imprint page usually comes immediately after the title page.)

PERSONAL REVIEW 10.5: Logging a Book Source

Look at Figure 10.3, where you will find the title page and the imprint page of a book. Get hold of some blank source cards and see if you can record on one of them the bibliographical information you would need for that book.

Then do the same for the present book that you are reading just now.

MULTILINGUAL MATTERS 30
Series Editor: Derrick Sharp

Introspection in Second Language Research

Edited by
Claus Færch and Gabriele Kasper

MULTILINGUAL MATTERS LTD
Clevedon · Philadelphia

Figure 10.3   Sample title/imprint pages

Library of Congress Cataloging-in-Publication Data

Færch, Claus.
   Introspection in second language research.

   (Multilingual matters ; v. 30)
   Bibliography: p.
   Includes index.
   1. Language and languages—Study and teaching—
Psychological aspects.   2. Second language acquisition—
Methodology.   3. Introspection.   I. Kasper, Gabriele.
II. Title.   III. Series.
P53.7.F34   1987   401′.9   87-7647
ISBN 0–905028–73–2
ISBN 0–905028–72–4 (pbk.)

British Library Cataloguing in Publication Data

Introspection in second language research.—
   (Multilingual matters; 30)
   1.   Second language acquisition
   I.   Færch, Claus   II. Kasper, Gabriele
   III. Series
   418′.007   P118.2

ISBN 0–905028–73–2
ISBN 0–905028–72–4 Pbk

Multilingual Matters Ltd,

Bank House, 8a Hill Road,	&	242 Cherry Street,
Clevedon, Avon BS21 7HH		Philadelphia, PA 19106–1906,
England.		U.S.A.

Typeset by Photo-graphics, Honiton, Devon.
Printed and bound in Great Britain by
Short Run Press, Exeter, EX2 7LW.

The cards you made for the last 'Personal review' section may have looked something like this:

Faerch, C. and Kasper, G. (eds.) (1987)
Introspection in Second Language Research
Clevedon/Philadelphia: Multilingual Matters

Wallace, M.J. (1998)
Action Research for Language Teachers
Cambridge: Cambridge University Press

Don't worry, however, if your cards didn't look exactly like this: the main thing is to get down the information you are going to need. Don't forget that the usual publishing convention is that titles are usually underlined or else printed in italics, as they have been here.

10.12   Book references: some problems

It is not always easy to get the information you need from imprint pages. Don't get confused between the publisher and the printer: the publisher's name is usually at the bottom of the title page. Some publishers have offices in several cities world wide: you can just choose the first city, or two if there are two. Also, it is not usual to record words like *Ltd.* or *Company* after the name of the publisher.

10.13   Source cards: Journals

For a *journal* the information you should record is:

– author's/authors' name(s)
– title of the article
– title of the journal in which it appeared

- month and year of publication (or exact date in the case of a news-paper, etc.)
- volume number and issue number
- pages of the article

Now let us try logging some journal articles.

PERSONAL REVIEW 10.6: Logging a Journal Source

Take a blank card and make up a source card for the article at the end of Chapter 5.

Make up another one for the *MET* article we were looking at earlier in this chapter. Remember that the page numbers must refer to the journal in which the articles were originally published. You will find this information in the introduction to the articles.

Your source cards might look something like this:

Arndt, V. (1987)
Six writers in search of texts: A protocol-based
study of L1 and L2 writing
ELT Journal Vol 41/4
October 1987
pp. 257–267

Buckeridge, D. (1994)
Forging links : an idea for reviewing superlatives
. . . and a bit more!
Modern English Teacher Vol 3/3
July 1994
pp. 40–41

10.14   Journal references: Some points to remember

Remember that the title of a journal is like the title of a book, so it should either be underlined or printed in italics.

The title of the article itself can be left plain (as in the examples above), or can be enclosed in either single or double quotation marks.

Different journals will require information displayed in different ways, so it is better to have too much information than too little.

The source card is for your own use, so you may decide that you want to display information differently (e.g. by recording the author's first name, thus: Valerie ARNDT). On the other hand, if you are writing a dissertation where you are going to have lots of references, it might be wiser to record them in exactly the way required by your University regulations. The main thing with the names of authors, editors and publishers is – get them right! It is very easy to misspell a name you are not familiar with.

All sorts of niggling problems of presentation can arise when you are recording references. Many of them can be resolved by looking at what other contributors have done. Some journals issue would-be authors with *style sheets* which explain exactly how references are to be written up. If you are writing a dissertation, etc., your university will no doubt provide detailed advice. Some useful guides in this area will be recommended in the 'Suggestions for further reading' section.

PERSONAL REVIEW 10.6: Listing References

We have just said that different publications have different rules, so it is worthwhile studying published reference lists to see 'how it is done'.

1. Go back again to Valerie Arndt's article (end of Chapter 5) and look at the list of references at the end of the article. Find an example of:
    – a journal article by one author
    – a journal article by two authors
    – a book written by several authors
    – a book edited by one editor
    – an article by two authors in a published collection of articles
    – an unpublished paper presented at a conference.

2. What seem to be the conventions for this publisher with regard to:
    – displaying the name of one author/two authors/several authors?
    – indicating the year of publication?

- displaying the title of an article?
- displaying the volume number, issue number and page reference of a journal article?
- recording an article in an edited book?

How did you do? As I have said, these are very niggling issues, but you will have to pay attention to such details if you think that you might eventually want to publish something about your action research.

10.15   Reading and reacting

So far we have been discussing the mechanics of finding sources and recording them, which is a necessary procedure, but not a very exciting one. The main reason for searching the literature is to find authors you can enter into a dialogue with, either by agreeing or disagreeing with them; by being informed, intrigued, excited, outraged and sometimes, we have to admit, baffled or bored. It is a dialogue, but something of a one-way dialogue: although the author can talk to you, there is no way that you can directly interact with him or her (until you have written an article of your own, that is). If you possess your own copy of the book, or a photocopy of the article, you can highlight bits that seem important, and/or write comments in the margin. This is probably the quickest and easiest way of reacting to a text. But note:

- you have to have your own copy of the text (which could be expensive if you have many references);
- this process can be *too* easy. I once came across a second-hand copy of a linguistics textbook, in which the student who had owned it had highlighted almost every line! Used indiscriminately, highlighting or underlining can become a mindless procedure which defeats its own purpose.

The next most popular technique which most people use is to take notes in a notebook. The problem with this approach is that it is not very flexible, if you are using many references. You may find that closely related topics are scattered in widely separated parts of the notebook.

People who anticipate that they are going to have a lot of references sometimes use *notecards*, with different cards for different topics. So after reading an article, you may end up with several cards, each with a different topic heading. The advantage of this system is that, after you have read several articles or books, you can rearrange the card *by topic*. The important thing to remember is that there must be enough information on the notecard to lead you back to the original source, and that means:

- author (etc.)
- year of publication
- page reference

The information could be displayed like this: Buckeridge (1994: 41). If you have got a source card for the article, or you have a photocopy of it, this should be enough to help you to identify it.

If you have a computer, it should also be possible to type entries straight into an appropriate database, which can then be copied and pasted as required. The usual precautions about making back-up discs apply.

There is no 'best' way of storing your reactions to your reading: it depends on a number of factors, some personal and some dependent on how many references you are actually going to store. Obviously, the more references you intend to have, the more systematic you are going to have to be.

PERSONAL REVIEW 10.7: Storing Reactions

You may have been a student once or you may be one now. What are/were your preferred ways of storing your reactions to what you read? Have you used any of the techniques we have been discussing? How effective were those techniques? If you don't already do so, would you consider using the notecard system or (if you have access to a wordprocessor) a computer database?

10.16 Ways of reacting

What is the nature of your dialogue with the writer? There are probably three ways in which you will want to react:

1. The writer has said something that you may want to *quote;*
2. You may wish to *summarise* part of what the writer has to say, or perhaps summarise the whole article, chapter, etc.;
3. You may wish to *record your own thoughts, views, etc.* on something the writer has said – this could obviously be combined with either of the first two ways listed here.

The third possibility is not problematic, and can be handled any way you like. The first and second possibilities require a bit more care:

1. **Quotations**   Make sure that you quote exactly from the text. If you decide to miss something out, use a certain number of dots (e.g. three or four). If you decide to put something in, to make the meaning of the quotation clearer, use square brackets.

    Here is a notecard which gives a short quotation from p. 41 of Buckeridge's article (from the section that begins 'Step three').

'While there is no specific time limit imposed on step two of this activity [i.e. moving around the class asking questions], it is a good idea to provide for some feedback time in the latter part of the lesson . . . Also, as a follow-up, they could write some short paragraphs about what they and other students have in common.'

Buckeridge, D. (1994: 41)

---

2. **Summaries**   Good summaries are not always easy to write. Make sure that your summary is a faithful reflection of what the writer actually said. Be careful to separate out your own views from his or hers.

PERSONAL REVIEW 10.8: References in the Text

Let us look at how writers incorporate references into their text. Turn back to Sara Cotterall's article at the end of Chapter 8, and look again at her first section: 'Why is autonomy desirable?'

1. Which of the possibilities that we have been discussing (i.e. quotations/summaries/own views) does Cotterall use in this section of her article? Give examples.

2. What 'rules' for using quotations could you derive from this extract?

3. What is Cotterall trying to do in this section, and how do her sources help her?

10.17   Commentary

This extract from Cotterall repays careful study, as it is a good example of the effective use of sources. She certainly uses the first two possibilities, and arguably also uses the third.

Cotterall seems to be trying to do two things in this section:

1.   to define what is meant by the term *learner autonomy*;   and
2.   to say why learner autonomy is a desirable thing.

The definition she takes care of by using a quotation (from Boud, 1988). But she also expands and clarifies Boud's definition, by adding some examples of her own.

In response to the question posed in her sub-heading (Why is autonomy desirable?), she advances three kinds of reasons: philosophical, pedagogical and practical. The philosophical argument she supports with summaries from Knowles (1975) and Littlejohn (1985). The pedagogical argument is supported by a quotation from Candy (1988), and a summary of a point made by Joiner, which was itself referred to by another writer, McCafferty (1981), who is Cotterall's actual reference. The practical argument for learner autonomy she makes herself, without reference.

Since the quotations are fairly long ones, they are given separate paragraphs, slightly inset from the rest of the text. The Boud quotation is discontinuous from the introductory phrase, so it is introduced by a colon(:); the Candy quotation runs on from what goes before it, so it is not separated from the preceding text by any punctuation marks.

10.18   Using the literature

OK, so now, you have something to share. You have a topic that interests you, some ideas of your own about the topic, and you have read some books and articles that seem to you to be relevant. You have in front of you a little pile (or perhaps a large pile) of source cards and notecards. There are two ways you can use them:

1.   in a spoken presentation
2.   in a written presentation

Whichever mode of presentation you choose, you will need to do a fair amount of preparation. Having source cards and notecards is not enough in itself! Let us start by looking at the preparation you will need to do for your presentation.

The most important thing to remember about using sources is that you have to use them – don't let them use you! What I am trying to say here is that whatever you say, or whatever you write, has to be driven

---

PERSONAL REVIEW 10.9: Using the Literature

Go back to the article by Eloise Pearson at the end of Chapter 7. In Task 4 associated with that exemplar article, you have already done some work on Pearson's use of sources, but let us take another look.

Read through the last section of Pearson's article again (i.e. the section beginning *Some conclusions*). As you are doing so, think about these questions:

1.   In what way does Pearson use her sources in this section?

2.   Does she accept everything they have to say uncritically?

3.   Who is 'in charge' here: Pearson or her sources?

---

and organised by your own ideas, and whatever message it is that you want to get across. This is true even of literature-review chapters in a dissertation, and of survey articles. You may have got some ideas from your reading, but now you must fit those ideas into your own framework. How do you relate to your sources: do you accept them or not? If the sources contradict one another, where do you stand? Examiners and readers complain that the most common fault in literature reviews written by students is that their reviews come over as lists of sources strung together, as it were, with very few signs of critical engagement with the ideas being quoted or summarised.

My own impression on reading this article is that the author is very much in charge, and is using her sources very well. In the final section she uses various authorities to corroborate the findings from her own data. But she does not accept their views uncritically. In the fifth paragraph of this section, for example, she quotes Larsen and Smalley (1972) to the effect that the only way to learn a foreign language is to devote a significant amount of time to it. This is undoubtedly true, but Pearson points out the practical difficulties encountered in attempting to do this. Finally, she aptly uses a quotation from Wenden (1985) to support her main point, which is the need to integrate 'learning training' with language training. For a summary of what I have been saying, see the SOURCES CHECKLIST which follows.

You might find it interesting to look at an attempt to show how

Valerie Arndt has used sources to develop her discussion in her article entitled 'Six writers in search of texts: A protocol-based study of L1 and L2 writing', the exemplar article for Chapter 5. I have used a 'mind-map' display (Figure 10.4) to show how the different readings are used to underpin the various sections of the article. If you are intending to use quite a few sources, as Arndt does here, you might find it useful to draw up a rough display like this to remind yourself where you intend to fit in the various quotations, etc. that you logged on your notecards (if that is the system you have been using). Now try PERSONAL REVIEW 10.9.

10.19   Presentation

It is actually very difficult to give general advice on presentation, as the form of presentation depends on the nature of your audience, and there is a huge variety of different kinds of audiences.

The best way of learning how to present to a certain audience is to watch others presenting to the same audience. Judge for yourself what techniques and approaches seem to be appropriate. As I have said before, the same goes for journals, magazines, etc.: familiarise yourself

---

Sources checklist

1. Read the sources carefully. You should attempt this difficult 'balancing act':
   - Be on the look-out for evidence that supports your point of view.
   - At the same time look out for new or different ideas and perspectives. If they seem to undermine your position, what is your response?

2. Make source cards for all sources read.

3. Make notes as appropriate.

4. Establish clearly in your own mind what your position, ideas, etc. are.

5. Make an outline of your talk, article, chapter, etc.

6. Locate your sources (name + date) at the relevant sections of your outline.

7. Are the sources supportive of your ideas or not?

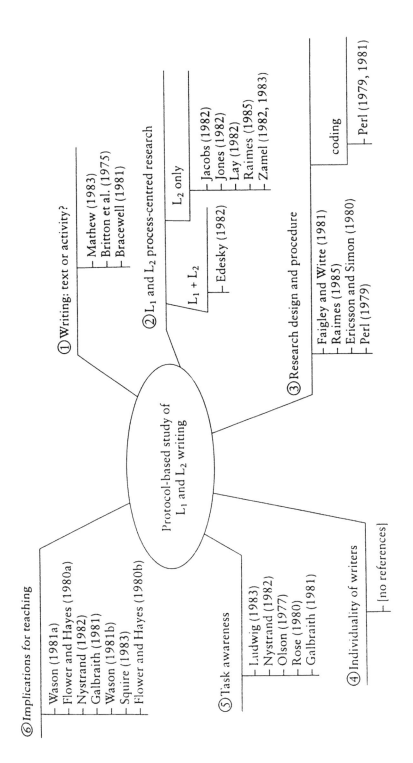

① Writing: text or activity?
— Mathew (1983)
— Britton et al. (1975)
— Bracewell (1981)

② L_1 and L_2 process-centred research

$L_1 + L_2$
— Edesky (1982)

L_2 only
— Jacobs (1982)
— Jones (1982)
— Lay (1982)
— Raimes (1985)
— Zamel (1982, 1983)

coding
— Perl (1979, 1981)

Protocol-based study of L_1 and L_2 writing

③ Research design and procedure
— Faigley and Witte (1981)
— Raimes (1985)
— Ericsson and Simon (1980)
— Perl (1979)

⑥ Implications for teaching
— Wason (1981a)
— Flower and Hayes (1980a)
— Nystrand (1982)
— Galbraith (1981)
— Wason (1981b)
— Squire (1983)
— Flower and Hayes (1980b)

⑤ Task awareness
— Ludwig (1983)
— Nystrand (1982)
— Olson (1977)
— Rose (1980)
— Galbraith (1981)

④ Individuality of writers
— [no references]

Figure 10.4 Sources mind-map

8. If they are supportive, decide how you are going to use them (e.g. by quotation or summary).

9. If they are not supportive, decide:
   - how you are going to represent their views (by quotation or by summary);
   - why you do not accept those views, and how you are going to present your arguments against them.

10. Finally, you can be selective, as long as you represent fairly the literature you have read. Just because fifty authors agree with you does not mean you have to quote all of them! On the other hand, if fifty authors disagree with you, you should probably present the views of at least some of them.

with the house-style of any journal you are thinking of contributing to. In these cases, familiarity breeds confidence!

Something else that breeds confidence is careful preparation. First, imagine yourself as a member of your own audience ('audience' here includes readership). If you were listening to a talk with this title, what sort of things would you be wanting to hear? What sort of style of presentation would you be expecting? Then think of your message. What are the main ideas that you want to leave your audience with? How are you going to ensure that these ideas are highlighted?

10.20   Oral presentation

I will be dealing with written presentations later, but, even if you are interested in writing rather than speaking, it is worth remembering that it is often a good plan to air your ideas in an interactive forum, such as a workshop or an informal talk, before you commit yourself to a written article. You will feel more confidence in your materials if you have previously rehearsed with an audience. You may also get useful feedback, and even new insights that will improve the quality of your article.

The first thing to think about is how to match your topic to your audience. Is the sort of thing you are talking about going to fit in with your audience's interests and expectations? If you were a typical member of the target audience, what would your reaction be to this topic? Can you slant the topic in a way that may make it interesting/

relevant to your listeners? Once you have sorted this out, you can think about the actual presentation.

Before an oral presentation, you will want to be as well prepared as possible, and this may well mean writing the full text of your talk. But this is not necessarily the form in which you are going to deliver it. In order to maintain eye-contact with their audience, most people prefer to deliver the talk itself from outline notes. These can be

- on a sheet of paper
- on cards (one card for each main idea)
- on an OHT (overhead transparency)
- prepared beforehand on a flip-chart or chalkboard
- on a prepared handout
- or by using some combination of these

Now for some tips about using these. They will sound very obvious, but there must be very few presenters who have not felt momentarily that they have 'lost their way' during a presentation, and often for the simplest of reasons:

- If you are reading from notes or cards, make sure that they are very legibly written or printed. If you use a wordprocessor, consider using 18-point size print, or even larger.
- If you are using cards, consider numbering them, stapling them together in one corner, or using some other method to ensure that they stay in the right order.
- If you are using an overhead projector (OHP) or a flip-chart/chalk-board, make sure that what you have written on it can be easily read, even from the back of the room. It is surprising how often this elementary point is overlooked by speakers, often to the intense frustration of the audience.
- If you are typing your outline OHTs on a wordprocessor, consider using type that is 24-point size or even 36. In this connection, remember that lower-case letters (like those you are reading now) are actually easier to read from a distance than upper-case letters LIKE THESE. Sometimes what you have to say can be summarised graphically, and this can make the presentation more interesting.

As far as delivery is concerned:

- If at all possible, familiarise yourself with the venue of your talk. Is there a convenient place for your notes, OHTs, etc.? Will you be sitting or standing, and, if so, where? If you are using any teaching aids will they be conveniently within reach? And so on.
- If you are using aids, make sure you know how they work, and that they are all set up to go. Also try to find out what your options are if

something goes wrong (e.g. if the bulb for the OHP fails, or if the video recorder starts acting up). Even if your presentation is very 'low-tech' things can still go wrong: if you are using a chalkboard, find out where the chalk is kept, if there is a duster, etc.

– Give your audience time to 'tune in' to you. Don't say anything too central to your talk in the first few minutes. (Some speakers use this time to introduce themselves, or tell the audience a little bit more about themselves.)

– As far as possible, maintain eye-contact with your audience.

– Be very clear. A useful procedure for achieving this aim is:
  – Say what you are going to say.
  – Say it.
  – Say what you have just said.
  (In other words: give a preview outline; deliver your message; give a summary outline.)

– Don't over-run. It is better to finish too early than too late. Your audience will probably forgive you if they miss one or two of your valuable points. They may not forgive you if they miss their coffee or lunch!

– Finally, even if your talk hasn't gone as planned (e.g. if you haven't managed to cover everything you intended to say), always try to finish on a clear, positive note. A good way of quickly rounding off a talk is to state briefly the most important thought you want to leave with your audience. You should carefully prepare this statement beforehand, so that you can finish confidently.

I have said nothing here about ways of organising audience involvement through tasks, group work, etc.: you will find useful suggestions on these and many other related issues in Gibbs and others (1987) *53 Interesting Things to do in your Lectures.*

PERSONAL REVIEW 10.10: Oral Presentation Style

The next few times you go to presentations, consider making notes not just on the content of the talks, but also on how the presenters deliver their message. You might find the checklist that follows useful.

Oral presentation checklist

1. How would you rate the talk overall for:

   effectiveness?   Very much ——————— Not at all

   (Circle number)   1   2   3   4   5   6   7

2. How would you rate the talk overall for:

   clarity? (Circle number)   1   2   3   4   5   6   7

3. What things did the speaker do that contributed to the effectiveness of the presentation?

   ....

   ....

4. Were there any presentation weaknesses in the talk?

   ....

   ....

5. What lessons have you learned for your own oral presentations?

   ....

   ....

10.21   Written presentations

As I have already said, there is a huge variation in different writing contexts, and the best way to learn about them is to read widely in a range of publications that you think you might write for. There are also many books to help you in this area, particularly if you are going to write for the more academic market, and an example text will be given in the 'Suggestions for further reading' section.

– As with oral presentation, make sure that your message is *clear*. This includes obvious things like explaining acronyms and abbreviations which have only a local significance, if you are writing for a wider audience. The advice given for oral presentation about clearly signalling your content may also apply here, so you could have a structure like this:
1. overview
2. main section
3. summary/conclusions and/or recommendations

- Consider 'signposting' the different stages of your article by the helpful use of headings and sub-headings.
- For some journals, and nearly all dissertations, you will have to provide an *abstract*. This is a kind of summary, which especially in the case of dissertations, should summarise your main findings.
- Before you submit an article for publication, consider asking some colleagues to read and comment on it.

PERSONAL REVIEW 10.11: Written Presentation Style

I have stressed several times the importance of the fact that good writing depends upon 'good reading' (i.e. wide and critical reading in the target area). As before, a checklist has been provided. Apply the checklist to any of the articles reprinted in this book, or to any article that is relevant to your needs.

Written presentation checklist

1. How would you rate the article overall for:

    effectiveness?   Very much ——————— Not at all

    (Circle number)   1   2   3   4   5   6   7

2. How would you rate the article overall for:

    clarity? (Circle number)   1   2   3   4   5   6   7

3. What things did the writer do that contributed to the effectiveness of the presentation? (Where appropriate, you can consider the effectiveness of the abstract, and headings/ sub-headings, layout, diagrams, etc.)

    ....

    ....

4. Were there any presentation weaknesses in the article? (For example, were you lost or confused at any point? Did the author sometimes make statements that should have been supported by evidence, but weren't? Was there unnecessary use of jargon?)

    ....

    ....

5. What lessons have you learned for your own writing?

    ....

    ....

10.22   Summary

In this chapter, I have tried to emphasise the importance of collaboration and networking in professional development, and how action research can be useful in this process.

I have tried to show how you can exchange ideas with other colleagues operating in the field of ELT. There are various ways of getting ideas and learning about other people's research, ranging from informal conversation to reading articles in journals.

You will want to reflect on these ideas, perhaps incorporate them into your way of thinking, and perhaps also use them as a basis for your own research. In this chapter, I have suggested some ways of doing this, and also how to share your thoughts and findings with others through either oral or written presentations.

10.23   Exemplar article

This chapter concludes with an opportunity to apply the checklist we have just discussed to a survey article on teaching L2 listening. The details of the article are as follows:

Rebecca L. Oxford (1993). Research update on teaching L2 listening. *System*, Vol. 21, No. 2, 205–211.

System, Vol. 21, No. 2, pp. 205–211, 1993
Printed in Great Britain

0346–251X/93 $6.00 + 0.00

RESEARCH UPDATE ON TEACHING L2 LISTENING

REBECCA L. OXFORD

University of Alabama, Tuscaloosa, AL, USA

Listening is a fundamental language skill, but it is often ignored by foreign and second language teachers. This article explains the complexity and importance of the listening skill, summarizes research on L2 listening, and provides a research-based consumer's guide to selecting and using L2 listening activities.

INTRODUCTION

The skill of listening should be a major area of concern to teachers and students of a second or foreign language (L2). Listening is a fundamental language skill that typically develops faster than speaking and that often influences the development of reading and writing ability in the new language (Scarcella and Oxford, 1992). Yet in many instances listening is treated like a neglected stepchild. It is "an overlooked dimension in language acquisition" (Feyten, 1991: p. 173). While the other three language skills receive direct instructional attention, teachers frequently expect students to develop their listening capability by osmosis and without help (Mendelsohn, 1984). "We have to teach our students HOW to listen," argues Mendelsohn (p. 63). Listening can no longer be relegated to the status of an enabling skill that simply helps students to speak (Nord, 1981) in the traditional, frenzied "Hear it, repeat it!," "Hear it, translate it!" mode so well described by Meyer (1984).

This article maintains that *listening, the most fundamental language skill, can be taught and that it should be a clear focus of classroom instruction.* This article discusses relevant research and provides research-based guidelines for the teaching of listening. These are the primary themes addressed:

(1) The meaning of listening in the context of input and intake
(2) The complexity of listening as a skill
(3) Research on L2 listening
(4) A consumer's guide to selecting and using L2 listening activities

THE MEANING OF LISTENING IN THE CONTEXT OF INPUT AND INTAKE

Listening is "the process of receiving, attending to, and assigning meaning to aural stimuli" (Wolvin and Coakley, 1985: p. 74). All aspects of listening involve a transformation of "input" into "intake"—a change from the whirling buzz of noise into a meaningful subset that is internalized by the learner (Cohen, 1990; Larsen-Freeman and Long, 1991; Ellis, 1986; Scarcella and Oxford, 1992). This distinction between input and intake is very important. Not everything to which a student is exposed becomes "intake," only the part that is significant and to which the student is paying attention.

THE COMPLEXITY OF LISTENING AS A SKILL

Listening is "a complex, problem-solving skill" (Wipf, 1984: p. 345). Listening is more than just perception of sounds, although perception is the foundation. Listening also includes comprehension of meaning-bearing words, phrases, clauses, sentences, and connected discourse.

Ordinarily listening is not an isolated skill. In normal, everyday communication, listening usually occurs together with speaking. Only in certain circumstances—for instance, in a lecture, at the theater, or when listening to the radio—does listening appear to be an isolated skill, not interacting with other language skills. Yet, even in those special situations, listeners often have support from the written word (lecture handouts, theater program notes, radio program listings) to figure out the meaning; moreover, skilled listeners in such circumstances apply what they know from other skills (e.g. from the sociolinguistic rules of speaking) to predict what is likely to be said next.

In almost any setting involving the native language, listening is the most frequently used language skill. Of the total time devoted to communicating, 45% is spent listening, 30% speaking, 16% reading, and 9% writing (Duker, 1971; Feyten, 1991). In our culture it is estimated that "close to 90% of class time in high school and college is spent listening to discussion and lectures" (Taylor, 1964).

However, people have trouble with listening in their own language, not to mention in a second or foreign language. Conaway's (1982) review of many studies showed that deficient listening skills were a stronger factor in college failure than were poor reading skills and low academic aptitude. After listening to a 10-min presentation, the average listener has heard, correctly understood, properly evaluated, and retained only about 30% of what was said, with the retention rate dropping to 20% after 48 m (Breecher, 1983).

Listening is sometimes difficult. The fleetingness of speech demands vigilance on the part of the listener. Listening—at least outside of the classroom or the language lab—usually requires understanding the meaning on the spot and instantaneously, without any chance to rewind a tape and listen again. In contrast, with the written word, the reader can simply go back and reread a passage that has been misunderstood or that did not gain sufficient attention (Joiner, 1986).

Ordinary speech, unlike the written word, contains many ungrammatical, reduced, or incomplete forms. It also contains hesitations, false starts, repetitions, fillers, and pauses, all of which make up 30–50% of any conversation (Oxford, 1990). On the other hand, the large amount of redundancy in everyday speech sometimes allows listeners to pick up the meaning later if they missed something. In certain situations, listeners can also ask for clarification or repetition from speakers.

Listeners must cope with verbal and nonverbal messages, which are sometimes mutually contradictory. For example, the (positive) statement "Let's get together for lunch sometime" might be contradicted by (negative) nonverbal messages of gesture and facial expression. As much as 93% of the total meaning of any interaction comes from nonverbal, often visual, clues.

RECENT RESEARCH ON LISTENING IN L2 DEVELOPMENT

Recent research has shown that listening is very important in developing a second or foreign language. The following discussion summarizes these research topics: listening as a predictor of L2 proficiency, L2 listeners compared with L2 readers, L2 sound perception, "bottom-up" and "top-down" L2 listening, simplification of L2 input, attention in L2 comprehension, memory in L2 comprehension, monitoring L2 comprehension, and affective aspects of L2 listening.

Listening
In Feyten's (1991) study, listening—understood as a set of related abilities—contributed significantly to the prediction of foreign language proficiency. Eleven to 38% of the variability in proficiency was explained by listening. In fact, listening skill contributed more to the prediction of proficiency than did sex, length of previous language learning experience, language being learned, and last contact with the language.

L2 listeners compared with L2 readers
Lund (1991) compared L2 listening and reading comprehension. He found that listeners and readers approached comprehension tasks differently, and their results were therefore different. L2 listeners recalled more main ideas than L2 readers and invented plausible contexts when uncertain. However, L2 listeners recalled fewer details than L2 readers.

L2 sound perception
Byrnes (1984: p. 325) noted that the task of the beginning L2 listener is, first of all, to perceive—to break out the important sounds from the ongoing stream, to differentiate "units in a previously undifferentiated sequence of noises." Perception of sounds is made difficult by the different pronunciations of words across versions of the same language (e.g. British, Indian, Pakistani, Canadian, Australian, and regional US Englishes). Sound perception is also made difficult by the different rhythms and tone patterns in the L2 compared with the rhythms and tone patterns in the students' native language (Ur, 1984).

L2 listening as "bottom-up" and "top-down" processing
L2 listening is not just a "bottom-up" skill in which the meaning can be derived from perception or comprehension of the sum of all the discrete sounds, syllables, words, or phrases (Ur, 1984). L2 listening does indeed involve some "bottom-up" processing, but at the same time it requires substantial amounts of "top-down" processing in which the meaning is inferred from broad contextual clues and background knowledge (Richards, 1983). To comprehend meaning, the L2 listener links what is heard to his or her internal schemata—mental frameworks in long-term memory (Byrnes, 1984).

Oxford (1990) lists a variety of clues to help L2 listeners infer meanings:

(1) Linguistic clues, such as suffices, prefixes, word order, stress, and cognates.
(2) Structural clues in the text, such as *first, second, third; the most important concept is . . .; we will now turn to . . .; so far we have covered;* and *in summary . . .*
(3) Social context clues, such as the likely purpose of the spoken input given the social situation, the meaning as related to the social status and age of the interlocutors, and the emotional tone of the conversation.
(4) Nonverbal clues, such as body movement (a grimace, a smile, a shrug, a rolling of eyes), the physical distance between speaker and listener, and background noise.
(5) General world knowledge possessed by the listener.

Simplification of L2 input
One of the most hotly contested aspects of L2 acquisition theory is whether listening input should be intentionally simplified for L2 learners. It is obvious that, in learning a first language, children initially receive simplified input ("motherese" as it is sometimes called), and some L2 specialists believe that L2 learners should likewise receive simplified input [see Scarcella and Oxford (1992) for a review of theoretical perspectives on this issue]. Advantages of simplified input include: (a) greater ease of comprehension for L2 learners, and (b) greater initial self-confidence in the protected classroom environment. Disadvantages include: (a) creation of an unrealistic expectation that all L2 input should be simple and easy to understand, (b) subsequent frustration (and even anger) at not being able to comprehend unsimplified, normal speech, and (c) loss of self-esteem in language settings outside of the classroom. By and large, simplified input is not useful as a long-term L2 instructional strategy (Scarcella and Oxford, 1992).

Attention in L2 listening comprehension
Lack of attention can be a significant problem in L2 listening. Cohen (1990) found that, on average, 50% of L2 students are attending to the content of a lesson at any given moment, and most are just repeating the material to themselves—rather than performing any higher-order functions on the material (such as making analogies to material already learned). Scovel (1991: pp. 3, 5) emphasizes the importance of attention as "central to the entire process of second language acquisition," as "the learner's window to the world," and as "the neuropsychological mechanism that promotes or prohibits acquisition."

Attention can be increased by active intention and action during the listening process. Attention can be raised through setting long-term goals and short-term objectives for L2 listening, making personally meaningful mental associations while listening, identifying the purpose of L2 listening in any given situation, and consciously deciding to look for clues while listening (Oxford, 1990; Scarcella and Oxford, 1992; Cohen, 1990; Mendelsohn, 1984).

Purposes of L2 listening
Research suggests that different L2 listening tasks invoke different kinds of listening behaviors on the part of students. *Listening for details* for the learner to pay selective attention to those details and filter out other information (Oxford, 1990). *Listening for the main idea* is a more global type of listening that centers on broader concepts and less on details and examples (Oxford, 1990). *Emphatic listening*, associated with the philosophy of Carl Rogers, requires focusing on the emotional content as well as the facts given by the speaker, and providing supportive verbal and nonverbal responses (Coakley and Wolvin, 1986). *Appreciative listening* (Coakley and Wolvin, 1986) involves listening to enjoy or gain a sensory impression of the material, and requires paying aesthetic attention to language style, musicality, and background sounds. *Critical listening* (Oxford, 1990) requires analyzing and determining the value of arguments presented. *Relational listening* (Farra, 1983; Feyten, 1991) involves paying attention to the whole environment as part of listening comprehension. Many other kinds of listening might also exist. L2 listeners must know what kind of listening they are expected to do at a given time, so that they can choose the appropriate listening behaviors.

Memory in L2 comprehension
Retention or memory is an issue in longer L2 discourse. The longer the discourse, the more the L2 listener must try to remember what has been said earlier in order to follow the flow of the meaning. The L2 listener who can remember what he or she has heard performs more effectively, and memory strategies (simple mnemonics such as using imagery, rhyming, personal associations, and physical response) can help listeners remember what was said (Oxford, 1990).

Monitoring L2 comprehension
Henner-Stanchina (1986) found that L2 listening involves frequent monitoring of one's own comprehension. L2 listeners must act as detectives who test out hypotheses about the meaning of what they hear. They must often guess the meaning from context clues, predict what comes next, assess the accuracy of their predictions, and make adjustments if the predictors are proved wrong [see also Ellis (1986) regarding the L2 hypothesis-testing process]. Based on her own research, Henner-Stanchina (1986) proposed a general program for improving learners' comprehension-monitoring ability.

Affective aspects of L2 listening
"Affective" refers to attitudes, beliefs, and emotions. Often L2 students have a negative attitude or belief about their listening ability—a "negative listening

self-concept" (Joiner, 1986). Anxiety frequently occurs when students feel they cannot handle an L2 listening talk. Highly visual learners are particularly vulnerable to anxiety when faced with complex listening activities (Oxford and Lavine, 1991). Anxiety is exacerbated when listeners think they must understand every word they hear, a very unrealistic goal. When anxiety strikes, it prevents learners from "transferring even the most basic first-language coping skills to the second language" (Meyer, 1984: p. 343) and creates a sense of failure and fatigue. Henner-Stanchina (1986) notes that few L2 listeners realize that they must extract meaning and mentally integrate new knowledge with what is already known; most L2 listeners believe that, in order to understand, they must define every word and apply every grammar rule, even though they do not have to do so to understand what they hear in their own native language.

More positive listening self-concepts can be created by helping students realize that word-for-word comprehension is not necessary and that guessing and hypothesis-testing are valuable (Oxford, 1990). L2 listening anxiety can be reduced through a variety of techniques, such as deep breathing, using music to relax, and saying positive affirmations (Oxford and Lavine, 1991).

A CONSUMER'S GUIDE TO SELECTING AND USING L2 LISTENING ACTIVITIES

Based on research by Mendelsohn (1984), Ur (1984), Meyer (1984), Oxford (1990), Scarcella and Oxford (1992), Cohen (1990), Henner-Stanchina (1986), and others, the following principles have been summarized for selecting and using L2 listening activities:

(1) The listening activity must have a real, communicative purpose.
(2) The activity must use authentic language without significantly slower or simpler speech than would normally be used in everyday life.
(3) Prelistening tasks (e.g. discussing the topic, brainstorming, presenting vocabulary, sharing of related articles) must be used to stimulate the appropriate background knowledge and help learners identify the purpose of the listening activity.
(4) The listening text must offer content that is personally interesting and motivating to learners.
(5) To allow listeners to infer meaning from body language and related context clues, the speaker must be visible whenever possible (unless the explicit purpose is to help students understand radio programs or audiotapes).
(6) The listening activity must offer many environmental clues to meaning, just as in real-life listening.
(7) When possible, the whole listening text should be given, and then it should be divided into parts that can be repeated. This sequence gives listeners time to think and rethink their hypotheses about the meaning of what is said.
(8) At the end, the whole text should be given again, and learners should have the opportunity to discuss their hypotheses and how they tested and altered them.

(9) The listening activity must require listeners to respond in some meaningful fashion, either individually or in small groups or pairs—by saying something, following a command or request, asking a question, taking notes, and so on.

(10) The listening activity must be fashioned so that listeners with normal background knowledge are able to understand the topic without doing specialized research, unless the class is focused on language for special purposes.

(11) The text of the listening activity must be typical for its own speech type; that is, an informal conversation must have short, redundant, rapid chunks of speech, while a lecture must be more formalized and orderly.

(12) The classroom climate surrounding the listening activity must be nonthreatening and positive, and simple affective strategies should be used to reduce anxiety if it is present before or during the listening activity.

CONCLUSIONS

L2 listening is a complex skill that deserves the attention of learners and teachers alike. Recent research offers many suggestions about how listening can be facilitated in the L2 classroom. Meaningful, interesting language tasks using ordinary, unsimplified L2 speech are valuable. Teachers can encourage learners to tap their own background knowledge, identify the purpose of the listening task, use hypothesis-testing and comprehension-monitoring strategies, and conquer their fears about listening in the L2.

REFERENCES

BREECHER, M. B. (1983) How to be a better listener and get more out of life. L.A. Times News Syndicate.

BYRNES, H. (1984) The role of listening comprehension: a theoretical base. *Foreign Language Annals* 17, 317–329.

COAKLEY, C. J. and WOLVIN, A. D. (1986) Listening in the native language. In Wing, B. H. (ed.), *Listening, Reading, and Writing: Analysis and Application*, pp. 11–42. Middlebury, VT: Northeast Conference on the Teaching of Foreign Languages.

COHEN, A. D. (1990) *Language Learning: Insights for Learners, Teachers, and Researcher.* New York: Newbury House/Harper Collins (now Boston, MA: Heinle & Heinle).

CONAWAY, M. (1982) Listening: learning tool and retention agent. In Algier A. S. and Algier K. W. (eds), *Improving Reading and Study Skills.* San Francisco, CA: Jossey-Bass.

DUKER, S. (ed.) (1971) *Listening Readings.* New York: Scarecrow.

ELLIS, R. (1986) *Understanding Second Language Acquisition.* Oxford: Oxford University Press.

FARRA, H. (1983) Relational listening. *Listening Post Supplement* 21–40.

FEYTEN, C. M. (1991) The power of listening ability: an overlooked dimension in language acquisition. *Modern Language Journal* 75, 173–180.

HENNER-STANCHINA, C. (1986) Teaching strategies for listening comprehension. Paper presented at the LaGuardia Conference on Learning Strategies, LaGuardia Community College, New York.

JOINER, E. (1986) Listening in the foreign language. In Wing, B. H. (ed.), *Listening, Reading, and Writing: Analysis and Application*, pp. 43–70. Middlebury, VT: Northeast Conference on the Teaching of Foreign Languages.

LARSEN-FREEMAN, D. and LONG, M. (1991) *An Introduction to Research on Second Language Acquisition*. Cambridge: Cambridge University Press.

LUND, R. J. (1991) A comparison of second language and reading comprehension. *Modern Language Journal* **75**, 196–204.

MEHRABIAN, A. (1971) *Silent Messages*. Belmont, CA: Wadsworth.

MENDELSOHN, D. J. (1984) There ARE strategies for listening. *TEAL Occasional Papers* **8**, 63–76.

MEYER, R. (1984) "Listen my children, and you shall hear ..." *Foreign Language Annals* **17**, 343–344.

NORD, J. R. (1981) Three steps to listening fluency: a beginning. In Winitz, H. (ed.), *The Comprehension Approach to Foreign Language Instruction*. Rowley, MA: Newbury House.

OXFORD, R. L. (1900) *Language Learning Services: What Every Teacher Should Know*. New York: Newbury House/Harper Collins (now Boston, MA: Heinle & Heinle).

OXFORD, R. L. and LAVINE, R. Z. (1991) Affective aspects of language learning. Paper presented at the Annual Meeting of the Modern Language Association, Chicago, IL.

RICHARDS, J. C. (1983) Listening comprehension: approach, design, procedure. *TESOL Quarterly* **17**, 291–340.

SCARCELLA, R. C. and OXFORD, R. L. (1992) *The Tapestry of Language Learning: the Individual in the Communicative Classroom*. Boston, MA: Heinle & Heinle.

SCOVEL, T. (1991) *The Role of Culture in Second Language Pedagogy*, Position Paper in Tapestry Program. Boston, MA: Heinle & Heinle.

TAYLOR, S. E. (1964) *Listening: What Research Says to the Teacher*. Washington, DC: National Education Association.

UR, P. (1984) *Teaching Listening Comprehension*. Cambridge: Cambridge University Press.

WIPF, J. A. (1984) Strategies for teaching second language listening.

WOLVIN, A. D. and COAKLEY, C. G. (1985) *Listening*, 2nd edition. Dubuque, IA: William C. Brown.

Forging links: an idea for reviewing superlatives ... and a bit more!

> *Douglas Buckeridge* teaches at Pitman College, London. He describes an activity to give learners practice with superlatives.

The idea for this activity was inspired, in general, by Gertrude Moskowitz's humanistic approach in *Caring and Sharing in the Foreign Language Class* and, in particular, by Exercise 3, Lots In Common, which appears in the Relating to Others section of that book.

Moskowitz defines the content of humanistic education as relating to 'the feelings, experiences, memories, hopes, aspirations, beliefs, values, needs and fantasies of students' (p14). She also stresses the importance of 'accentuating the positive' and fostering feelings of cooperation and unity within the classroom. Consequently, I have tried to incorporate some of these elements into an activity which also provides a review of superlative adjectives.

The activity

This activity is intended for students who have already been introduced to and had extensive practice in using superlative adjectives.

Step one   Each student is given the following list of questions:
1. What kind of movies are the most enjoyable?
2. What's the most delicious foreign food?
3. What's the most interesting sport to watch?
4. What's the best time of year?
5. What's the nicest thing about studying English?
6. What kind of person is the easiest to get on with?

Ask the students to take a minute or two to think about *their own* answers to these questions (along with reasons to support them), possibly with some soft music playing in the background to help them relax and focus on the task in hand.

Step two   Having done this, they stand up and move around the class, mingling with the other students, asking and answering the above questions. Whenever they find someone who has an answer which is the same as one of their own, they should try to develop a conversation on that topic. For example if they

come across someone who likes the same kind of movies, they can ask each other further questions such as:
Why do you like them so much?
How do you feel when you watch them?
How often do you go to (that kind of movie)?
Have you seen (name of movie)?
What did you think of it?

As soon as they have discussed that topic satisfactorily, they see if they have any other common answers and, if not, they separate and continue to mingle. Encourage them to talk to as many other students as they can in the time available. Again, playing soft background music tends to relax the students and facilitate communication.

Step three While there is no specific time limit imposed on step two of this activity, it is a good idea to provide for some feedback time in the latter part of the lesson. During this time the students can – in groups or as a whole class – share, in a lighthearted way, some of the links between themselves and their classmates.

Also, as a follow-up, they could write some short paragraphs about what they and other students have in common.

Points to note

- Superlatives can be worked on at different times, e.g. they are aimed at elementary students in books such as *Streamline Departures* and at intermediate students in ones such as *Interchange 2*, so this activity is not confined to a particular level.
- While the initial questions on the questionnaire are prescribed, the students are free to develop conversations in ways which are relevant to them, i.e. although the topics are chosen for them, they can exploit them in any way they wish.
- The importance of *intrinsic* interest in the topic to success of conversational/ opinion-gap activities is emphasised by materials developers like Klippel and Ur. Therefore my list of initial superlative questions only serves as an example. It is certainly open to change depending on the needs and interests of various groups of students.
- This activity can be used with either large or small classes.

References
Klippel, F. (1984) *Keep Talking*, CUP
Hartley, B. & Viney, P. (1978) *Streamline Departures*, OUP
Moskowitz, G. (1978) *Caring and Sharing In The Foreign Language Class*, Newbury House
Richards, J. (1991) *Interchange 2*, CUP
Ur, P. (1992) *Grammar Practice Activities*, CUP

lll *Douglas Buckeridge*

Concluding remarks

The main theme of this book has been to place action research firmly within the area of professional development. I have presented it as one of the ways in which teachers can solve professional problems and improve their practice through reflection-on-action. In action research this reflection is done through the systematic collection and analysis of relevant data, and by applying the results of these investigations of classroom practice.

I have deliberately used the phrase 'one of the ways' because it has not been suggested here that every teacher can or should be a researcher. Teachers have a big enough job to do by teaching, without having other responsibilities thrust upon them. It is essential that such an important area to society as teaching should be thoroughly and competently researched, but the vast majority of teachers have neither the time nor the resources, nor (in many cases) the specialised expertise to undertake this task on any significant scale. The appropriate authorities will have to see to it that selected professionals are trained to do that job and funded to carry it out. What we *are* saying is that the limited and highly-focused kind of investigation which we have described here, and have called 'action research' is a possible way forward to professional self-development.

Nor is it being suggested that the only or the best way of professional development is through action research. This book began with a discussion of a whole range of possible avenues of professional development. In spite of these caveats, it has been suggested that action research is an important avenue for professional development and for several reasons.

Firstly, it supposes that one way of solving professional problems is through collecting relevant data in some systematic way and subjecting those data to reasoned analysis. The results of this analysis can then become the basis for decisions about further professional action. This is the basis of action research. (Other ways of dealing with problems might include discussion ['talking things through'], reasoning from first principles, appeals to authority, complaining to a sympathetic listener, etc.)

Secondly, Action Research encourages collaboration. The isolation of teachers has often been noted.

'The problem of [teachers'] isolation is a deep-seated one. Architecture often supports it. Overload sustains it. History legitimates it.'

(Fullan and Hargreaves, 1992)

The 'objective' aspect of action research (i.e. discovering facts rather than making judgements) can facilitate collaboration. The pooling and sharing of ideas can demonstrate the rewards of collaborative action research. (Again, though, a word of caution. Collaboration has to be voluntary: it should not be imposed. Co-operatives have had a pretty good track record: collectives have not been so successful . . .)

Thirdly, action research can both draw on academic research (thereby providing it with a professional rationale), and also feed into it by exploring areas of professional concern.

There are also pragmatic reasons for considering action research in the context of teacher training. In some countries, serious moves are being made in the direction of continuing professional education linked to formal in-service qualification, which are in turn linked to promotional prospects or financial rewards (or both) *within the area of teaching* (as opposed to management, training, inspection, etc.). For most teachers, it is highly desirable that this kind of formal training is firmly rooted within their professional experience and action research is highly suited to that purpose.

There is every indication that these developments in on-the-job training will be facilitated by the development of electronic communication through the Internet (see, for example, Carrier 1997). Not only will communication between trainers and trainees themselves, as well as among trainers/trainees, become easier, but also the whole issue of access to library sources will be simplified. In time, access to sources on a world-wide scale will become virtually unlimited. Thus the collaborative sharing of ideas discussed in Chapter 10 will take on a new dimension.

Finally, with regard to pre-service training, action research is ideally suited to the development of reflective practice through reflection-on-action. Through it, trainees can be provided with a flexible but powerful means of professional development. With the right kind of institutional and management support, they could use action research to improve their own teaching and perhaps also to help raise the level of performance generally in their working situation.

Glossary of research terms

abstract brief version or summary of an article, talk, thesis research paper, etc.; it should give an outline of the main issues and conclusions.

action research method of professional self-development which involves the systematic collection and analysis of data related to practice.

affective data factual information relating to feelings or emotions.

analysis (1) process by which research data are examined and conclusions drawn from them; (2) report on this process.

author catalogue list of books, etc., which is organised alphabetically according to author.

autobiography a person's (professional) life story as told by himself or herself.

bibliography list of books, articles and other sources; list of references. (Note: a list of references includes only books, articles, etc. which are referred to in the text; a bibliography may include other sources which are relevant, but not directly referred to.)

biography a person's (professional) life story as told by someone else.

case study an in-depth study of one particular student, teacher, class, school, etc.

closed questions questions which allow only a limited range of answers (e.g. 'yes' or 'no').

computer-accessed catalogue list of books, articles, etc. that can be retrieved through a computer.

concurrent validity extent to which research or test results or findings are confirmed by other results acquired about the same time. See also *validity*.

confidentiality act of keeping findings, sources, etc., private.

construct validity extent to which test or research results are consistent with what is known about some psychological quality (construct) that cannot be directly observed, e.g. an aptitude for languages. See also *validity*.

content validity type of validity in which a test represents accurately the content it is supposed to measure. Thus, a test would not have content validity if it tested something that had not been taught. See also *validity*.

control group   in an *experiment*, the group which is not given any special treatment. See also *experimental group*.

convenience sample   kind of *sample* which is chosen because it is relatively quick or easy to get access to.

criterion   standard by which something or someone can be evaluated or judged.

critical incident   an event which is chosen for investigation because it has a special (professional) significance.

data   observations or information (e.g. facts, measurements) which can be used for research or which are available as the results of research. See also *raw data*.

database   an organised collection of *data* from which information can be quickly extracted.

data collection   the process of gathering *data*.

deductive inquiry   form of investigation in which conclusions are arrived at by reasoning from general or universal principles. See also *inductive inquiry*.

dependent variable   see *variable*.

diary   private account of a person's actions, thoughts and feelings written by the person himself or herself, usually on a daily basis.

discussant   someone who takes part in a discussion.

empirical data   factual information which is acquired through experience or observation (e.g. by doing carefully controlled experiments).

empirical research   method of investigation in which factual information is acquired through experience or observation, usually by performing an *experiment*.

evaluation   process of assessing the worth or value of something.

experiment   investigation conducted under controlled circumstances, usually involving subjecting someone or something to some kind of treatment and measuring the results.

experimental group   in an *experiment* the group which is subjected to some kind of special treatment. See also *control group*.

external validity   extent to which the results of a research study correspond to the reality outside the research study which the study purports to be informing us about. For example, a research project which purports to show us how learners learn foreign languages in the classroom may be so carefully controlled that its findings are difficult to relate to real classrooms: it therefore lacks external validity. Compare with *internal validity*. See also *validity*.

face validity   extent to which test/research results appear to measure what they are supposed to measure, without providing evidence that they actually do so. See also *validity*.

field notes written comments made in the course of professional action.

findings what has been discovered as the result of research.

focus with reference to an *interview*, something which is provided to stimulate or structure discussion; key aspect of a topic.

follow-up interview procedure when someone who has previously been interviewed is interviewed again (e.g. in order to clarify something, explore an issue in more depth, etc.).

hard data information which is completely factual and objective (e.g. a measurement). See also *soft data.*

heuristic research type of investigation which is exploratory rather than trying to prove or disprove a certain *hypothesis*. Heuristic research is usually more concerned with discovering the right questions to ask rather than the right answers.

hypothesis suggested explanation which may be later supported or disproved through (experimental) evidence.

illuminative research type of investigation which is intended to simply throw light on a topic rather than come to generalisable conclusions.

imprint page page in a book in which the key publication details are recorded.

independent variable See *variable.*

inductive inquiry form of investigation in which conclusions are derived from experience or empirical evidence. See also *deductive inquiry.*

informant someone who supplies a researcher with information.

inquiry systematic investigation. Also spelled *enquiry.*

inter-library loan system whereby books can be borrowed from another library through one's own library.

internal validity extent to which the results of a research study are logical and coherent because of the careful design and management of the research. Compare with *external validity.* See also *validity.*

interview conversation or meeting intended to gather certain information.

interview schedule list of questions prepared by someone who is conducting an *interview.*

introspective data information which is acquired from a person's account of his or her own thought processes, feelings, ideas, etc.

journals shared account of a person's actions, thoughts and feelings written by the person himself or herself, usually on a daily basis.

learner product term used for what is produced by a learner through performing study tasks in the form of written essays, test answers, etc.

life history person's account of his or her professional life.

literature   what has been written about an academic topic, usually in the form of books and journal articles.

literature search   the process of reading through academic books, journal articles, etc., to find information relevant to one's research topic.

log   record of professional action which is set out in a systematic way.

matching group   in an *experiment*, a group which is as far as possible identical to another group in one or more specified aspects. Groups may be matched for sex, age, qualifications, etc.

mentalistic data   information which is acquired from a person's account of his or her own thought processes, thoughts, feelings, etc.

narrative   an account from personal experience of a sequence of events of professional interest.

notecard   card on which a researcher keeps notes on what he or she has read for future reference.

observation   process of watching or listening to professional action either while it is happening, or from a taped sequence.

open(ended) question   type of question to which the range of possible answers has not been specified in advance.

personal account   statement by someone on some aspect of his or her professional life (e.g. a narrative of professional experience, etc.).

pilot   trial research done on a small scale in order to anticipate problems.

plagiarism   act of using someone else's ideas or writings without acknowledgement and passing them off as your own.

population   a group of people that you want to find out about by doing your research. This is often larger than the number of people that you can actually investigate (the *sample*). See also *sample* and *target population*.

predictive validity   extent to which what is predicted by research or by a test is actually confirmed later. So, for example, research findings would have predictive validity if they predicted that everyone being taught by a new method would increase their scores in an examination and they actually did so. See also *validity*.

prompts   with reference to an interview, follow-up questions that have been prepared beforehand with the intention of eliciting more information, should that be necessary.

protocol   written record of everything that has been said or done when taking part in a research process (e.g. the *transcript* of what someone has said during a *think-aloud* session).

protocol analysis   the act of submitting *transcripts* and similar written records to systematic examination.

qualitative research   type of investigation in which there is a substantial subjective element. See also *quantitative research*.

quantitative research type of investigation which is intended to be objective, using only, or mostly, data that can be accurately measured or counted. See also *qualitative research*.

questionnaire form on which there is a set of questions to be answered by a number of people so that information about those people which is of interest to the researcher can be discovered. Questionnaires are usually answered in writing, but may also be used in an *interview*.

random sample selection of people from a given *population*, chosen by chance.

rationale (1) the set of ideas which explain why a piece of research has been undertaken and why it has been done in a certain way; (2) part of a thesis, dissertation, etc., in which these underpinning ideas are explained.

raw data factual information which has been collected but not yet organised or analysed.

reliability extent to which research can be repeated and show the same or similar results; stability or consistency of test results.

replicable used to describe research processes which can be repeated by another researcher and would be expected to give the same or similar results.

research form of investigation in which *data* is collected and analysed.

researcher ethics standards of moral conduct as applied to research (e.g. not revealing the names of people that you have promised to keep confidential).

respondent someone who replied to a research enquiry (e.g. by filling in a *questionnaire*).

sample group of people who are investigated because they are considered to be representative of a larger group (*population*) from which they are drawn. See also *population; convenience sample; random sample; stratified sample*.

sampling the process of gathering a *sample*.

self-observation process by which someone monitors or examines his or her own behaviour.

self-report account given to a researcher of one's own behaviour, thought processes, etc.

semi-structured interview formal conversation or discussion for which the researcher has prepared the key questions, but is also able to ask supplementary questions, depending on the responses received.

shelf-mark number given to locate a book, etc. in a library collection. Shelf-marks are organised according to topic. Various ways of organising shelf-marks are in existence (e.g. the Dewey Decimal system, the Library of Congress System, etc.).

significance level see under *significant*.

significant with reference to research findings not caused simply by chance. Significance is usually expressed by means of a *significance level*, so for example, comparison of two scores may be 'significant at the .05 level' (expressed as $p<.05$). This means that the likelihood of the findings being simply due to chance is less than 5%.

soft data information that is derived from research that is subjective and/or not amenable to precise measurement.

source card card which gives publication information about an article, book, etc. that has been used to provide you with information for your research.

story informal account of some aspect of one's professional life.

stratified sampling procedure that ensures that the group that is taken is representative of a larger group (*population*) because it reflects the composition of the larger group in certain specified ways. For example, it may have the same percentage of males and females as the *target population*. See also: *population; target population; sample; random sample.*

structured interview formal conversation conducted for research purposes in which all the questions that are asked have been prepared beforehand. See also *semi-structured interview; unstructured interview.*

structured reflection process of thinking about one's professional activities in a systematic, organised way.

style sheet information provided by an editor or a publisher which explains to you how you should present your manuscript in terms of layout, etc.

subject catalogue list which enables you to access books from a library according to topic.

survey method of getting information on certain selected topics from a number of people (usually a large number and often chosen at random).

survey article piece of writing which summarises selected examples of what has been published on a certain topic.

target population a specific group of people that you want to find out about, although you may be actually able to investigate only a small number (*sample*) of them. See also *population; sample.*

think-aloud research procedure which involves people attempting to articulate (express) what is actually going through their minds as they attempt some task (e.g. writing a composition, reading a text). This process is usually taped and transcribed. See also *protocol; protocol analysis.*

title catalogue list which enables you to access a book from a library if you know the title of the book.

transcription   written version of what has been said (e.g. in an interview or during a lesson).

trialling   way of finding out how worthwhile, useful, etc. something is by making use of it and observing the results: textbooks, methods and teaching aids can all be trialled.

triangulation   method of making your research findings more *reliable* by collecting and analysing the *data* using more than one research method. So you could research someone else's teaching by *observation* of the teacher, *interviewing* the teacher, and getting the pupils to fill in a *questionnaire*.

treatment   something that is done to an *experimental group* which is expected to have some measurable result. An example of a treatment would be a new method of teaching reading which is expected to have the result of improving reading skills.

unstructured interview   conversation or meeting which is conducted for research purposes but for which there is little or no fixed plan or organisation: the researcher follows through on any topics that seem interesting or worthwhile as they arise.

validity   quality of a test or research procedure whereby it does what it is supposed to do. So a valid test of reading comprehension will test reading comprehension skills and not (say) writing skills. There are several different kinds of validity. See also *concurrent validity; construct validity; content validity; face validity; predictive validity; internal validity; external validity.*

variable   element in a research study that can vary or change (e.g. test scores, amount of time spent studying, etc.). Sometimes a researcher will modify one variable to produce an effect on another variable. For example, a researcher might want to show that an increase in the amount of time studying a language caused an improvement in test scores for that language. The variable causing the change (study time) is called the *independent variable*; the variable that is affected by the change (test score) is called the *dependent variable.*

verbal categories   in a questionnaire, scale options which are expressed in words rather than numbers (e.g. 'excellent – good – average – poor').

verbal reports   accounts given by individuals of their thought processes, feelings, ideas, etc.

verification   process by which research findings are, or are not, confirmed (e.g. by doing an experiment again or by using a different research technique).

working title   title used for a research study, article, etc. until such time as an exact title is found, which may not be until a substantial amount of work has been done in the study, etc.

Suggestions for further reading

General texts

You could easily collect a whole library of books on various aspects of research, so the few suggestions are highly selective and personal. I have tried to suggest books which are reasonably approachable and down to earth.

Let us start with a book that is specifically aimed at classroom teachers. It is:

> Hopkins, D. (1993). *A Teacher's Guide to Classroom Research*. 2nd ed. Buckingham/Philadelphia: Open University Press.

Another book which is more general in its appeal, but very user-friendly is:

> Bell, J. (1993). *Doing Your Research Project: A Guide for First-time Researchers in Education and Social Science*. 2nd ed. Buckingham/ Philadelphia: Open University Press.
>
> Bell's book contains many useful checklists for the different research techniques and procedures.

A more advanced book, and one which is in the foreign language/ second language context is:

> Nunan, D. (1992) *Research Methods in Language Learning*. Cambridge/New York: Cambridge University Press.

Finally in this section, I will mention a standard text book on education research. It is:

> Cohen, L. and Manion, L. (1994). *Research Methods in Education*. 4th ed. London/New York: Routledge.
>
> As well as giving authoritative accounts of the techniques that I have mentioned in this book, Cohen and Manion also describe techniques that have not been mentioned here such as Historical Research and the use of Personal Constructs.

Specific techniques:

Diaries and verbal reports

The best way into these is by looking at actual examples. Most are also interesting to read. Some examples:

Freeman, E. (1983). *Teacher Thinking: A Study of Practical Knowledge*. London: Croom Helm.

An early and very readable study.

Bailey, K. M. and Nunan, D., (eds.) (1996). *Voices from the Language Classroom*. Cambridge/New York: Cambridge University Press.

This book actually exemplifies a wide range of techniques, but there are several examples of diary studies.

Thomas, D. (1995). *Teachers' Stories*. Buckingham/Philadelphia: Open University Press.

This book is not specifically for language teaching, although the first 'story', by Elizabeth Thomas, is entitled 'My language experience . . .'

Most diary studies have been kept over a fairly limited time. The following book records a language teacher's development over many years. It is quite fascinating:

Appel, J. (1995). *Diary of a Language Teacher*. Oxford: Heinemann.

Observation techniques

There are many useful books in this area, but I will just mention two:

Wajnryb, R. (1992) *Classroom Observation Tasks: A Resource Book for Language Teachers and Trainers*. Cambridge/New York: Cambridge University Press.

This is a very practical 'how to' book with lots of ideas for *ad-hoc* observation schedules.

A book which gives a more narrative account of developments in observing the language classroom, and gives details of some of the well-known observation systems is:

Allwright D. (1988). *Observation in the Language Classroom*. London/New York: Longman.

Interviews and Questionnaires

A comprehensive guide to interviewing techniques is:

> Powney, J. and Watts, M. (1987). *Interviewing in Educational Research*. London: Routledge and Keegan Paul.

> As well as giving detailed guidance in the techniques involved, this book also provides six case studies of actual interviews, with transcriptions, and also supplies useful checklists.

Case studies

A book on this topic which manages to be at the same time fairly technical, but also accessible and interesting to read is:

> Yin, R. K. (1994). *Case Study Research: Design and Methods*. (2nd ed.) Thousand Oaks, California/London: Sage Publications.

> One of the helpful aspects of Robert Yin's book is that it contains 39 'boxes' describing various examples of actual case studies.

Evaluation

Evaluation is a huge area with many sub-specialisms depending on the kind of area that is being evaluated. A very accessible introduction to the whole topic is:

> Rea-Dickens, P. and Germaine, G. (1992). *Evaluation*. Oxford: Oxford University Press.

For a useful guide to textbook evaluation, see:

> Cunningsworth, A. (1995). *Choosing your Coursebook*. Oxford: Heinemann.

Publication and presentation

There are many guides available on how to write up research, especially for theses and dissertations. As far as articles are concerned, the best method is to study carefully back issues of the magazine or journal you intend to write for. Some journals have 'style pages' which tell you how they expect articles to be presented. Universities usually publish their own guidelines.

A general book on academic style, which you might find useful for reference is:

American Psychological Association (1994). *Publication Manual of the American Psychological Association*. (4th ed.) Washington DC: American Psychological Association.

As far as presentation is concerned, again the best advice is to familiarise yourself with the kind of groups and/or associations that you might be talking to. Even if you intend to give an informal talk, and not a lecture, you will probably find some useful ideas in:

Gibbs, G., Habeshaw, S. and Habeshaw, T. (1983). *53 Interesting Things to do in your Lectures*. Bristol, England: Technical and Education Services.

Personal and time management

There is a large and ever-increasing number of books on 'time management', 'personal effectiveness' and 'self management'. The fact that so many books of this kind exist is probably a bad sign: if there was a simple and effortless method of achieving success in this area, it would probably be common knowledge by now. The truth is that most of us are caught between the things we would like to do or spend more time on, and the amount of time available to us. Since the scope of the former is virtually infinite, and the scope of the latter is very strictly limited, tension between the two is inevitable.

Having said that, much sensible and helpful advice is available. Since these books are usually aimed at business managers, you might find some of the advice irrelevant. The best way to using these books may be to search through them until you find something that meets your needs: then act on it. You may also find it useful to put the book aside and come back to it from time to time. The advice stays the same (it is still good) but your circumstances, attitudes, etc. may have changed.

So, here are three titles:

Godefroy, C. H. and Clark, J. (1990). *The Complete Time Management System*. London: Piatkus.

Timm, P. R. (1987). *Successful Self-management*. London: Kogan Page.

Pedlar, M. and Boydell, T. (1985). *Managing Yourself*. London: Fontana/Collins.

Bibliography

(Note: the references listed here are those, and only those, which relate to the main text of the book. References derived from the 'exemplar articles' will be found in the lists of references attached to the appropriate articles.)

Allwright, D. (1988). *Observation in the Language Classroom.* London: Longman.

American Psychological Association (1994). *Publication Manual of the American Psychological Association* (4th ed.). Washington, DC: American Psychological Association.

Appel, J. (1989). Humanistic approaches in the secondary school: how far can we go? *ELT Journal*, 43, 4, 261–267.

Appel, J. (1995). *Diary of a Language Teacher.* Oxford: Heinemann.

Arndt, V. (1987). Six writers in search of texts: a protocol-based study of L1 and L2 writing. *ELT Journal*, 41, 4, 257–267.

Bailey, K.M. (1983). Competitiveness and anxiety in adult second language learning: looking *at* and *through* the diary studies. In R. Scarcella and S. Krashen (eds.), *Research in Second Language Acquisition: Selected Papers of the Los Angeles Second Language Research Forum.* Rowley, Massachusetts: Newbury House.

Bailey, K.M. (1993). The use of diary studies in teacher education programs. In J.C. Richards and D. Nunan (eds.) *Second Language Teacher Education.* Cambridge: Cambridge University Press.

Bailey, K.M. & Nunan, D. (eds.) (1996). *Voices from the Language Classroom.* Cambridge and New York: Cambridge University Press.

Bell, J. (1993). *Doing your Research Project: A Guide for First-time Researchers in Education and Social Science* (2nd ed.). Milton Keynes, England / Philadelphia: Open University Press.

Bellack, A.A., Kliebard, H.M., Hyman, R.T. & Smith, F.L. (1966). *The Language of the Classroom.* New York: Teachers College Press, Columbia University.

Brock, M.N., Yu, B. and Wong, M. (1992). 'Journaling' together: collaborative diary-keeping and teacher development. In J. Flowerdew, M. Brock and S. Hsia (eds.) *Perspectives on Second Language Teacher Education*. Hong Kong: City Polytechnic of Hong Kong.

Brown, G., Anderson, A., Shillcock, R. & Yule, G. (1984). *Teaching Talk: Strategies for Production and Assessment*. Cambridge: Cambridge University Press.

Buckeridge, D. (1994). Forging links: an idea for reviewing superlatives . . . and a bit more! *MET, 3*, 3, 40–41.

Calil, R. (1995 a & b)
(a) Professional Development in TEFL: the electronic list experience.
(b) The Internet and its electronic resources.
Both reported in *IATEFL Annual Conference Report 1995*, 28–29. Whitstable, Kent: IATEFL.

Carrier, M. (1997). ELT online: the rise of the Internet. *ELT Journal, 51*, 3, 279–309.

Cohen, A.D. (1987). Using verbal reports in research on language learning. In C. Færch and G. Kasper (eds.) *Introspection in Second Language Research*. Clevedon England/Philadelphia: Multilingual Matters.

Cohen, A.D. & Hosenfeld, C. (1981) Some uses of mentalistic data in second language research. *Language Learning, 31*, 2, 285–313.

Cohen, L. & Manion, L. (1994). *Research Methods in Education* (4th ed.) London and New York: Routledge.

Cotterall, S. (1995). Developing a course strategy for learner autonomy. *ELT Journal, 49*, 3, 219–227.

Cunningsworth, A. (1995). *Choosing your Coursebook*. Oxford: Heinemann.

Ellis, G. & Sinclair, B. (1989). *Learning to Learn English: A Course in Learner Training*. Cambridge: Cambridge University Press.

Fanselow, J.F. (1987). *Breaking Rules: Generating and Exploring Alternatives in Language Teaching*. New York and London: Longman.

Flanders, N.A. (1970). *Analyzing Teacher Behavior*. Reading, Massachusetts: Addison-Wesley.

Fortune, A. (1992). Self-study grammar practice: learners' views and preferences. *ELT Journal, 62*, 2, 160–171.

Freeman, E. (1983). *Teacher Thinking: A Study of Practical Knowledge*. London: Croom Helm.

Fullan, M. & Hargreaves, A. (1992). *What's Worth Fighting for in your School*. Milton Keynes, England: Open University Press.

Gibbs, G., Habeshaw, S. & Habeshaw, T. (1987). *53 Interesting Things to do in your Lectures*. Bristol, England: Technical and Educational Services.

Godefroy, C.H. & Clark, J. (1990). *The Complete Time Management System*. London: Piatkus.

Goodson, I.F. (1992). Sponsoring the teacher's voice: learners' lives and teachers' development. In A. Hargreaves and M. Fullan (eds.) *Understanding Teacher Development.* New York: Teachers College Press

Hancock, R. and Settle, D. (1990). *Teacher Appraisal and Self-evaluation: A Practical Guide.* Oxford: Blackwell Education.

Hopkins, D. (1993). *A Teacher's Guide to Classroom Research* (2nd ed.). Buckingham, England/ Philadelphia: Open University Press.

Huberman, M. (1992). Teacher development and instructional mastery. In A. Hargreaves and M. Fullan (eds.) *Understanding Teacher Development.* London: Cassell/New York: Teachers College Press.

Jordan, R.R. (1990). Pyramid discussions. *ELT Journal, 44,* 1, 46–54.

Kumeravadivelu, B. (1991). Language learning tasks: teacher intention and learner interpretation. *ELT Journal, 45,* 2, 98–107.

Laufer, B. (1991). The development of L2 lexis in the expression of the advanced learner. *Modern Language Journal, 75,* 4, 440–448.

Lowe, T. (1994). An experiment in role-reversal: teachers as language learners. *ELT Journal, 41,* 2, 89–96.

Luft, J. (1969). *Of Human Interaction.* New York: National Press Books.

Malamah-Thomas, A. (1987). *Classroom Interaction.* Oxford: Oxford University Press.

Matsumoto, K. (1993). Verbal-report data and introspective methods in second language research: state of the art. *RELC Journal, 24,* 1, 32–60.

Moskowitz, G. (1971). Interaction analysis: a new modern language for supervisors. *Foreign Language Annals, 1,* 3, 211–221.

Murdoch, G. (1994). Language development provision in teacher training curricula. *ELT Journal, 48,* 3, 253–264.

Nunan, D. (1992). *Research Methods in Language Learning.* Cambridge and New York: Cambridge University Press.

Oxford, R.L. (1993). Research Update on Teaching L2 Listening. *System, 21,* 2, 205–211.

Pearson, E. (1988). Learner Strategies and Learner Interviews. *ELT Journal, 42,* 3, 173–178.

Pedler, M. & Boydell, T. (1985). *Managing Yourself.* London: Fontana/ Collins.

Powney, J. & Watts, M. (1987). *Interviewing in Educational Research.* London: Routledge & Kegan Paul.

Raimes, A. (1985). What unskilled ESL students do as they write: a classroom study of composing. *TESOL Quarterly, 19,* 2, 229–258.

Ransdell, D.R. (1993). Creative writing is Greek to me: the continuing education of a language teacher. *ELT Journal, 47,* 1, 40–46.

Rea-Dickens, P. and Germaine, G. (1992). *Evaluation.* Oxford: Oxford University Press.

Reed, B. & Nolan, S. (1994). Survey review: two series of Business English materials. *ELT Journal, 48* , 1, 80–89.

Sergeovanni, T.J. & Starratt, R.J. (1983). *Supervision: Human Perspectives*. New York: McGraw-Hill.

Sinclair, J. McH. & Coulthard, R.M. *Towards an Analysis of Discourse*. Oxford: Oxford University Press.

Thomas, D. (1995). *Teachers' Stories*. Buckingham, England/Philadelphia: Open University Press.

Vincent, S. (1990). Motivating the advanced learner in developing writing skills: a project. *ELT Journal, 44*, 4, 272–278.

Wajnryb, R. (1992). *Classroom Observation Tasks: A Resource Book for Teachers and Trainers*. Cambridge and New York: Cambridge University Press.

Wallace, M.J. (1991). *Training Foreign Language Teachers: A Reflective Approach*. Cambridge: Cambridge University Press.

Wallace, M.J. (1993). Towards creating and maintaining a professional dynamic in ELT. Paper presented at the ITTI conference on *Future Directions in Teacher Education*, held at International House, London, March 1993.

Widdowson, H.G. (1993). Innovation in teacher development. *Annual Review of Applied Linguistics, 13*, 260–265.

Woods, P. (1987). Life histories and teacher knowledge. In J. Smyth (ed.) *Educating Teachers: Changing the Nature of Pedagogical Knowledge*. London: Falmer Press.

Wright, T. (1992). L2 classroom research and L2 teacher education: towards a collaborative approach. In J. Flowerdew, M. Brock and S. Hsia (eds.) *Perspectives in Second Language Acquisition*. Hong Kong: City Polytechnic of Homg Kong.

Yin, R. K. (1994). *Case Study Research: Design and Methods* (2nd ed.). Thousand Oaks, California / London: Sage Publications.

Subject index

Note: Index items cover only the main text and not the exemplar articles.

Author index